Do it

1. Think twice before buying anything on credit. Ask yourself, what's the real cost if I don't pay cash?

2. Compare your bank's checking account fees and terms with its competitors' for better rates.

3. Write a will.

4. Invest in your employer's 401(k) or IRA plan; if self-employed, open a SEP-IRA or Keogh.

5. Investigate a term life insurance policy if you don't already have one.

*One luxurious
bubble bath*

*Access to most comfortable
chair and favorite TV show*

*One half-hour massage
(will need to recruit spouse, child, friend)*

*Time to recline and listen to a favorite CD
(or at least one song)*

cut

6. Cut your discretionary spending by 10 percent a month and bank the money you save.

7. Make saving a family affair. Involve your spouse and kids.

8. Calculate your taxes and income so your withholding is accurate.

9. Read one financial publication a week.

10. Set aside an emergency stash of money equal to at least three months' expenses.

COUPON

COUPON

COUPON

COUPON

Build Your Financial Future

B.J.
We know its not
easy to be a
poor college student,
but we hope you
can make millions
someday!

Erik & Jen

Build Your Financial Future

Terry Meany

Macmillan • USA

Macmillan Publishing books may be purchased for business or sales promotional use. For information please write: Special Markets Department, Macmillan Publishing USA, 1633 Broadway, New York, NY 10019.

International Standard Book Number: 0-02-862648-6
Library of Congress Catalog Card Number: 98-88082

01   00   99   8   7   6   5   4   3   2   1

Interpretation of the printing code: the rightmost number of the first series of numbers is the year of the book's printing; the rightmost number of the second series of numbers is the number of the book's printing. For example, a printing code of 99-1 shows that the first printing occurred in 1999.

Printed in the United States of America

Book Design: Madhouse Studios

Page creation by David Faust and Heather Pope.

Special thanks to Tom Siedell who worked as a collaborator on this book.

You Don't Have to Feel Guilty Anymore!

IT'S O.K. TO DO IT *THE LAZY WAY!*

It seems every time we turn around, we're given more responsibility, more information to absorb, more places we need to go, and more numbers, dates, and names to remember. Both our bodies and our minds are already on overload. And we know what happens next—cleaning the house, balancing the checkbook, and cooking dinner get put off until "tomorrow" and eventually fall by the wayside.

So let's be frank—we're all starting to feel a bit guilty about the dirty laundry, stacks of ATM slips, and Chinese take-out. Just thinking about tackling those terrible tasks makes you exhausted, right? If only there were an easy, effortless way to get this stuff done! (And done right!)

There is—*The Lazy Way*! By providing the pain-free way to do something—including tons of shortcuts and time-saving tips, as well as lists of all the stuff you'll ever need to get it done efficiently—*The Lazy Way* series cuts through all of the time-wasting thought processes and laborious exercises. You'll discover the secrets of those who have figured out *The Lazy Way*. You'll get things done in half the time it takes the average person—and then you will sit back and smugly consider those poor suckers who haven't discovered *The Lazy Way* yet. With *The Lazy Way,* you'll learn how to put in minimal effort and get maximum results so you can devote your attention and energy to the pleasures in life!

THE LAZY WAY PROMISE

Everyone on *The Lazy Way* staff promises that, if you adopt *The Lazy Way* philosophy, you'll never break a sweat, you'll barely lift a finger, you won't put strain on your brain, and you'll have plenty of time to put up your feet. We guarantee you will find that these activities are no longer hardships, since you're doing them *The Lazy Way*. We also firmly support taking breaks and encourage rewarding yourself (we even offer our suggestions in each book!). With *The Lazy Way,* the only thing you'll be overwhelmed by is all of your newfound free time!

THE LAZY WAY SPECIAL FEATURES

Every book in our series features the following sidebars in the margins, all designed to save you time and aggravation down the road.

- **"Quick n' Painless"**—shortcuts that get the job done fast.

- **"You'll Thank Yourself Later"**—advice that saves time down the road.

- **"A Complete Waste of Time"**—warnings that spare countless headaches and squandered hours.

- **"If You're So Inclined"**—optional tips for moments of inspired added effort.

- **"The Lazy Way"**—rewards to make the task more pleasurable.

If you've either decided to give up altogether or have taken a strong interest in the subject, you'll find information on hiring outside help with "How to Get Someone Else to Do It" as well as further reading recommendations in "If You Want to Learn More, Read These." In addition, there's an only-what-you-need-to-know glossary of terms and product names ("If You Don't Know What It Means/Does, Look Here") as well as "It's Time for Your Reward"—fun and relaxing ways to treat yourself for a job well done.

With *The Lazy Way* series, you'll find that getting the job done has never been so painless!

Series Editor
Amy Gordon

Cover Designer
Michael Freeland

Editorial Director
Gary Krebs

Developmental Editor
Doris Cross

Production Editor
Robyn Burnett

Director of Creative Services
Michele Laseau

What's in This Book

The Simple Path to Wealth

You've heard or read the stories all of your life. Uncle Bob who bought Polaroid when it first hit the market and he retired to Florida rich and happy. Aunt Hazel who wore frayed dresses and mildewy winter coats and died with three million in stocks and bonds at the local Dean Witter office, which she then left to her church choir. Or the 16-year-old high school junior who invested his money from delivering newspapers—most likely your paper—and now drives a new Porsche. And you wonder what you're doing wrong.

In a panic, you look ahead to your retirement and you see yourself working at a fast-food restaurant, your days spent bussing away mushy concoctions of french fries and ketchup and wiping tables topped with puddles of soft drinks. Your kids, who tried to put themselves through school bussing these same tables, are paying off their college debts and barely speaking to you. Congress is still debating Social Security reform, but the argument is kind of a moot one since they borrowed all the funds to pay for the National Sports Stadium referendum you voted for years earlier (motto: "When people get old, they'll be glad we built these. Whatever.").

Americans have always been fascinated with money and getting ahead. Our history is filled with stories about Rockefeller and Carnegie and now Gates, who became richer than everybody, even richer than some small countries. We've been the industrial powerhouse of the world and now we're the software center of the universe, at least until Neptunians invade us with a really cool operating system à la the old Star Trek series. Despite this fascination, few people really take the time to learn how to manage their money or even understand the nature of money or markets. Consequently, we always worry about it and are often ineffective when dealing with it.

Every day, we are bombarded with news of the stock markets, the Dow Jones Industrial Average, NASDAQ, the price of gold, and the never-ending predictions of analysts and brokers, all of whom you presume to know more than you.

At some point in time, everyone of these prognosticators will be proven correct. Eventually. Someday. It could be tomorrow, it could be in the next century. If the crystal ball doesn't work this time, well, let's try version 2.0 and see what happens. Smart investing means you read widely and ignore the hype. Lazy investing means you understand there will be ups and downs in the market and that you will live to see a richer day.

A lazy investor doesn't have to spend every waking minute poring over market returns and annual reports. She knows that at any given time, there will always be an investment that will give her a higher yield, but that she can't be forever pursuing it. She knows that so-called experts who do devote most of their waking hours to the market still take losses from time to time, sometimes huge ones.

For most people, solid investments, held for a long period of time, will pay off better than fretting and trading and paying commissions to brokers. This book will point the way to a secure future without spending all of your present time worrying about it.

Part 1

Getting Organized Without the Agony

Are You Too Lazy to Read Getting Organized Without the Agony?

1 The only organizing skill you've been able to master is separating your socks, which are all the same color, into pairs. ☐ yes ☐ no

2 You think a quick take is a really, really short movie preview. ☐ yes ☐ no

3 Money usually follows you and then it keeps going, leaving you holding the bill. ☐ yes ☐ no

Chapter one

Start Counting It Up

*"A journey of a thousand miles
must begin with a single step."*
—Chinese proverb
"Cash Only."
*—Uncle Hank's Golden Pheasant
Cantonese Restaurant*

Hank had his priorities in order and order in his life. Cash in, cash out, no waiting for checks to clear or credit card companies to pay up. He always knew how much money he had in the bank and the cash register—to the penny! Not too many of us are that organized. But you must start somewhere. It gets easier after you take the first step.

Planning your financial future without knowing your current financial condition is something like having your physician guess what's wrong with you and prescribe a treatment without first doing an examination. The results can be quite interesting—you could end up hobbling around on a plaster cast when all you're suffering from is an earache.

Some people can get away with less scrutiny in their lives than others. "One of the advantages of being disorderly," wrote A. A. Milne (alter ego to Winnie the Pooh) "is that one is constantly making exciting discoveries." Easy for him to say; his books are still selling and pulling in royalties. He could afford exciting discoveries. Before you can get your financial life in order, you'll first have to sort through, probe, and examine your financial situation. That is, unless you're a best-selling author of children's books about fussy bears.

Figuring up your assets, liabilities, and cash at hand is not exactly computer science, although you may want your computer to keep track of it all. Doing this is actually the start of the lazy life. *The Lazy Way* means you can find out what your financial position is at a glance of your records, instead of being unpleasantly surprised! Think of it as financial cruise control: You put your papers in order, easily check them at a glance—they'll be neatly filed away, after all—and readjust your speed when the road conditions change. Lazy means you don't spend your nights and free time poring over obscure financial reports and have a paging service call you with the London price of gold every morning. Your finances will be far simpler. Boring even.

Your first step involves sorting through all the papers you keep stashing in your desk: pay stubs, bank statements, tax returns, loan statements, anything with a "$" sign on it. You don't have to include your spare penny jar or check pay phones for loose change, however.

QUICK 🔘 PAINLESS

One of the most basic money management techniques is keeping your checkbook balanced as you go. Many people don't do this and are regularly surprised—and not for the better—when their monthly statement arrives.

TAKING STOCK

Self-knowledge is more than a philosophical ideal, and financial self-knowledge has very practical uses, such as:

- As a homeowner, you'll know if your home is adequately insured. Your current equity will determine if you can take out a home equity loan, a low-cost means of borrowing.

- A quick look at your emergency fund will let you know if you need to add to it or whether you've put aside an adequate amount for those unexpected surprises.

- Thinking of retiring? An easily monitored retirement account will determine how much gold you'll have in those golden years.

For investors, it can mean the difference between enjoying success and being very sore from kicking yourself over bad decisions. Being honest with yourself—and knowing your assets and liabilities—will help you determine:

1. Down-to-earth goals

2. How much money you can and want to invest and save

3. The degree of risk you can live with

4. A realistic financial future

In recent times, too many baby boomers have found themselves 20 years older and shopping for bifocals. The approach to money they took in college (buy now, buy

IF YOU'RE SO INCLINED

As a backup, you can always scan your monthly bank and brokerage statements and save them on your computer's hard drive or separate disk.

YOU'LL THANK YOURSELF LATER

Making an inventory of your assets and figuring your net worth will give you a good idea of how much you can safely invest and how much of a margin of error you can live with. Pay attention to these figures or you can needlessly overextend yourself in the market.

later, pay for it eventually) now leaves something to be desired. They've discovered mutual funds and have been pouring money into them, partly accounting for their high returns in recent years. Retirement and college costs are hot topics of conversation, with an agitated need to fund them both. This doesn't have to be you. No running around like a last-minute Christmas shopper trying to find that elusive new toy for your kids. You'll know what you can and cannot afford. You're going to sit down quietly with your financial tools of the trade, including your:

1. Financial records and statements

2. Checkbook, bankbook

3. Notebook, file folders, pencils

4. Calculator

5. Computer and appropriate software (can take the place of 3 and 4)

You don't have to do this all at once, especially if your desk and papers are, you know, organizationally-challenged. Take your file folders and:

- Label them (bank statements, tax records, etc.)
- File appropriate papers in them
- Put them aside until all papers are filed

More Than You Thought

Consider all of your assets. Do you own a home? A coin collection? Savings bonds from your bar mitzvah? Even if some of these aren't liquid—that is, readily exchanged for cash—they still determine your net worth, so include them all.

In your notebook—or on your computer—you should start listing: Money, Property, Investments, Valuables, and General Assets. Use the following list as a guide:

- Savings account
- Checking account
- Savings Bonds
- Brokerage account/money market
- Certificates of deposit (CDs)
- Treasuries (T-bills, bonds, and notes)
- Stocks, bonds, mutual funds
- Pension and profit-sharing plans
- Retirement accounts: IRA, 401(k), Keogh, etc.
- Cash-value life insurance policies
- Annuities
- Real estate/home
- Business interests and partnerships
- Notes receivable
- Automobile(s), boat, etc.
- Jewelry and antiques
- Other (e.g., coin or stamp collection)
- Other (e.g., rainy day fund*)
  This is a meaningless term if you live in Seattle.

Be honest, don't exaggerate the value of your '88 Honda Prelude even if you have nicknamed it "Precious." You're trying to establish a base to work from.

QUICK n PAINLESS

Establish a simple filing system for all your important records, including non-net-worth items such as insurance policies and recent tax documents. A good filing system makes periodic review much easier.

Estimating, as in, "I think my collection of 1960–90 Rolling Rock beer cans is worth at least $5,000," doesn't count and won't help you if you were to ever actually depend on its cash value only to find you can only get about $35 for it. And no fair appraising your 286 computer as a valuable antique. Gas stations give away free calculators with more computing power if you fill up with eight gallons or more of regular.

Working up your net worth statement can, rightly or wrongly, become a self-worth statement. Despite what self-help books say, we're probably not going to evade the notion that what we're worth asset-wise is often tied up with what we feel we're worth person-wise. It's tough to escape that when you're living in the richest culture in history replete with overnight billionaires who could never get dates in high school. Money is just one facet of your life, albeit a major one. Follow the direction of this book—starting with your net worth statement—and you'll find dealing with your money to be a less fretful experience.

Of course, if you were the author who made a quizzillion dollars telling your readers that money isn't everything and they should like themselves for who they are, easy for you. Even if you're not, you may be worth more than you think.

I'd Rather Hear Fingernails on a Chalkboard

Think of your net worth statement as your first step. You know how this is the information age and knowledge is power and power is liberating and liberation is

QUICK ⬭ PAINLESS

Office supply stores sell simple household accounting systems to keep track of money in and money out. It's a lot quicker to jot it down when it happens than to look for pay stubs and receipts months later. Rather do it on your computer? Try Quicken or Microsoft Money. These software programs may take a while to set up, but they can simplify nearly all aspects of your financial life later on.

_____ (fill in your own cliché)? And self-empowerment, besides being a wretched catchall phrase of the consulting industry, is really something to strive toward? Well, welcome to your own private self-empowerment session and be thankful you don't have to listen to some obnoxious, hack "empowerment coach" with bleached teeth blather on about the power within and maximizing your envisionment.

Your next step is figuring up your debts and expenses.

Where does it all go?

Adding up income and net worth has a vague connection to the philosophical notion of relativism. That is, once you look at the totals, you might feel relatively wealthy. Add in your liabilities and you might feel relatively different.

When you bite this bullet (or Swiss chocolate, which is a lot tastier and less potentially lethal) you should have a list that includes:

- Mortgage
- Automobile loan
- Boat loan
- Credit card debt
- Student loans
- Medical debt
- Other major debt (e.g., past tax debt)

It's a potent list, and it may be longer depending upon your circumstances. Maybe you and the bank own a motorcycle or a Bayliner that sleeps six. Maybe your

Now that you've got the asset and income side of your net worth statement done—and you're feeling pretty good about yourself— set it down for a day and do something fun. No, I don't mean flying first class to Italy, which would definitely be fun, but maybe buying a nice bottle of wine, something with a cork instead of a screw top.

The Lazy Way

goal was to become a walking art form in progress, for instance, and you owe your tattoo artist big time—and you don't want to think about what repossession would entail! It's far easier to get on with your investments and savings goals once you get all your financial data out in the open. Honesty is the best policy here, even if you're not a boy/girl/other scout. So list everything.

Hidden Away

This book is about securing your financial future. A few simple steps, taken one at a time, can make tomorrow and next year, as well as the ensuing decades, a lot more pleasurable. It means looking ahead and maybe putting off some enjoyment today for bigger payoffs later—not exactly the message you get from "Make no payments for 90 days/60 months' financing D.O.C." sport utility vehicle ads.

The key to your financial security is understanding that no one is likely to take your financial situation as seriously as you do. The current debate about Social Security and health care reform have probably made you aware that you really can't depend on anyone else to take care of you as you get older except yourself. Even your doting parents might find you less than adorable when you're middle-aged and still living with them in the same bunk bed you had as a five year old. So much for that weekly allowance you've been getting.

I strongly advocate, promote, espouse, tell you to do it or else, that you contribute heavily for your retirement years. The government (rightfully for most people) mandates some participation in the Social Security system.

Although they aren't part of the bottom line on your net worth statement, retirement accounts, and Social Security will play a key role in your long-range retirement planning.

Social Security payments—that's the FICA (Federal Insurance Contribution Act) column on your pay stub—shows how much you've paid into the fund for Social Security and Medicare. And, your employer matches this amount (unless you're self-employed, in which case you pay the entire tab). This is a very lazy way to save, albeit an involuntary one, and, in the opinion of many, one which doesn't bring a very competitive return. Nevertheless, the money is there and it's yours, but who keeps track of it? The Social Security Administration, that's who.

To get a current accounting of your social security account—you'll probably be pleasantly surprised at how much you've put aside—contact the Social Security Administration (800-772-1213 or www.ssa.gov). Ask for Form 7004, "Request for Personal Earnings and Benefit Estimate Statement." This form can also be downloaded from the Internet, and, yes, as usual, you'll have to download Adobe Acrobat Reader if you don't already have it.

If you've participated in a traditional retirement program at work (called defined-benefit plans because employers have basically set up an annuity that will pay you a certain amount in retirement, based typically on your years of service), your employer's (or perhaps a past employer's) benefits office can provide you with a current accounting of your benefits when you retire.

YOU'LL THANK YOURSELF LATER

Keep in mind that while the recent past has had very little inflation, this can always change. Don't base your retirement financial needs on today's prices or you'll wind up selling yourself short.

Both the government and your employer can make mistakes. Check your retirement benefits periodically to be sure they are correct and current. Social Security should be confirmed every two to three years or after you change employers. Some small businesses fail to pay into the fund. You don't want to be caught short!

ADDING IT ALL UP

You may be surprised at your net worth, whether it's more or less than you expected. Sometimes more is better and this is one of those times. If your addition leaves you a little short of your expectations, this is the time to find out—not when you're thinking of retiring. It's easy to spend in America. It's a national pastime. Maybe your net worth statement will guide you to another hobby.

You could take the easy way out. You can hire all kinds of helpers—accountants, tax attorneys, stockbrokers, financial planners. They will happily sort through your papers and receipts, for an hourly rate or set fee, and guide you on your way. It's hard to justify all these hands grabbing for your financial pie if you have modest assets. And then there are those pesky questions, such as:

- Am I getting my money's worth?
- Am I giving up too much control of my finances to others?
- Do the results justify the expense?

There are all sorts of advisors, stockbrokers, and fund managers out there who can't beat or even meet broad market returns, yet they remain at their jobs, some of them investing millions and millions of dollars every day without spectacular results. You can do better on your own and keep the fees for yourself!

THE LAZY WAY

Buying time can be very expensive if you have to pay someone else, in the form of financial planners, accountants, or tax preparers, to provide it for you by sorting through a Birkenstock shoe box full of receipts and financial statements. Taking the time to count it all up, arrange your files, and keep your affairs orderly throughout the year is hands-down faster—with less screaming and desk pounding— than discovering you've been barely treading the financial waters for longer than you want to know.

How much time are we talking? For starters, take a Sunday afternoon during football season—or the night of the Miss America Pageant, if you prefer—turn on the TV, and start arranging the past year's bank statements, pay stubs, and credit card payments. Put each in a file folder and you should have it done without going into overtime, or when Miss Ohio gets the crown. In an age of multitasking, this won't be any challenge for you.

Rather use a computer? It will take longer to input the data into all of those irksome columns, but once your spread sheets are done, you can add new information each month when you balance your checkbook. Instant record keeping—neat and professional—just be sure to keep a file copy on a separate disk. Computers are great tools until you get a message reading, "File Doesn't Exist No Matter What You Say."

With either system, paper or computer, you'll always be on top of your finances. You'll be especially thankful at tax time. And, you can watch your progress as you move toward a bright financial future.

IF YOU'RE SO INCLINED

If you do hire a professional, such as an accountant, planner, or lawyer, have your papers and records in order first. Your reward will be fewer billable hours on their part and lower fees for you.

Getting Time and Money on Your Side

	The Old Way	The Lazy Way
Sorting through your paper piles and trying to figure out your finances vs. opening up a ledger or computer file where you've regularly stored everything:	Okay, I'm almost up to year 1992 now.	Another minute out of my life.
Using a shoe box as your filing system vs. a convenient, ready-made bookkeeping system:	Hey, when you cleaned out the closet you didn't throw out the box marked "Important Stuff" did you?	This 10 minutes a month I spend writing in checks and receipts is a real killer.
Hoping you can live on Social Security vs. building your own retirement fund with an IRA or 401(k):	I like the idea of living in a rooming house when I retire. It'll be a welcome change of pace.	Dear, should we go to Spain or Italy for lunch this weekend?
Neglecting to write out a net worth statement and hoping your finances are okay vs. writing it all down and knowing where you stand:	It looks like we've got −$57 in the bank. Hey, I finally understand the concept of negative integers.	Good thing we caught this shortage in Mindy's college fund early.

Chapter two

Math Lesson: Bills × Money = Less Money

There's a reason that the word "debt" rhymes with the word "bet." In a sense, you and your creditor are engaging in a wager that you will pay money back in the future for goods or services that you enjoy today. The creditor looks at your ability to pay and decides whether it's a good bet or a sucker bet. Sometimes they don't look very closely, which is why credit counseling services exist.

Almost anything can be billed monthly these days, including groceries, dry cleaning, concert tickets, meals out, and Zippy's veterinary care. There's little reason to pay cash when you can have the convenience of automatic withdrawals from your bank account or simply writing checks once a month to pay a credit card company. In a sense, this convenience makes it easier to accumulate debt and lose track of our expenses. The more physical distance we have between the money itself and the goods and services rendered, the more tenuous the connection between the two. If we had to peel off a roll of twenties to pay our bills, I guarantee as individuals we would adopt an entirely different consciousness about our money and where it goes. Think what it would be like if we used cattle or bales of hay for our currency. How exactly do you give change for a heifer?

In the last chapter, we uncovered your assets: cash, equities, property. That's the fun part when you consider tipping your barrista a buck because you feel like a hot shot. Time to poke a few holes in your bubble and bring you back to earth. Depending on how you spend your money—an easy thing to do—this won't be a complete deflation, but enough to get you to see your expenses in a new light.

In this chapter we're going to discover where your money goes, instead of, "Oh, you know, rent, groceries, stuff like that." We're going to construct a kind of cash-flow statement, something your mother would have called a household budget. For many people, the word "budget" has unhappy connotations, and why not, it's full of "oughts:"

- You ought to pay these bills sooner.
- You ought to spend less money on those silly clothes.
- You ought to save more money for a rainy day.
- You ought to marry a nice doctor. Your cousin did.

Okay, the last one isn't exactly a budget item, unless the mythical doctor is a plastic surgeon working in Beverly Hills. Then you won't need a budget.

The problem with budgets is that they often are an idyllic conception of where your money goes. Something

QUICK **n** PAINLESS

Charging the everyday expenses which you normally incur is an excellent way to simplify your bookkeeping. But this only works if you earmark money in your checking account to pay when the bills come due.

along the lines of, "I'll only spend $1 a day on lunch. It can't cost more than that." What we want is a description of where it actually goes—especially those $5-club sandwiches at the deli down the street from the office.

Getting a handle on your cash-flow—knowing where your money really goes—is the next step to getting your finances in order. Instead of scratching your head at the end of the month while staring at that $79.63 checkbook balance when your budget said it would be $700, you'll know where all of your hard-earned dollars have gone. Then you can start working on keeping those dollars from going anywhere except into furthering your goals and financial security. A wasted dollar poorly spent is one less dollar toward a secure future.

CASH-FLOW KNOW-HOW

Cash-flow? Isn't that for a business? In America, everything is a business. It's our paradigm, main chakra point, dream center, you name it. It is what we do. Even individuals who disdain capitalism and material wealth still have to figure out ways to pay the Copies 'R' Us center for printing revolutionary diatribes.

Treating yourself, and your household expenses, like a small business isn't an automatic condemnation to a life of emotional aloofness. Who knows, maybe you live in a software lab 24 hours a day and have already accomplished this. But it does take some of the emotion out of money so you can deal with it rationally instead of reacting to it impulsively.

YOU'LL THANK YOURSELF LATER

Spend less than your budget could allow. This is living under your means and a great way to save.

Think of yourself as an office manager and your money as part your yearly budget. Anything left over will be your bonus. This makes the challenge of budgeting more objective—and obtainable!

Cash-flow is simply an accounting of money in and money out. Money in includes:

- Salary
- Interest and dividend payments
- Alimony and child support
- Pensions
- Disability Payments
- Receivables (loan payments, business interest)
- Rent from investment property

Money in, as discussed in the previous chapter, is the easy part. It's easily accounted for since it normally arrives in the form of a check every other week, monthly payments, or quarterly distributions from investments. Laundromat owners dealing with sacks of quarters may have a slightly different perspective.

Money out—the often faster flowing part of cash-flow—is a little more complicated.

Pretty Soon You're Talking About Some Real Money

Think about the many and myriad places your money goes. Maybe you pick up a morning paper on the way into work along with a Danish—the pastry, not a resident of Denmark—and something to drink. You hate packing a lunch so when noon rolls around it's a sandwich, chips, and a drink. There's a book sale down the street, hardbacks 30% off, so you grab a best-seller. There's dry cleaning to pick up on the way home and groceries, too. After dinner, you start attacking that stack of monthly bills, including the orthodontist for the braces you never had as a kid but now have as an adult.

Many of these are discretionary expenses, that is, you have some control over them. You have to eat, but you can choose lentils instead of steak. Books can be checked out at the library. Dry cleaning isn't necessary if you choose clothing that can be tossed into a washing machine, although this kind of limits your ability to dress for success. The braces? As long as you can chew your food and your teeth aren't falling out, everything else is optional from a survival point of view. Socially, you might find more than a few people—vampire wannabes excluded—put off by your fangs, however.

Aside from discretionary expenses, you have involuntary—i.e., if you want to stay out of jail—costs such as taxes, maybe child or spousal support after a divorce, as well as general overhead (housing, utilities, etc.). Just be thankful you're not paying with cattle—unless you're really put off by your ex, in which case paying up with a couple of old dairy cows may be strangely satisfying.

The Mother of All Lists

The following list should include most common expenses. Hobbyist beekeepers, ceramic collectible addicts, and guys who must have a new computer every six months may have to add some additional categories.

Most people will have ongoing, fixed expenses, including:

- Credit card balance(s)
- Mortgage/rent

QUICK n' PAINLESS

Want to simplify your checking account ledger? Round off to the nearest dollar when paying bills. You'll get a slight credit on your next bill, or change back if it's your grocer, and you eliminate dealing with odd amount of cents.

- Medical
- School loans
- Automobile loans
- Other

In addition, most of us pay Uncle Sam and his various state and local relatives something as well in the form of taxes.

- Federal taxes
- Social Security
- Medicare
- State and local taxes
- Other

After the big monthly bills and taxes are paid, most everything left over is in your hands. It can either head to your favorite northern Italian restaurant or to the pasta section of your grocery store. Many of these expenses aren't really up for discussion—who isn't going to have a phone?—but you do have some control over how much each costs.

Some of these expenses include:

House Stuff

- House/rental insurance
- Real estate taxes
- Electric
- Gas
- Water, sewer, garbage

- Telephone
- Internet connection
- Cable TV
- House/yard maintenance
- Home improvement loans

Eating

- Groceries
- Fast food
- Espresso, pastries, fun food
- Meals out
- Drinks and alcohol
- Other

Cars and Getting Around

- Insurance
- Gas and oil
- Repairs
- Parking
- Bus/train/ferry passes
- License tabs renewal

Kids

- School
- Daycare
- Clothes
- Books, toys
- Dance lessons, soccer, etc.
- Other

YOU'LL THANK YOURSELF LATER

Carry a small notebook to write down easily forgotten expenses. This will give you an accurate record of your monthly costs.

Medical

- Insurance premiums
- Cash out for uncovered costs
- Alternative medicines, vitamins, etc.

Fun stuff

- Movies out
- Video rentals
- CDs, stereo upgrades
- Concerts, plays
- Sporting events
- Zoo, museums, fairs
- Skiing
- Vacations, airfares
- Software purchases
- Family outings
- Other

Clothes

- Yours
- Partner/spouse
- Kids

Miscellaneous

- Union/professional dues
- Holiday, wedding, birthday gifts
- Pet expenses, veterinary bills

IF YOU'RE SO
INCLINED

Look seriously at your need for an automobile. Car ownership is one of our single biggest expenses. Do you use it enough to justify the cost?

- Tobacco
- Newspapers, magazines, newsletters
- Hair care
- Personal care
- Therapists
- Lawyer, accountant
- Other loans
- Health club

Okay, you've done enough and you're probably wondering why you're not living in the poorhouse like a Charles Dickens character. Go out for the evening. One more fling is probably a good idea at this point.

A Closer Look

Although these categories can give you some idea of where your money goes, chances are you really can't give a thorough accounting of your money. Not many of us can. Even the most obsessive and least lazy of us rarely keep track of how much we spend on grande skim-milk decaf lattes. Here's a little exercise that takes only a few minutes of your time each day but can be a real eye-opener: For one month, carry a small notebook and jot down every cash or debit-card purchase, from the newspaper you buy at the commuter station to the last-minute birthday card you pick up on your lunch hour. There are no moral imperatives here. No one's looking over your shoulder and tsk-tsking your spendthrift ways. There's nothing wrong with skim-milk decaf lattes (except perhaps that they don't have caffeine). What you want to know is where the cash really goes.

Month up? Now you should know where all the green stuff is going. As I said 30 days ago, this isn't a

moral lesson. As far as I know, the only moral commandments concerning money are that you shouldn't steal it or try printing it at home. But as we continue with this lazy guide to finances, you'll discover that there are priorities—your priorities, that is to say your goals: The things you really want to do in life, next month, next year, 20 years from now. The quality of that later life may well be determined by your actions today. As we all have learned once we left the nest, if you want "Y," you may have to give up "X" to get it. Or at least you may have to postpone "X" for a while.

In the next few chapters we'll make use of this cash-flow statement to get your finances on firm ground. To get you in the mood, take a look at some of the categories. It's kind of like playing 20 questions with yourself. For instance, consider your mortgage:

- Am I getting the best rate?
- Are there any advantages to refinancing?
- Should I consider moving to a less expensive home?

How about those credit cards?

- How many purchases did I make this month that I forgot about until I got the monthly bill? How many were restaurant meals, now long gone?
- What is the interest rate on my card? How does it compare with my next-door neighbor's rate?
- What has been my total interest payments vs. principal this past year?

And then there's all the rest:

- Do I really need to be driving a new RX-7 with its high payments and insurance costs?

- What if I cut back my meals out to once a week instead of every other day?

- Am I taking advantage of all the tax breaks available to me?

- Does my cat really need all of those massage sessions?

The point is not to live the life of a monk. Besides, all of those monasteries have been turned into high-end condominiums. But unless you're living off of a generous, inexhaustible trust fund or are otherwise independently wealthy, every dollar matters. You know that much or you wouldn't have picked up this book.

A single dinner out at a casual restaurant runs between $10–$20. Twice a week, and you've spent more than $40–$80 a month, $520–$1,040 a year—all in after-tax dollars that aren't being invested! Double those figures if you're chivalrously courting a potential spouse and picking up the tabs. A similar amount of money invested in any number of highly appreciating stocks the past 10 years would have given you enough money to eat out at your whim. If you see yourself as a small business, you've just spent a lot of money on entertainment without bringing in any additional revenue.

But I want to have some fun, you say. What's wrong with a night of clubbing it around town? Nothing, as long as you understand the cost, both now and in your

IF YOU'RE SO
INCLINED

Look for entertainment coupon books. For a fixed price, you can buy discount coupons for many restaurants, which can cut down your dining out costs.

Remember to view your expenses in pre-tax and after-tax dollars. Your true cost will be a higher percentage of your income than you thought.

future. Once you've spent those dollars, they're gone forever. The experience remains, you say. Big ones maybe, like your honeymoon or a trip to Aspen, but try and recall a memorable meal at your local steak and beer joint.

I hate to break the news to readers under the age of 30, but unless you work in the human cannonball business, you're going to be around for a long time, like another 50 years or so. What you do today will influence how you live later. Why assume that these years are the only ones that matter? It could all end tomorrow, but it probably won't, so strike a balance. Have some fun, save some money. As certain nationally syndicated advice columnists would say, you don't need a lot of money to have fun. The fact that they probably are wealthy has no bearing whatsoever on their advice. Well, maybe a little.

NOW WHAT?

These first two chapters cover the most boring part of finances: not difficult, just tedious. It's something like shopping for and preparing Thanksgiving dinner—the fun comes in the eating. But you should have a good idea of how much money is coming in and where it's all going. This is your starting point for building your financial future, and it's where we'll pick up in the next chapter. But before you move on . . .

So far you've determined how much you're worth, monetarily, at least, and you know where your money goes. Ask yourself a few more questions based on what you've done in these first two chapters:

1. Does knowing your current net worth make you feel content or dissatisfied? Do you feel like you're making progress or spinning your wheels?

2. How about the cash going out? Does knowing how much you spend leave you panicked?

3. Do you feel in control of your finances, but think you can do better? Or have your finances never seemed so out of control?

If you've got your spending contained, if your credit card bills and other debts under control, congratulations. You're way ahead of most Americans. You can even skip the next chapter, although I don't recommend it. There's a lot of information for even the most financially astute. But if you have too much month and too little money, the next chapter will get you started in the right direction . . . the laziest way possible. Either way, relax. Managing your finances isn't that difficult. Some people manage to get by on very modest salaries their entire lives and end up millionaires when they retire. They are not magicians nor do they have anything to do with the computer industry. They are simply intelligent people who steadily invested while controlling their expenses. Pretty easy stuff for anyone.

THE LAZY WAY

Knowing where your money goes—and deciding to keep more of it on your side of the table—allows you to put time on your side. Time is the Merlin of the financial world. If you have enough of it, even modest invest-

YOU'LL THANK YOURSELF LATER

If you hold yourself to a penny-pinching budget, you may have some problems meeting your goals. Give yourself an allowance for some treats and rewards, in moderation, of course, in case your kids are watching!

ments can grow to astounding amounts. A few thousand dollars invested in Coca-Cola when it went public in 1919 and the biggest decision of the heirs these days would be which island to buy off the coast of Maine to build their next summer vacation cottage. Knowledge of your cash flow, and a growing control over it, will put you light years ahead of people who ignore it at their peril.

Getting Time and Money on Your Side

	The Old Way	**The Lazy Way**
Ignoring the principals of cash flow vs. recording and understanding where your money goes:	C'mon, there's gotta be some spare change under one of these cushions.	Sure, we can afford to buy a new couch. Our cash-flow statement says go ahead.
Treating your household expenses following the principle of whatever happens, happens, vs. running it like a business:	Looks like we've got a happening here: we're out of heating oil.	Hey, we've made a profit this month.
Attaching a lot of emotion to money vs. looking at it objectively:	I hate not having money! I love having money! Why don't I have more money?	Money isn't everything, but I have to have it to pay the bills. It isn't going to control my life.
Feeling you have no control whatsoever over your expenditures vs. cutting back voluntarily on your spending:	It's not my fault my new CD player cost $2,000. What can I do about it?	You're nuts if you think I'm going to pay more than $400 for a CD player. I don't care if the cabinet is built out of Koa wood.

First Things First

Are You Too Lazy to Read First Things First?

1 You're afraid to eliminate your debts because you'll miss your creditors' Christmas cards. ☐ yes ☐ no

2 Real investors just close their eyes and go "eenie, meenie, minie, moe" to pick an investment. ☐ yes ☐ no

3 You're too busy putting your cash into empty salsa jars so you can bury them in the back yard. ☐ yes ☐ no

Chapter three

Play Now, Pay Later

William Shakespeare—sharp dresser and suspected front man for an unknown playwright—said, "Neither a borrower or lender be." We all have the lender part down pretty well and often avoid it at all costs, especially with certain relatives. Unfortunately, the borrower part only requires a signature or two-cent piece of plastic with the word "Visa" or "MasterCard" written across it for any of us to slip into that role with a capital "B." Debt has its place. We might well be singing "God Save the Queen" and watching weird television comedies if the colonists hadn't been able to borrow a buck or two to kick the British out after throwing that tea party in Boston.

Debt isn't automatically evil. A mortgage keeps a roof over your head while you build equity in your home. A college loan will, hopefully, help give Junior well-paying career skills. A business loan can help you set up your new Dog and Cat Plaza Hotel—a hot area of business these days. A home equity loan might pay for an additional bedroom to house an elderly parent. Credit card debt to pay off last year's first-class trip to the Kentucky Derby is another matter.

QUICK n' PAINLESS

Use debt to your advantage, not for indulgences you can't pay off when the bill arrives. If a major purchase or debt isn't going to advance your wealth, you probably don't need it.

Until your debts are under control, you have little business investing. What good does it do to get a six percent return on a bond if your discretionary debt payments—read credit cards or certain installment loans—are costing you over 16 percent? It's like putting a shiny new paint job on the top side of your boat while it's flooding below from unplugged holes. Get some jaunty clothes—with your credit card, of course—and you can go down in style!

If your net worth and cash flow statements reveal a debt problem, or you just want to better manage your debts, this chapter will help pave the way.

A HOUSE OF CARDS

Jean Piaget was a Swiss developmental psychologist who viewed kids as developing in stages. He would explain (when he wasn't doing typical Swiss activities like yodeling or shopping for lederhosen) that at certain stages, children engage in egocentric behavior ("I want . . . "), which they eventually grow out of. In America, I'm afraid M. Piaget would find a massive case of arrested development.

Few of us are independently wealthy. Debt, which is a calculated risk assumed by both the borrower and the lender, allows us to acquire everything from houses to strange food dehydrators advertised on late-night television. These latter purchases are almost always paid for with a credit card—a plastic companion for just about every consumer old enough to see over a store's display counter. The problems arise when we say "I want . . . " too often and too indiscreetly.

Credit cards have almost become a necessity in modern-day commerce. Try and rent a car without one. Pay cash for an airline ticket and be prepared for a pre-flight interview by guys wearing opaque, black sunglasses and t-shirts declaring, "Anti-Terrorist Squads Never Smile." Credit cards are even used as a second form of identification.

Credit cards offer:

- Convenience
- Safety
- Some consumer protection
- Free short term use of the issuer's money

"Congratulations! Because of Your Outstanding Credit . . . "

You can't beat a credit card for convenience or safety—as long as you don't lose it! No need to carry a lot of cash. If your card is lost or stolen, your potential losses from unauthorized charges are limited. Some cards also offer some protection if an item you purchased is damaged or stolen. In addition, you may also be eligible for free rental car insurance and travel assistance. And then there's the float. Finally, get convenient monthly statements—easier than messing with a checkbook.

The float on a credit card purchase is the time between your purchase and the date the payment is due. It's free use of the card issuer's money—if you pay your bill in full every month! And therein lies the rub with credit cards.

YOU'LL THANK YOURSELF LATER

If you're trying to establish credit, department store and oil company credit cards are relatively easy to acquire. Paying these bills on time will help show your general creditworthiness.

Credit card debt is probably the most expensive debt you'll ever encounter, unless you deal with guys named Rocco who operate out of your local pool hall. How expensive? Let's run some numbers.

Take a $5,000 debt at 17.9 percent APR (annual percentage rate)—the interest you're paying the issuer—with a minimum monthly base payment of $20 with a two percent minimum payment. If you only paid off the minimum, your first monthly payment would be $100, which will decline over time, but it will take you 34 years to pay off the debt. Your interest total alone will be $12,600! That's just for the original $5,000! Keep charging concert tickets and Dockers and you'll be passing these debts off with your estate.

If you only pay the minimum amount every month, the price of whatever you buy can increase incredibly. Suddenly that bargain suit costs as much as one that's tailor-made. How do you reconcile easy credit, a voracious consumer culture, and controlling your debt load? Get lazy.

- Put your credit card repayment on automatic: Take the minimum payment on your most recent statement and pay that much this month and every month until the balance is paid, even though the minimum required payment will go down each month. Using the example above of the $5,000 balance, pay $100 every month—after all you can make that payment this month, so why not every month—and you'll cut 26 years and over $8,300 in interest from your loan.

QUICK ⬭ PAINLESS

Talk with your card issuer about eliminating the yearly maintenance fee. There are enough "free" cards around that your issuer may be willing to drop the fee instead of losing you as a customer.

- Or: Tack on whatever amount you can afford—$25, $50, $100—to the minimum payment. Again using the same example, an additional $25 per month will cut 23 years and $8,000 from your repayment schedule.

- Quit using the card(s) until your debt is paid off. You'll never retire the debt if you keep adding on purchases.

There's nothing lazy about scrambling to pay an ever-increasing credit card debt or watching that debt grow month by month. This is more like indentured servitude—of your own making! You can simplify your financial life, and free up a lot of cash for other purposes, by following these tips for wise credit card use.

- Limit the number of cards you sign up for. One all purpose card like Visa or MasterCard should take care of most of your purchases, even gasoline and groceries.

- If you have more than one card, pay off the highest interest rate card first while maintaining minimum payments for the other card(s).

- Reduce your interest rate by either (1) negotiating with your card issuer for a lower rate, or (2) switching to another issuer. Compare rates by checking newspapers and financial magazines. Computer users can find up-to-date card rates at www.bankrate.com or www.ramresearch, as well as any unsolicited offers you receive in the mail. Check your rates regularly and switch your balance whenever it's to your advantage.

A COMPLETE WASTE OF TIME

The 3 Worst Ways to Handle Credit Card Debt:

1. Only pay the minimum amount due.

2. Run up your spending to your credit limit.

3. Hold multiple credit cards and spend on all of them.

■ Don't shop unless you really need to. Shopping as entertainment and using a credit card as your admission ticket is a lot of work. Stay home and read a book instead.

Think of it this way: is it simpler to figure out how to pay for those unused roller blades you just had to have or think first before buying them. Do you want to advance your own financial future or that of the retailers at the mall?

Controlling discretionary spending should provide some automatic debt control. What if you're in too deep? Maybe you took all of those unsolicited offers in the mail to heart and thought, "I must be doing great! Look at the credit lines these complete strangers are offering me. No need to insult Corn Huskers Savings and Loan in Omaha after they went to all the trouble to send me a personalized invitation to sign up for a gold MasterCard." Now you're looking at a huge monthly bill, maybe as big as your parents' first mortgage—or even your first home mortgage!

If you're really overextended on your credit cards, you can:

■ Take out a tax deductible home equity loan

■ Consider borrowing against your 401(k)

■ Try and renegotiate your debt with your card issuer

Borrowing against your home or retirement accounts can be a risky strategy if you continue unchecked spend-

YOU'LL THANK YOURSELF LATER

When you switch credit card accounts, be sure to close your old account(s) out. Too many open credit lines can hurt your credit rating.

ing with your credit cards. Recent studies show that more than half the homeowners who take out home equity loans to consolidate credit card debt end up charging new card debt up to the same levels as before. So although the numbers may tell you that it makes financial sense to borrow against your home or retirement account to rid yourself of credit card debt, for all but the most disciplined borrowers—and if you were disciplined, you probably wouldn't have run up that debt in the first place—the best and simplest plan is simply to bite the bullet and pay off the card debt by making additional payments each month.

If your credit card debt seems overwhelming, and the solutions above seem too little, too late, consider these alternatives:

- Debt Counselors of America (800-680-3328, www.dca.org) can help you work with your credit card issuer to help you set up repayment schedules.

- Debtors Anonymous (see local listings), like other 12-step programs, recognizes that chronic credit card abuse may be a deeper problem that requires long-term treatment.

If your debt problem is serious but manageable, consider tearing up your credit cards. Some people take credit card destruction to certain creative heights by fusing them together with propane torches, or melting them in the oven on a piece of aluminum foil. Hole punchers work well, too.

IF YOU'RE SO
INCLINED

Extreme credit card debt can be paid off with a home equity loan or by borrowing against your 401(k). These are exceptional measures and should be taken only after careful consideration.

Read your credit card agreement carefully! Avoid cards that use a two-cycle method for determining your monthly balance as this is the most expensive approach.

Remember, credit card issuers make most of their money from your interest payments. It behooves them—and beguiles you—to have you stretch out your payments. It's almost like a second mortgage, but at a much higher interest rate. But if you are disciplined enough to pay off your balance monthly, then go ahead and charge as many of your normal purchases (e.g., groceries, drug store items, dry cleaning) as possible. Writing one check at the end of the month—while using the issuer's money interest-free—is a very lazy way to handle your monthly bills! And some cards offer rebates or frequent flier miles to make this use even more attractive.

Credit card issuers are in the business to make money and recently some of them have not taken kindly to customers who pay off their bills without carrying a balance. One in particular—no names, please—rewards your good financial management with a $25 a year fee if you don't incur any interest charges. If your issuer decides to follow suit, find someone else. One thing the world does not lack is new credit card issuers.

CUTE DOLLHOUSE, ONLY $400,000, BRING PAINTBRUSH

A home mortgage is probably the biggest loan you'll ever take out—unless you really have a thing for Rembrandts. It's also some of the cheapest money available. A mortgage is a loan against a very bankable asset: your home. It gives the bank or mortgage company something they can grab if you're unable to pay and they have to foreclose—an action they have little interest in doing—which can be to your advantage should you have to renegotiate the terms of your loan due to, shall we say, income-challenged circumstances.

Mortgage debt—and a home purchase—make sense for most people if:

- The real estate market is appreciating and is likely to do so in the immediate future (never a sure thing)

- The down payment is low, allowing you to control an expensive asset with little money out of pocket

- You'll stay in your new home long enough to recover your purchase and estimated sales costs, as well as the cost of any home improvements

Once you've decided that home ownership is for you you'll have to decide on the type of mortgage and the amount of the loan that you can comfortably live with. The rule of thumb calls for a mortgage payment not to exceed 28 percent of your monthly income and total debts, including your mortgage payment, not to exceed 36 percent of your income. Does this rule of thumb fit your financial profile? If you accepted these percentage limits, would you:

- Have enough money left over every month for savings and retirement?

- Be able to adequately pay for any emergencies that might arise?

- Be emotionally comfortable with that debt level?

Just because the bank says you can borrow it—and is willing to loan it to you—doesn't mean it's such a hot idea to take them up on the offer.

IF YOU'RE SO
INCLINED

Consider carrying two all purpose cards: (1) a no-fee card (regardless of the interest rate) for purchases you'll pay off immediately, and (2) a low-interest card for emergencies that may require more time to pay off.

Lots-O-Loans

There are numerous loan programs to choose from. Mortgage brokers have access to many lenders and can shop around to find you the best loan for your circumstances. The mortgage business is very competitive; what you're mainly buying from brokers is service with a smile. You can always go down the street to someone with a bigger smile who has access to the same lenders.

The mortgage payment isn't the only debt you take on when you buy a home. Home purchases come with fees (those pesky closing costs), property taxes, and improvements. Window coverings, shower curtains, rugs—even this small stuff starts adding up! If you have to borrow to pay for it, your debt increases and you can find your budget has become a financial free-for-all.

Can you lessen the blow from your new home, sweet home? It's as easy as reading the Sunday paper

1. Periodically, the Sunday real estate section runs a comparative table of local mortgage rates. Check for the low interest lenders.

2. Talk with a mortgage broker who may have more resources.

3. Compare the closing costs and fees, as well as the interest rates.

4. Compare adjustable rate mortgages (ARMs), 15-year, and 30-year programs for the one best suited to you and your budget.

QUICK 🅝 PAINLESS

Discuss your mortgage questions with a mortgage provider well in advance of actually needing a mortgage. This will help determine what you can realistically afford. If you're getting ready to buy, go ahead and get pre-qualified for your loan.

5. Calculate any advantage of a larger down payment—up to 20 percent—over a smaller one of three to five percent.

    If possible—and if the cost is to your advantage—roll some of the fees into the loan itself.

As you build equity in your home, you can take advantage of it in the form of a home equity loan, but be careful! Bet wrong when you borrow against your home and you may relive the joys of renting a studio apartment as you did in your college days. On the other hand, judicious use of a home equity loan has some advantages, such as:

- Interest is generally tax deductible.
- Interest rates are lower than many other types of loans.
- If taken out as a line of credit, it can be a ready emergency fund.

Some financial advisors recommend paying a home mortgage off early. How? By sending in additional principal payments every month or by taking out a 15-year loan. Just as with credit card debt, years and thousands of dollars in interest can be cut over the life of the loan by paying it off early. Other advisors think the guys recommending this are old fuddy-duddies who think the next Great Depression is always just around the corner.

YOU'LL THANK YOURSELF LATER

Prequalification for a mortgage can be a big help if you have to quickly put an offer down on a house. This often happens in a hot real estate market so you want to be prepared.

It's an easy strategy to carry out, and may make sense if you expect to stay in your home for years and years. Roughly speaking, if you double the principal payment every month, you eliminate one future payment from the loan. Think of it this way: a thirty year loan has 360 payments. Double up on the principal with your first monthly payment and say adios to payment number 360. It's not quite that exact, but you get the idea—and the interest savings is tremendous. Home security is yours that much sooner. Are there drawbacks? Of course, including:

- You have a lot of equity, or cash, tied up in an asset that may not be appreciating as fast as it would if invested elsewhere for a higher rate of return.
- Few people actually stay in one house long enough to make paying it off worthwhile.
- Your mortgage interest rate is comparatively cheap—and it's tax deductible.

In the end, this is a personal decision. If you're more comfortable owning a mortgage-free house sooner rather than later, then follow the advice of the fuddy-duddies—after all, they've seen hard times, which is a perspective many people today don't have.

HOT WHEELS AND A COUPON PAYMENT BOOK

Americans' love affair with the automobile often becomes the stuff of self-help personal psychology books, that is, a dysfunctional, abusive relationship. We buy cars that:

1. Are bigger than we need.

2. Go faster than every legal speed limit in the country.

3. Are usually unaffordable without loans or leases.

You want to cut down your automobile-related debt? Simple. Sell the BMW and buy a used Honda. Simpler yet, don't buy the BMW, at least not until your new software program is bought out by Microsoft and you're suddenly rich. Letting your car become an ego extension is an expensive proposition.

Think twice before leasing! To make a valid comparison between leasing and buying, you'll have to compare:

- Total up-front cost.
- Total costs at the end of the loan term and lease.
- The lost interest or investment value of your down payment for a purchased car or acquisition costs and security deposit on a leased car.
- The value of the car to you at the end of the loan/lease.

The last one is easy: nothing if you've leased it, something if you've purchased it. If you must take out a loan to buy a car, consider a home equity loan, which at least has some tax advantages.

ALL IN THE FAMILY

Personal loans between family members or friends can have big emotional costs associated with them unless all

IF YOU'RE SO
INCLINED

Carefully consider the value in paying off your mortgage early. You'll save thousands of dollars in interest, but tie up a lot of cash in a non-liquid asset. It may be worth doing for the comfort factor, however.

parties involved treat them the same as they would a bank loan. Well, this holds true unless the borrower regularly reneges with their bank and the lender regularly brings it up over Thanksgiving dinner.

If you take out a personal loan with a family member or friend:

- Spell out all the terms—amount, interest rate, and payback period—in writing.
- Sign a promissory note.
- Treat the loan as seriously as any commercially obtained loan.

If you're on good terms with your family and friends, stay that way if you borrow money from them. Pay your loan back on time and according to agreed upon terms. These loans are debts just like any other.

SCHOOL DAYS

With the exception of certain espresso-and-junk-food-fueled Internet start-up company executives who skipped college, a post-secondary degree is usually the ticket to higher earnings and more choices in occupations. But it doesn't come cheap, even if you go to state universities. College takes money and, for most people, loans. This falls under the category of good debt.

There are entire books and websites (see Resources) dedicated to financing a two- or four-year degree. If you're going to be financing your own or someone else's education through loans, it will effect your credit rating—how much you'll be able to borrow for, say, a home

YOU'LL THANK YOURSELF LATER

Keep any loans between family members strictly impersonal and businesslike. If you're borrowing the money, sign a loan agreement and pay it back on time. If you're the lender, the loan is between you and the borrower so don't mention it to anyone else.

or a car. If it comes down to a new car or college, skip the fancy wheels and get the degree. You can always buy a car.

YOU CAN'T DO THIS WITH SOCIAL SECURITY

One peculiarity of 401(k) retirement plans is the option of borrowing against them. Taking money out of a retirement plan goes against the idea of the fund, which is to put aside tax-deferred money, leave it alone, and let it grow and increase until you need it in your retirement years. Best to consider this only in the case of a real emergency so you don't shortchange your future.

Loans against a 401(k) are normally at lower rates than other types of personal loans, but there are some caveats associated with them:

- If you leave your job before the loan is repaid, it falls due immediately. If you cannot repay in full, it is considered by the IRS to be a premature withdrawal on which taxes are due—along with a 10% penalty.

- Money taken out of the account doesn't grow or benefit from long-term investing until it's paid back.

- You can jeopardize your retirement if the loan isn't repaid.

A loan against your 401(k) isn't exactly an attack on mom and apple pie, but just be sure to pay it back as quickly as possible. The same goes for borrowing against your life insurance policy. Do it if you have to, but reinstate your full coverage as soon as possible.

IF YOU'RE SO
INCLINED

You can ease the pinch of student loans. Sallie Mae offers those Stafford Loan borrowers who make timely payments over their first two to four years up to a two-percentage point reduction in rates. Call your lender about similar incentive programs.

MARGINAL MARGINS

Buying securities—mainly stocks—on margin is like having a line of credit in a casino. Everything is great while you're winning, but when the cards decide you're not worthy of "21" at the blackjack tables, you have to pay up.

Margin buying is based on the stock brokerage firm loaning you money to buy securities, usually 50 percent of the value of stocks. If you want $10,000 worth of YippeeKiAy.com, you only have to put up $5,000 to buy on margin. The broker puts up the rest, charging you interest, of course. You can control a large block of stock and only put up half of its purchase value with your own cash. If the stock increases in value, you can make a tidy profit since you only put up half the money!

The downside raises its ugly head if the stock drops. Remember, you still owe that other $5,000. Not only that, if the stock drops enough, you can be subject to a margin call. Your friendly broker wants to be sure you maintain a minimum maintenance or security balance in the account. You may have to cough up the money a lot sooner than you expected—especially since you believed YippeeKiAy.com was going to take off big time. And you still owe interest on the money you borrowed!

Unless you're a very sophisticated investor and are prepared to take some losses, keep margin debt out of your life. This is suppose to be easy, not ridiculous!

YOU'LL THANK YOURSELF LATER

Loans taken out against 401(k) accounts are like home equity loans: only to be considered if absolutely necessary. Weigh all the pros and cons before borrowing against your retirement account.

THE LAZY WAY

Debt has its place and that place is under your control, not the other way around. Debt that advances you along in life—i.e., home mortgage and school loans—should definitely be considered and researched for the best deals. Home equity loans have a limited place, as well, but keep in mind you are exposing your home to risk. Credit card debt should be kept to a minimum, especially if you cannot pay off the balance in full at each billing. Paying off your credit card bills every month should become as automatic as paying your rent or mortgage.

Loans against your 401(k) and life insurance policy should be considered emergency loans or very short-term loans. You don't want to lose sight of the purpose of either your life insurance policy or your retirement investments by diluting them with loans.

Borrowing money on margin to buy equities can be very iffy. If you want to gamble that badly, consider getting a penny ante poker game together with your friends. It's a lot cheaper and usually good for a few laughs.

YOU'LL THANK YOURSELF LATER

Forget about buying stocks on margin. Even experienced traders take losses doing this. This is anything but lazy investing.

Getting Time and Money on Your Side

	The Old Way	The Lazy Way
Incurring debt up to your eyeballs vs. controlling your spending and limiting it to what you can afford:	Man, my eyes are killing me.	I can see clearly now the pain is gone.
Borrowing against your 401(k) to pay for your new nuclear-powered, oversize barbecue vs. paying cash for a standard, charcoal-powered Weber:	So I have to work until I'm 75. Look at this grill!	Early retirement looks closer all the time.
Taking out a seven-year loan for a sports utility vehicle you'll never take off the road vs. a two-year loan for a used Toyota:	Well, you never know when I might run into a really deep pothole.	After investing the money I saved I'll be looking at a Porsche when I retire.
Paying minimum payments toward credit card debt vs. larger payments to pay off the bill sooner:	Hey, I finally paid off the Christmas '75 bills.	Hey, I paid off the bills from last Christmas.
Buying stocks on margin vs. paying cash:	Now I know why they call this margin buying— it's been very marginal.	This seminar pushes margin buying. This guy must think I'm really stupid.

Building a Nest Egg Without Going Into Labor

After many banks closed around the country during the Great Depression, the federal government established the FDIC (Federal Deposit Insurance Corporation) as kind of a massive public anti-depressant. A good number of people, including my wife's grandfather, had continued misgivings about the safety of banks. They placed some of their money in jars and cans and buried them in their backyards. Texas soil and its various subterranean inhabitants did not treat these newly placed vaults kindly and much of Grampy's money disintegrated to the point of being unrecognizable. Just as well; he couldn't remember where much of it was anyway. His sons found some of the errant jars years later when Grampy got around to mentioning them. A digging frenzy failed to find all of the forgotten jars. But Grampy had the right idea: he put some money away for a rainy day—even if the rain did rust out his jar tops.

QUICK ⟨n⟩ PAINLESS

Your very first step to securing your financial future—after paring down your debt—is to put aside funds for unexpected use, those times when you may have little or no income, and especially for emergencies. But I can always borrow, you say. What if you're out of work for three months? Loans usually have to be paid back on a monthly basis, unless they come from an indulgent uncle. Who's going to loan you any money if you have no income?

Human beings need some degree of security. That's why we have social conventions, commerce, and buy really offensive car alarms—especially the ones that talk to you, warning that you're too close to the car. Money figuratively in the bank—once, literally, your only real option—will help provide that security and allow you to get on with your investing. (By the way, if you have one of those talking car alarms you can quit wondering why your fenders keep getting kicked in by irate passersby.)

A PENNY HERE, A PENNY THERE

How much should you put aside? What's the worst case scenario? Many advisors suggest putting aside three to six months' living expenses. You may believe this is excessive, that you're immune to economic downturns because you're a hot Java programmer or nail artist who can always find work.

Nothing is as certain as uncertainty. Consider:

- You could be struck with a severe illness—or struck by a bus—and out of work for an extended period of time.

- Family circumstances could cause you to take an unpaid leave of absence from work for months.

- In the ever-changing world of technology, today's hot prospect software or programming language could be tomorrow's also-ran (Remember IBM's OS2?).

- Downsizing occurs in all industries.

Capitalism isn't all that forgiving and doesn't focus much on individual circumstances. It's pretty much a sink-or-swim attitude. You're on your own, so listen to the Boy Scouts—be prepared!

Do You Feel Lucky?

Accidents, layoffs, and family troubles can happen to anyone. An emergency fund allows you and your family to carry on and deal with the disruption without worrying about paying the bills. Leave your assumptions of invincibility at the door and start putting some dollars aside.

Okay, you're convinced. Where does the money come from? Take a look at your cash-flow statement. Every discretionary expense can be squeezed to wring out some savings.

- A fast-food lunch can run around $3.50–$4.50, a deli lunch $5–$7 or more. A lunch from leftovers or food already at home might cost you $1.50, a possible $2–$5.50 daily savings. That's $10–$27.50 a week.

- Same holds true for all those espressos, cookies, and muffins at the coffee shop with the cool,

YOU'LL THANK YOURSELF LATER

Calculate how much money you would actually need to get by for 3–6 months. This is the bare-bones amount you should put away. It should cover general overhead—housing, insurance, food—not entertainment, which can always be cut back.

QUICK 🔵 PAINLESS

retro-nouveau artsy name. We're a nation of coffee addicts, but at $2 a pop—plus food costs—it really adds up.

- Pay off your credit card bills. Take the monthly money you were paying and put it aside as savings. Look for a lower-rate card.

- Do you really need to replace your stereo? Hold off for a year or two and put the money aside.

- Do you drive to work? Is there a convenient bus or train available, hence eliminating parking and wear and tear on your car? Does your employer offer a subsidized bus pass?

- Check your automobile insurance deductible. Is it too high for the value of your car? A higher deductible—if appropriate—can save you some money.

- Do you really need to buy out the store every Christmas to avoid being rejected forever by your family and friends? This is an expensive fantasy; the average gift purchase per American is way beyond anything reasonable. Stick with homemade cookies and small presents. If you're rejected, find some new friends and take your cookies back. Put the money you didn't spend in the bank.

- Going to the movies? The museum? Stick to the matinees or reduced-price days.

- Do your kids really need designer clothes? Young kids won't care if you don't buy them. Besides, they'll outgrow them before you get home from the store. Stick with the basics or try some of the second-hand clothing stores for children.

Many of these suggestions won't radically alter your life or pull the rug out from under your social standing. Once you've paid off your credit cards, for instance, continuing to pay the same amount of money each month into an emergency fund will simply be life as usual. You won't even notice it—and this is the essence of *The Lazy Way*—as you secure your financial future.

DULL IS GOOD

Emergency money has to be easily accessible in safe, boring, fuddy-duddy cash-equivalent parking spots. Sometimes boring is Okay! Look where it got Al Gore. Would you rather be living in the Rocky Mountains (an area normally not associated with active volcanoes) or next to a modern-day Mt. Vesuvius? Seeing the glow of the lava rivulets every night might be very captivating until the big one comes. There's a reason land in the volcano's path on the big island of Hawaii is cheaper than beachfront lots on the Kona side of the island.

With your emergency money, the goal is not necessarily to get the highest return (higher return usually implies higher risk) as it is in getting a steady, reliable return without any loss of principal, that is, the money you're putting into the account. You can look for higher returns with your other money, but put your crisis cash aside first.

QUICK 🔘 PAINLESS

Did you get a raise or bonus recently? Bank this and continue living on your old income. This is living under your means—an excellent way to put money aside.

Aside from Fort Knox, do such secure places exist? Absolutely, and you have a number to choose from, including:

- Savings accounts
- Certificates of Deposit (CDs)
- Money market accounts/money market mutual funds
- Short-term U.S. Treasuries
- Savings Bonds

These are all money instruments that will pay a fixed interest rate, although that rate may change periodically except in the case of treasuries and CDs. Their interest rates are fixed for the length of their maturity.

You have a lot of choices, but this is an easy decision. You'll spend more time sorting through the salad dressing section of your grocery store than you will finding a place to park your cash.

A Better Version of Your Childhood Piggy Bank

When many of us were kids—all right, this is one of those inter-generation observational biases—parents, schools, and banks conspired to get us to open our first savings account. Tellers would dutifully take our allowances and crisp, new $5 bills we received from grandparents for our birthdays and then note the deposit in our bank books. Tightly clutching those passbooks, we would watch our bottom line grow at a glacial pace, invisibly affected by the two percent interest rate so generously paid by the bank.

Kids are very kinetic: the trip to the bank, physically handling the money and the passbook, and writing in the totals were all important rituals and helped establish the reality of their savings. You don't have to stand in line for a teller anymore—automatic transfer will take care of that—but one thing hasn't changed much: the interest rates. They're currently around two percent or less on savings accounts. For those nostalgically looking for the imagined simplicity of yesteryear, you don't have to look any further than passbook savings. Who wants to live with these kinds of returns?

Now that you're grown up, you have a better choice.

OFF TO THE MARKET

Imagine some androgynous banker walking down an aisle in a grocery store called The Money Market. The aisle is marked "Short-Term Debt Goodies." The banker, who is pushing an enormous cart, tosses in certificates of deposit, U.S. Treasury bills, commercial paper, borrowings from the Federal Reserve Bank, and other money products. Bagged up with a smile and taken back to the bank (or savings and loan or credit union) these goodies will become the basis for federally insured money market deposit accounts—usually referred to simply as a money market account. When you deposit your money, you're buying into this basket of goods.

The advantages of a money market account include:

- Liquidity (the money is available without penalty)
- A higher interest rate than most checking or savings accounts
- They are FDIC insured

These accounts normally require higher minimum opening deposits and balances than most savings or checking accounts. Check writing is limited. These are good, insured places to keep excess cash that you don't want to tie up in a time-sensitive investment such as a bond or CD.

Rate shopping is important because the difference between banks can be significant. As an example, in mid-1998, when the average bank was paying 2.5 percent on its money market account, Chase Manhattan Bank (800-635-7837) offered a three-tiered money market account with a minimum initial deposit of $1,000:

- 4.65% (APY—annual percentage yield) paid on balances up to $15,000
- 5.15% on balances from $15,000–$25,000
- 5.65% on balances of $25,000 or more

A thousand dollars may be more than you can commit right now, but there are alternatives. At the same time, Atlanta Internet Bank (also a member of the FDIC) advertised a 5.50 percent annual percentage yield on money market accounts with a minimum opening balance of only $100. Contact them at www.atlantabank.com/mmda.htm or 888-BKONWEB.

Another alternative to the $1,000 or more minimum is a money market mutual fund.

It May as Well Be Guaranteed

It's easy to confuse money market accounts with money market mutual funds. The latter invest in all kinds of safe debt including:

- Government securities

- Certificates of deposit

- Commercial paper (short-term, unsecured debt, usually backed by bank lines of credit)

Some money market mutual funds invest only in government debt, which is safer yet. Despite the lack of insurance against losses, these are safe funds. No money market mutual fund marketed to individuals has ever defaulted. In fact, in most brokerage accounts, any cash you have floating around is normally placed into a money market fund until you decide what to do with it. Relax, this is a good place for any cash that isn't tied up in an investment. In terms of risk, money market funds are in about the same category as your getting hit by a meteor while jogging. Besides, most meteors seem to land in Midwest cornfields, not exactly prime jogging areas, but watch out if you drive a tractor.

Unlike money market accounts, money market funds usually have more liberal check writing privileges and are designed to always be valued at $1 a share; interest is paid in the form of new fund shares. Although the interest rate changes according to market conditions, money market mutual funds will almost always beat the returns on your local bank.

How about the minimums? Some are quite reasonable.

- The Munder Funds (www.munder.com/mmmf.html) start at a $250 minimum with $50 subsequent investments.

A money market account or money market mutual account tied with an automatic withdrawal from your regular checking account will easily build up your emergency account.

The Lazy Way

- TIAA-CREF (www.tiaa-cref.org/orient.html; 800-842-2733, ext. 5509), which stands for Teachers Insurance and Annuity Association/College Retirement Equities Fund, requires a $250 minimum initial investment, but accepts $25 if you start with an automatic investment plan (that is, automatic withdrawal from your current bank account).

- Strong Funds (www.strong-funds.com; 800-359-3379) offers a No-Minimum Investment Plan that allows you to deposit as little as $50 a month through automatic withdrawal until a minimum balance is obtained. Strong requires a $2,500 minimum balance for the majority of their funds.

These automatic account builders are by far the easiest way to build up an emergency fund. Fill out the fund application (if the money is coming from your checking account, you'll be asked to send along a blank, voided check) and the money is automatically transferred in electronic bits to another part of the world—the same way your salary is probably transferred from your employer to your bank. You don't have to do anything but monitor it through your monthly statements. The money is withdrawn before you think about spending it on a night out at the latest Swedish-Peruvian fusion restaurant, but it's not disappearing from your life. It's your personal salary—something you pay yourself first-that's being put aside for future use.

Among money funds, the main difference in yield comes from expenses. The highest-yielding funds are often those that waive some or all of their fees in order

IF YOU'RE SO
INCLINED

After your emergency fund is built up, continue to put extra cash into your money market/ mutual fund account unless it's being invested elsewhere. There's no point in keeping cash in non-interest or low paying checking accounts elsewhere.

to attract investment. Take advantage of this bonus, but watch for any announcement that the fund plans to stop waiving fees. That may be a signal to switch to another fund. Both money market funds and money market mutual funds have varying check-writing policies. Some only allow three checks a month for no less than $500 per check. Investigate several accounts and compare terms and conditions before signing on the dotted line.

In This Corner, the Government . . .

Money market deposit accounts and money market mutual funds are hands down the easiest way to build up your emergency fund, or park cash in general that you don't immediately need. A personal checking account should have only enough funds to cover your monthly bills and the bank's minimum balance requirement. If you need to keep some additional money available for regular, but periodic expenses, use a checking account that pays interest. Or use the savings account portion of your checking account and transfer funds as needed. You're trying to avoid tying up any more money than necessary in low yielding bank accounts while at the same time not going beyond any check-writing limits with your money market/mutual fund account.

We've established that money market mutual funds aren't insured, but are extremely safe and sound. Insured deposits or instruments (e.g., savings accounts, Treasuries, U.S. Savings Bonds, certificates of deposit, and the previously mentioned money market deposit accounts) are also available for building your emergency fund. The FDIC covers your savings and CDs for up to

YOU'LL THANK YOURSELF LATER

Remember to subtract your automatic withdrawal from your checking account register each month—they're easy to lose track of! Do it at the beginning of each month and get it out of the way.

$100,000 per banking institution. Treasuries and savings bonds are insured without limit.

A GREAT TRADITION . . . FOR THE BANKS

Savings accounts have been around forever and are at the bottom of the barrel when it comes to paying interest.

That said, a savings account does have some advantages:

- Your cash is liquid and immediately accessible.
- It's insured up to $100,000 per banking institution.
- You can immediately add to it at any time.
- Savings accounts require lower minimum balances than money market accounts

Most banks are FDIC-insured. Be certain that yours is covered! Your total accounts in any individual category type, for instance, single name accounts or joint accounts, at any single banking institution are insured up to $100,000. If you've got that much sitting in passbook savings and checking, you're either really rich or suffer from a kind of economic agoraphobia—a fear of the financial marketplace!

There is rarely any good reason to maintain a savings account unless, as noted, it's a very short-term parking place for extra cash needed in an everyday checking account. Put this childhood memory to rest and maintain a money market/mutual fund instead.

YOU'LL THANK YOURSELF LATER

A savings account is an easy way to begin saving, but not really a long-term vehicle for your money. For young children, though, it's a good way to start the savings bug—something you'll be glad for when they're older.

CDS WITH GUARANTEES

A certificate of deposit is a bank-issued, interest-paying debt instrument. Give them the money and they'll pay you a higher rate of interest than they pay on savings accounts. Unlike a savings account, which you can freely access without any penalties, CDs have established maturity dates, i.e., the time at which you can redeem the certificate and get your original investment plus interest returned to you. If you need the money prior to the maturity date, you'll be penalized. Unless you can find a short-term CD that pays better than a money market/mutual fund, there isn't much reason to buy one. You can buy CDs:

- Direct from a local bank
- From out-of-state banks
- At brokerage houses

QUICK ⬤ *PAINLESS*

Except for very limited purposes, don't put your money in a savings account with its low interest rate—less than half of the interest of money market accounts!

You have many choices besides your local bank. Brokerage houses will also sell you CDs, looking nationwide for competitive rates, but charge a transaction fee, so do some comparison shopping. CDs are an okay place to park your money for the duration of the maturity if you really need the assurance of insurance! Before buying, compare rates with those offered by more liquid investments, such as money market accounts. Minimum deposits can start as low as $1,000.

Comparative CD rates from banks around the country can be obtained from:

- *The Wall Street Journal*
- Financial magazines

- Brokerage firms
- Internet sites such as www.bankrate.com or www.banx.com

UNCLE SAM'S MONEY STORE

Treasuries and Savings Bonds (see Chapter 13) are the most guaranteed investments you can purchase, unless you own a pawn shop. They're okay for setting aside long-term money if you absolutely insist on 100 percent security. Otherwise, if you need to redeem them before their maturity dates, you can be hit with penalties.

Another drawback—one which is true for all fixed-rate bonds—is inflation. If interest rates go up, you can be locked into a low return for the duration of the term of the bond. Conversely, if rates drop, you can be looking pretty good. Given the low interest rates we are currently experiencing, it's impossible to say when inflation, and rates, may head upward.

Given the current rates being paid by money market/ mutual funds, there is little reason to bother with government bonds for your emergency funds. Emergency money needs to be accessible and as liquid as possible—two key traits of money markets.

THE LAZY WAY: HEY, HANDS OFF THAT CASH

The whole point of an emergency fund is to have it available when you need it, not when you want to buy a new kayak or take a week's cruise to the Virgin Islands. Think of it as having a highly contagious disease that will

IF YOU'RE SO INCLINED

Buy short-term CDs (six months to two years) so you don't get locked into an interest rate and penalty risks if you have to redeem early. Long-term CDs work best at the peak of an inflationary spiral, which no one can predict.

condemn you to listening to mindless, early morning disc jockey patter 24 hours a day while you lie in a coma, unable to tell your caretakers to turn it off, if you dare touch it for an impulse purchase.

Setting up an emergency savings fund is about the simplest bit of business you'll learn about in this book, and monitoring your emergency account is just a simple. Once a year, compare your bank or money market fund's yield to other bank's or fund's to see if it's still offering a competitive rate. Otherwise, forget about this account's existence—until you have an emergency.

IF YOU'RE SO
INCLINED

In the case of a big emergency, you can always use a cash advance on your credit card. It's an expensive, but expedient, way to get cash in a hurry—just use it as a last resort.

Getting Time and Money on Your Side

	The Old Way	The Lazy Way
Commingling your emergency money with your checking account money vs. setting up a separate account:	I could swear our emergency money was in here somewhere.	I know just where my emergency fund is and I never touch it unless I absolutely have to.
Hoping some extra money presents itself to start an emergency fund vs. squeezing money out of your current expenses:	All right, I found a quarter and a dime in the dryer.	We've got a million places we can cut back. Does the dog really need a weekly manicure and facial?
Thinking that you'll never have any catastrophes or sudden changes of fortune vs. understanding that everything can change when you least expect it:	I don't need no stinkin' emergency fund.	One more merger and I'll be looking for a job. Good thing I've put away six months' expenses as a cushion.
Putting some "rainy day" money aside in a savings account vs. making regular deposits to a money market/ mutual fund:	This account is really growing. I've got $126.98— and $2.98 is interest!	At a $100 a month per deposit and over five percent interest, I'll hit my goal sooner than I thought.

Chapter five

Painlessly Planning Beyond Your Next Paycheck

Cash-flow statements. Net-worth statements. Budgets. Emergency funds. And now Goals. Slowly, you're doing something you swore you would never do: you're sounding like your parents! Worse yet, you're the object of your own admonitions. If your folks had known you'd come to this, they could have spared everyone all that nagging every time you got caught sneaking a beer with your friends. Now that you've got a better idea of where you stand, you need to figure out what you want—and then how to get it.

Goals can include anything: wealth, raising a family, home ownership, or something as simple as paying off your school loans. Retirement—or having the means to live comfortably should you choose retirement at some point—usually makes the list, too.

You may decide to fly blindly, end up in the right place at the right time, get the girl/guy/other, and be fabulously wealthy with barely a whisper of an effort. This happens to fictional characters, but not often in the real world. Hedge your bets: set a few goals and make some plans. It's easier than you think!

WE'RE NOT TALKING HOCKEY GOALS HERE

Everyone's situation is different. Marriage and home ownership, for example, may be of no interest to you. You may want to retire at 40 and spend your days sailing around the South Pacific. Money may have very little personal appeal, but unless you're going to live off the land in the Yukon and eat caribou meat, you're going to have to deal with it.

Other considerations include:

- The desire or need for additional schooling.
- The possibility of taking care of aging parents in the future.
- Planning for and caring for a family.
- Raising a disabled child who will always require a caretaker.
- Career choices and mobility.

And then there's the issue of time. Where will you be, or where would you like to be, in:

- 5 years
- 10–20 years
- 20 years/retirement

IF YOU'RE SO
INCLINED

Decide which goals are primary and which are secondary, so you'll know which to concentrate on first. These will be the big ones—retirement and college funds—which should get most of your attention.

These are approximate time spans. Yours may be different, depending on your age and situation, but now is always the time to start thinking about things.

The objectives you establish don't have to be set in stone. You can move the goalposts any time you want to, but it's easier if you start out realistically and stay consistent. The idea of getting a new car every three years might turn into one every five years instead. Vacationing at a top Virgin Islands resort could morph into a week in the Florida Keys in a rented cottage. Will sending Junior to the University of Texas instead of to Harvard threaten his chances of ever getting a good job? Who knows, it may be to his benefit. He may end up with a boss who lives on barbecued chicken, talks like Ross Perot, and hates Ivy Leaguers.

Lumping all of your goals into one giant "I-want-a-house-college-funds-for-two-kids-$1.5-million-in-retirement-and-a-non-retirement-brokerage-account-and-a-townhouse-in-the-Canary-Islands" is a sure way to miss out on just about all of them. Separate, isolate, and allocate—starting with your most important goal.

College for Missy or a New BMW?

It can be a tempting decision, especially if you like German cars and fantasize about your daughter getting a full scholarship to Cal Tech after she proves Einstein was a con artist physicist. Figure out what you want and prioritize. Then go back to your cash-flow statement (while keeping anticipated future increases in salary and income in mind) and start writing up your plan.

YOU'LL THANK YOURSELF LATER

Be realistic! Set goals that will force you to stretch yourself, but not so grand that you're bound to be disappointed. If you're able to go beyond what you originally set, all the better.

Each of your goals will have a time frame attached to it. For example, you might want:

- To purchase a house within five years.
- Four years of college expenses put away within 18 years.
- Full retirement funds within 40 years.
- To pay off your car loan within two years.
- $10,000 in an emergency fund within three years.

Which is the most important to you? If you have a young family and are still renting, a home of your own may be a top priority. But the additional expense of saving and paying for a house may crimp your efforts at establishing a college fund. In an age of mergers and management changes, you may feel more secure with an emergency fund put aside, but that means you can't fund your retirement as fully as you would like to. How can you do it all?

Time Is on Your Side

If Missy is filling out her college applications as you read this paragraph, it's unlikely you'll come up with the tens of thousands of dollars needed for her schooling by the time fall semester rolls around if you're just getting started on it. You could try and invite the Sultan of Brunei over for coffee and baklava in the hope that a few dozen $1,000 bills might slip out of his pocket and end up under the cushions on your sofa, but his social calendar is probably packed. An earlier plan—hatched about the same time your daughter was hatched—would have rendered this goal a lot more obtainable. Put time—and the effect it has on investments—to work for you. Even modest amounts of money can add up to some amazing sums.

For example, you might not think saving $50 a month would amount to much. Think again! (Terms: $50 a month at eight percent return, no allowance for taxes.)

Saving $50 a month at eight percent

If you start at age:	You'll have this much by 65
25	$174,550
30	$114,694
35	$74,518

(Source: The Ayco Company L.P., Albany, New York)

Your time frame will effect how you save and invest toward your goals. Different investments—stocks, bonds, and savings accounts—have different degrees of risk over certain time periods. Before we get into that, let's discuss how your views of the future will affect your investment goals.

MADAM LAZONGA READS YOUR TEA LEAVES

Much of your investing, saving, and planning will be based on your view of the future. What do you see? What do you expect? If you think the year 2000 is going to bring about floods, armies of locusts, fried computer

YOU'LL THANK YOURSELF LATER

Let time do its job and make you wealthy at the same time. Start salting money away early—when you're in your twenties or even earlier—and rest easy about your retirement.

networks, and even more Beanie Babies, then head for Wyoming—trust me, there's plenty of room! After you build your bunker, stock up with canned goods and freeze-dried omelets and wait it out. That route is as easy as it gets; you don't have to worry about any dumb investments.

On the other hand, you may foresee a world more and more connected via the Internet and cellular phone systems, with a gradual increase in the standard of living going on everywhere. This increase brings with it more demand for soap, machinery, frozen waffles, and everything else we take for granted. Companies that provide all of this stuff-of-life will prosper, and so can you as an investor.

But the key to lazy finances and lazy investing—in fact, any investing—is accepting a simple fact: Nobody Knows. No one, not even a 90-cents-a-minute TV psychic, knows what will happen next week let alone 20 years from now. This doesn't mean that we should view ourselves as living in a huge, surreal casino, without an inkling of what will happen next as some invisible hand spins the roulette wheel. Fatalism works okay for squirrels who figure it's been a good year if they put a few acorns away for the winter. We're different, most of us anyway, in that we can look over long time periods and adjust our actions accordingly.

For instance, you know that some day you will need to make use of the services of a doctor or hospital. That's why you have medical insurance. Cloning and megavitamins aside, someday you're going to die. That's why you

YOU'LL THANK YOURSELF LATER

A big rule of investing (and one featured in advertisements for mutual funds) is that future performance can't be assured by past performance. Regardless of how you see the future—or how well an investment has done—be prepared for the some setbacks.

have life insurance and a will. (And if you don't have those things you will after you read the next few chapters.) And we also know that over the long haul, that is, when you're as old as your parents, some investments will make you more money than other investments. Disconcertingly, these same great long-term investments have a good chance of losing money over a short period of time, but that's no reason to panic and hide your money in a safe-deposit box!

(By the way, the contents of your safe-deposit box are not insured by the bank. A number of Key Bank box holders found this out recently in Seattle when robbers spent the early morning hours drilling through the reinforced concrete roof of the bank before making their way into the vault. You must insure the contents of your safe-deposit box through your own insurance company.)

By making use of this accumulated knowledge, you can establish a plan that gives you an advantage over the house odds—a sure way to prosper in an uncertain world.

Draw a Money Map

Think of saving for your financial future as a personal relationship that has its ups and downs but never involves leaving dirty towels on the floor. No arguments over vacation destinations, no putting up with a hissing cat that came with your girl/boyfriend, and no half-hour discussions over where to go for dinner. True, you can't snuggle up with your brokerage statements (although I'm sure some people do) but saving up, like any lasting

A COMPLETE WASTE OF TIME

The 3 Worst Ways to Plan for the Future:

1. Assume everything will stay the same as it is now.

2. Figure you don't have a clue and make no plans at all.

3. Expect the government to take care of you if you can't take care of yourself.

relationship, requires a regular commitment from you and more than just feigned interest when you look at your monthly brokerage statement.

The usual risk rule-of-thumb is the younger you are, the more exposure to risk you'll be able to handle. That's one reason you don't see too many seventy-somethings doing slingshot style reverse bunji jumps at state fairs, but you will see lines of twenty-somethings raring to give it a try. Riskier investments, by nature, should pay a higher rate of return than conservative investments. If you're young and you lose, you have years before retirement to make up the losses. This is certainly less true if you're 60 and have five years to retirement. At that point in your life, as tempting as Russian penny stocks may be ("Double your rubles overnight! And, we'll throw in one of those cool fur hats."), you're better off with something more reliable. This is especially true since the ruble was devalued by 34 percent the day prior to this writing.

The Market Says Come On In

With your cash-flow statements in hand, your debt under control, and your emergency fund established, you're ready to hit that street called Investment Boulevard. But which way do you go?

Pick just about any study you want and one fact seems to hold true: Ever since the first Neanderthal investment banker floated an initial public offering for the Acme Strike-'Em-Once-Flint Company, stocks have been the consistently highest paying investment available—in the long term—when compared to bonds or cash. Well, legally anyway. The guy named Big Harold who loans out $100 bills—and does all of his paperwork in a little black book—probably gets a better return than the historical 10–11 percent that stocks produce annually.

Stocks work regardless of your age, but with some caveats! Stocks, and interest rates, are like romance, presidential approval ratings, and soap bubbles: they go up, they go down, and sometimes they burst. In the long run, if history is any teacher, you will make money owning stocks. In the short run, you may not want to take the chance if you absolutely have to have the money safe and available. That's why your emergency money should go into money market funds of some kind.

Stocks give you ownership in the issuing company. You can rightfully fill up your car with Exxon gasoline and casually remark to your date how you prefer using that brand since you own part of the company. The return you get from owning stocks, sometimes called shares, comes from two components:

- Appreciation in the price of the shares
- Dividends paid on the stock

Stock prices are listed in the financial section of your newspaper (complete listings are available in papers such as *The Wall Street Journal* and *Barron's*). The prices change throughout the day based on supply and demand, which isn't necessarily rational. This is true of everything you purchase, which explains why some people will pay thousands of dollars for fake pearls once worn by Jackie Kennedy while something useful and edible like potatoes and wheat can wholesale for less than their production cost.

YOU'LL THANK YOURSELF LATER

An ancient warning that probably started with the beginnings of alchemy holds true with any investment: If it sounds too good to be true, it probably is! Don't be seduced by promises of unreal returns which are bound to be disappointing.

You buy your shares at a given price and hope to sell them at a later time—anywhere from a few hours to many years—for a higher price. The difference between your purchase price and a higher selling price is called appreciation. Unfortunately, appreciation has an evil twin called loss, the result of selling for a lower price than your purchase price. Unless you're a time-travelling investor from the future with the next 50 years of stock prices on a computer disk, some losses will be inevitable. Follow the advice in this book and you'll keep them to a minimum.

Like a Big Allowance

Large, successful companies add to your return in another way: by paying dividends. Dividends are a distribution of the company's profits (paid quarterly or annually) to its shareholders, calculated as a percentage of your share price at the time of distribution. A $50 stock paying a yearly $2.50 dividend gives you a yield of five percent. The best companies have a history of unbroken dividend payments, often with regular increases in the size of the dividend.

Dividends are paid automatically; you don't have to ask for them or do your chores first. As the payments accumulate in your account, they provide you with cash to purchase other investments, including more stock.

A small dividend or absence of a dividend, however, doesn't mean you should avoid buying stock in a particular company. Intel pays a whopping .12/share dividend and Microsoft pays nothing, but both are powerhouse corporations and have proven to be great investments.

A COMPLETE WASTE OF TIME

The 3 Worst Ways to View the Market:

1. Believing that the last 10 years' returns—which have been phenomenal—will automatically continue.

2. Trying to time the market (guess its direction and deciding whether to buy or sell).

3. Avoiding the market completely, thinking a crash is always just around the corner.

While stock shares represent ownership in a company, bonds are loans, just like the IOUs you gave your little brother when you were kids after you conned him into loaning you money. Unlike those IOUs—which he's probably still holding—bonds have very defined terms for:

- Purchase price
- Interest rate paid
- Maturity date

Bonds are issued by corporations, the federal government, and state and local governments. If you hold a bond until maturity, you know exactly how much you'll receive over the life of the bond. You'll receive:

- Regular interest payments; the rate is stated when the bond is purchased.
- Your principal back—the money you paid for the bond.

Together, these tell you the total return on your bond. but only if you hold it to maturity. If you must sell the bond prior to maturity, it can be sold on the "secondary" market. These are the listings in your newspaper's business section. There, all bets are off regarding your return. Why? Because interest rates change. If they drop lower than the rate of your bond, which is fixed until maturity, the market will pay a higher price for the bond you own. For example:

A $1,000 bond paying 10 percent will yield $100. If interest rates drop to nine percent, your bond is now

IF YOU'RE SO
INCLINED

Some brokerage firms, such as Charles Schwab, allow for automatic dividend reinvestment at no charge to the shareholder. This can be a worthwhile way to increase your share holdings.

worth closer to $1,100 (the $100 interest payment is the equivalent of $1,100 paying nine percent).

Terrific, you think, "Go bonds"—as long as interest rates drop. If rates go up, you're on the receiving end and your bond loses value. Now it's not paying enough.

$1,000 at 10 percent = $100 payment.

If interest rates go to 11 percent, your bond is now worth a little over $900 (the $100 interest payment is the equivalent of $910 paying 11 percent)

If you buy bonds with the idea of keeping them to maturity, you'll be able to plan your returns accurately. The drawback to bonds, as you can see, is locking into a long-term interest rate only to have the rates increase after you've made your purchase.

Federal government bonds (the various Treasuries listed in Chapter 13) are guaranteed, backed by the full faith of the U.S. government. The only way they're going to fail is if Disney makes a successful hostile bid for the Treasury Department and decides to issue bond holders free tickets to the Epcot Center instead of interest payments. Other bonds, including corporate and municipal, aren't guaranteed, although some of them are quite conservative and safe.

THE BIG THREE

Now you know the basic triumvirate: Stocks, bonds, and cash. Over the long term, owning stocks will make you more money than bonds, and bonds will make you more than cash. But over the short term, stocks are more

QUICK ⬤ PAINLESS

Just remember this rule: as interest rates go up, bond prices—on the secondary market—go down. Interest rates go down, prices go up. Bond prices act the opposite of interest rates.

likely to lose money (though they may very well make money) than bonds. Bonds can lose value, too, if interest rates change. Cash won't lose value, but you may have opportunity costs if you stick with cash when there are better paying long-term investments available. Short-term critical goals—usually five years or less—are often best financed more by money market/mutual funds, or maybe bonds or CDs, if you hold them to maturity. That's why you keep your emergency funds in the safest investment vehicles. If stocks tank and you lose some of your money, your five-year goal may become a 10-year goal. So much for buying that bungalow and getting away from the tango instructors renting the apartment upstairs.

Stock advocates will point out that the same amount of money put into successful stocks will usually yield a higher return than bonds. This is true except for the vexing adjective "successful." It wasn't that long ago that IBM—computer colossus of the universe—dropped from 100 to 40; the climb back didn't happen overnight. What if you had bought it right before the plunge? Peter Lynch, a.k.a. famous mega-investor for Fidelity Magellan, advocates stocks even for older investors, arguing that they can be used as a source of income as they increase in value by simply selling some of your shares. After the money he made at Fidelity, Peter isn't exactly a coupon clipper for local grocery store specials and probably doesn't have to fret too much about his investment mix.

YOU'LL THANK YOURSELF LATER

Just remember what your emergency money is for: emergencies! You can't afford to lose it or worry about getting a higher return in stocks instead of a money market. Use automatic deposit and forget about it.

SUMMING UP

You've decided to take the financial bull by the horns and face your situation. You won't be able to depend on Social Security for all of your post-career needs, so you need a retirement account. Your third landlord in a row is thinking of going condo with your building so it's time to buy or live in your car. Unless your kids are whizzes at gene splicing using everyday kitchen utensils, they probably won't get full academic scholarships to Yale. And even though you're an ace programmer, there are seventh graders who think your programming language is for babies and they can do it faster than you can anyway.

By identifying your existing conditions, you can determine your basic goals and give them a time frame. We've looked at how the three basic kinds of investments have done over time. It should be a simple matter of matching your goals to their appropriate time frame. That's what you did when you put together your emergency fund:

- You identified a need.
- You found a way to cut your expenses and systematically put money into your emergency fund.
- You chose a safe, easily accessible vehicle—a money market account—to deposit your money.
- You will regularly contribute to this account until your goal amount is reached.

Figuring out goals smacks of social planning, something Americans are always suspicious of, but you've done it anyway and the FBI hasn't swooped down to investigate you. Your next goal is to go do something fun and forget about college funds for awhile.

The Lazy Way

This approach will be no different with your other goals, including:

- Insuring your family and yourself from sudden catastrophe (covered in Chapters 6 and 7).
- Protecting your family in case of your death.
- Providing college funds for your children.
- Home purchase.
- Retirement.

By this time you're figuring you've got a lot of monthly contributions to make: retirement, college funds, house down payment, and reducing your debt! Before you throw your hands up in the air and yell at your dog, "What's the point, this is impossible!" and head for that quart of Ben and Jerry's in the freezer, relax! You've gotten this far. Just take it one step at a time.

Work the necessary monthly contributions into your budget one by one. Remember, debt reduction (from discretionary spending) should come first! It's tough to make the same percentage gain in the market that you're paying for credit purchases—about 16 percent on up. Paying off credit card debts will easily free up dollars for all those other goals hanging over your head.

Is a house down payment a strong number two? Be realistic! A modestly priced home is a more manageable first purchase than a leap right up to the dream castle level. (You can ignore this advice if you've got a fairy godmother.)

QUICK ⬭ *PAINLESS*

Contribute money regularly to your various funds— emergency, retirement, college—with automatic deposit through your checking account. You'll be less tempted to spend it if the invisible hand of electronic banking whisks it away first.

Even if a home purchase is a year or two down the road, familiarize yourself with the market. Watch price movements. You may want to consider moving to a less expensive area, even another state! If so, this will involve a major career or job change, so start planning early!

College funds? Well, if you don't have any kids, you've got one less thing on your list. Otherwise, you should figure on your little bundles of joy going off for some post-secondary education.

College funds should not take complete precedence over your own retirement funding. After all, if your kids end up with degrees in 17th-century French literature and are living with you again, you'll have some interesting literary discussions, but you'd better have something put aside for yourself. Just remember that you and your children can always take out loans for school costs—but no one's going to loan you money to retire on!

Saving for all these goals doesn't have to be overwhelming! Examine your expenses, decide where you're willing and able to cut back, and save the difference. Don't want to cut anything out? Okay, then you'll need to bring in some more bucks. Do you need more training to advance your career, and therefore your income? More education may be your best investment yet, even if you need to go into debt to pay for it.

Review your goals annually. Do you need to change your time frame? Did your doctor call saying, yep, you're expecting . . . twins? As the time frame changes, you may have to change your investment approach.

Any new goals? Have your horizons broadened? Maybe you're ready to leave school after three degrees and 12 years in the same dormitory. Forget those Buddhist tenets about only being able to end your suffering through meditation and righteousness in your behavior—you need a place to live!

Now you can head for the Ben and Jerry's. While you're absorbing all of that butter fat, you can think about our next chapter: insurance.

QUICK ⬭ PAINLESS

Figure out your most basic goals first, like home ownership, and start working towards it. It can be overwhelming—and self-defeating—to list 50 years worth of goals all at once.

Getting Time and Money on Your Side

	The Old Way	The Lazy Way
Muddling your way through your finances vs. making and following up on some basic plans:	Time for college already? Just when did we have kids, anyway?	We started your college fund the day we brought you home from the hospital.
Understating the time frame for a particular financial goal vs. a realistic appraisal:	You mean I gotta save for more than five years so I can retire?	A little bit every year I'm working and I'll retire in style.
Working toward the easiest goal first vs. prioritizing them:	All right, I've saved enough to see a double feature and buy a whale size tub of popcorn.	I can live with the car a few more years if it means I'll save enough to buy a condo.
Ignoring risk factors vs. calculating risk and then deciding on an investment:	Well, I thought our retirement would be okay tied up in Ukrainian government bonds.	I've broken up my portfolio into stocks, bonds, and some cash to weather all kinds of markets.
Keeping all of your retirement money in bonds when you're still young vs. stock mutual funds:	Hey, hey, looks like I'm making enough money in my 401(k) to retire at 87.	I hate these decisions. Retire to Aspen or Maui?

Part 3

Taking Your Finances to the Next Level

Are You Too Lazy to Read Taking Your Finances to the Next Level?

1 Your last name is Gates and you received this book as a gag gift.
☐ yes ☐ no

2 A former late night talk show sidekick has sent you a letter stating that you're the big sweepstakes winner. ☐ yes ☐ no

3 The aliens who just released you from captivity told you not to worry, you won't need any money when they come back for you later.
☐ yes ☐ no

Chapter six

So That's Why It's Called Insurance

A major unreleased study done by anonymous researchers and provided to me by undisclosed sources has concluded that no one on the face of the earth fully understands their insurance policies. And no one likes paying for insurance either (this isn't news). As civilization advanced, the insurance business, rightfully, came right along with it. Insurance has its place in advancing society. Just think how much happier the owners of the Leaning Tower of Pisa would have been if their builder had an insurance company to sue!

As you get older and start accumulating the stuff of life, you have more to lose—and more exposure to situations which can help you lose it. Think of insurance as a necessary evil, something like taxes, with volumes of mysterious, impenetrable regulations and clauses, but without the chilling IRS letters that start with the sentence, "We disagree with your deduction on line . . . "

Proper insurance coverage may not keep you out of harm's way, but it will keep you legal—in the states that require, for instance, automobile insurance—and a little safer from the injuries and lawsuits that might come your way. Life insurance, perhaps the most basic coverage of all, isn't required by any law, but is strongly recommended, especially if you have a family to support. It can't protect your life—living in a concrete bunker can't even fully do that—but it can help preserve much of what you've spent your life building and accumulating.

GET A LIFE

The last thing any of us think about—even after attending a funeral for someone who died unexpectedly—is life insurance. If you're twenty-something, you're indestructible! We are living longer these days, but no one's going to be around forever, claims of reincarnationists notwithstanding.

Life insurance serves two main purposes:

- It absolves any survivors from unexpected expenses due to your untimely death.
- It provides for your dependents and surviving spouse.

Providing for your dependents is the big one. If our children were some other species—okay, sometimes you might think they are another species—just about all you'd have to do is show them how to hunt and then kick them out of the family home at a relatively young age. Because we have these big cerebral cortexes and opposable thumbs, the only hunting we do is in the kitchen. The kids stick around the house until they're 18 or so, by which time they should have learned to shop, bathe themselves, and quote all the lyrics from the Smashing Pumpkins Greatest Hits CD. The benefits of life insurance will help ensure that these skills are developed and passed on if anything happens to you. Life insurance takes care of those who depend on your earned income.

Life insurance is also an odds maker's game. If you're young, in good health, and don't work in a dangerous occupation, the chances are you're going to be around for a long time. Given these circumstances, a policy can be relatively inexpensive. If you're 50, smoke two packs of unfiltered cigarettes a day, and are a human tester for new pesticides, well, let's just say your premiums will be higher.

How Much Is Enough?

Your circumstances will determine how much coverage you'll want from your policy. These circumstances include:

QUICK **n** PAINLESS

Even the most basic life insurance policy offered by your employer is better than no policy at all. This is an easy way out until you're ready to look into different coverage.

- Any dependents
- Your budget (how much can you pay for insurance)
- Debts, liabilities, and income replacement you want covered

If you're single, living alone, and want to cover your funeral costs and your Visa bill for your last trip to Cancún, a nominal policy with $25,000 coverage may be plenty. Families, especially young ones, bring along other considerations such as:

- Income replacement (yearly take–home salary times, say, 20 years)
- Mortgage or future rent costs
- Existing debts
- Children's education
- Funeral costs

Now it really starts adding up! Consider the 28-year-old tech worker breadwinner. Try these numbers on for size:

- $60,000 salary
- $160,000 mortgage
- $5,000 in existing debts
- Two children's school costs through college—don't even ask the price!
- $3,000–$5,000 funeral costs

And these figures don't account for inflation, salary increases, or a spouse's salary should anything happen to your better half. What if he or she is a stay-at-home parent? You would need a policy to cover the worst scenario:

- Single-income family, thus a monthly pre-tax income of $5,000
- House payments, including mortgage, taxes, and insurance, of approximately $1,250 per month
- Existing debt being paid off at an aggressive $200 per month

YOU'LL THANK YOURSELF LATER

Figure the worst case/ best case scenario for your life insurance policy and then decide on how much coverage you can afford—and hope your family will never need to use it!

- Food, utilities, clothing, etc. at $600+ month
- College fund contributions of $200 per month

If you really want to cover all those costs and leave your surviving spouse unburdened (except for the effects of inflation) you could need at least $1 million to cover anticipated expenses through college. A million-dollar lump sum earning six percent will provide your family with $60,000 a year without touching the principal and account for unrealized future salary increases. You can always get lower coverage—many people do given the cost—especially if a surviving spouse is working. Before you start reminiscing about your bachelor/bachelorette days in a one-bedroom apartment furnished by Pier 1 Imports, consider the different types of life insurance available and the price of the policies.

Making You Whole With the Universe

There's a life insurance policy for everybody, from daredevil, sole provider motorcycle stunt riders with 12 kids to 60-year-old, mineral-water-sipping, single librarians who walk three blocks to work in their sensible shoes. Some policies are purchased for their protective features only, and some for their presumed investment properties. It can be a little bewildering!

Life insurance is broken down into several categories:

- Term
- Whole life
- Universal life
- Variable life

A COMPLETE WASTE OF TIME

The 3 Worst Approaches to Life Insurance:

1. Drastically lacking sufficient coverage.

2. Paying for more coverage than you need when you could be investing the money elsewhere.

3. Having no coverage and having a family to support.

All of these policies can take care of any unfinished business, like paying off the house or your kids' schooling. How do they differ?

Term insurance offers protection for a specified period of time—one, 10, or 20 years or more, for example, which gives you a level or consistent yearly premium (your cost). This policy will pay a specific amount of money if you die during the term. There is no cash value built up under this policy.

Whole life is cash value insurance. It stays intact for your entire life, as long as you pay the premiums! It pays a death benefit—or the policy's face amount—which kicks in whenever you die. A cash reserve is set up by the insurance company using any earnings from the invested premiums that are above and beyond what are needed to pay the death benefits. The insurance company guarantees a portion of the cash value return.

Universal policies allow the insured to set the premium and the death benefit. This is a flexible policy whose return on accumulated cash value is tied to interest rates. There is no guaranteed return by the insurance company.

Variable life is a cash-value insurance policy whose return comes from mutual funds that the insured selects. The premiums are fixed, but the returns, or the cash value, are up to you and your choices of investment funds. The death benefit will not fall below a stated minimum amount, but if the market

QUICK ⬭ PAINLESS

Many advisors recommend term insurance for a good reason: it's a good deal for the price and doesn't tie up your money in a questionable investment vehicle. A term policy should be your first consideration when purchasing life insurance.

sinks and you picked the wrong funds, you can lose money. Always compare the cost, risk, and returns of variable life insurance with a universal life policy.

Now that life insurance is crystal clear, maybe we should have a lecture on DNA mapping! Term insurance is the simplest coverage to understand. This policy has a lower premium—a plus when your funds are tight—and affords larger death benefit for the price. Term insurance is a good choice when you need coverage for a limited period of time, say, the length of a mortgage or college costs for your kids. You want the money there if you're not around to pay these expenses. If it's no longer necessary to protect your income for your survivors—the house is paid off, the kids have flown the coop, and you've invested successfully—you should reconsider your need for any life insurance.

Insurance can be as complicated as you want it to be. For Internet information, go to http://insurance. yahoo.com/life.html and click those links! For price comparisons, head for www.Quotesmith.com, 800-556-9393. Be sure to weigh the cost of comparable policies!

Prices vary with your age, the amount of coverage you're seeking, your state of residency, and your health (or anticipated health, in the case of cigarettes). A 28-year-old non-smoker in Ohio will pay less than the same aged guy in New York. That's at least one good reason to move to the Buckeye State. He'll even pay less than a New York smoker! Quotesmith accounts for all these variables; just plug in yours and start your search. It provides numerous insurance companies' policy costs with

QUICK ⬛ PAINLESS

If you're single and have no dependents, the main reason to take out life insurance is to pay for your funeral costs and tidying up your affairs after you're gone. An inexpensive term policy should suit your purposes.

Internet price quotes can be very low, but be sure to compare with a local independent agent—referred by a friend or colleague—for more in-depth information. Then compare policy to policy.

links to the companies themselves for further information.

Renewing term insurance will be costlier to you as time goes on—after all, you're getting older! There's a better chance you won't make it to the end of the term and the company will have to pay off. Since you're only buying a death benefit, you will have to invest your money for growth and return elsewhere. On the plus side, as you age, you may have less need for term life insurance. Once your major financial commitments are out of the way (e.g., home mortgage, children's education, other debts) it may be less necessary to protect your income stream. You can invest the money spent for ever increasing insurance premiums in equities such as mutual funds.

The Whole Enchilada

A whole life policy is often used as a form of protection during an insured's income-producing years. You pay a set premium and the insurance company guarantees the death benefit and invests the earnings from the premiums into investments of its choosing. The returns are conservative and are sometimes drawn off when the insured retires. Think of it as buying insurance on the installment plan. The policy ends at age 100, at which point the cash value of the policy is expected to equal the face amount or the amount paid at the death of the insured. Make it to 100, and you get everything back.

Universal life is a little more dicey. If interest rates are high, your premiums will gain more than enough return to maintain the death benefits guaranteed by the policy. If rates drop—oops!—your premiums may have to be increased to cover the anticipated cost of the death benefit. There is a possibility that the policy could lapse if the premiums fall short.

A variable policy allows you plenty of choice for investments, but also the greatest opportunity for loss.

DECISIONS, DECISIONS

Strenuous arguments are made in favor of term insurance for its simplicity and cost. Buy a cheap policy and invest your money elsewhere. If you have a fatally toxic reaction to some wretched food like creamed corn—always a possibility and, please, no protesting letters from the Creamed Corn Lovers of America—your family is covered.

Advocates of whole life stress its dependability and cash value, kind of like savings bonds: a modest return, but secure. Besides, you never know when you might need the death benefits. They're always there, waiting in the background.

Universal life and variable universal life offer you a better return, but at greater risk.

Reading the policies may not be simple, but there are some easy ways out of the insurance maize:

1. If you're in your twenties or thirties, and your budget is tight, consider a term policy with an option to convert to a cash value policy later.

2. As the cost of renewing a term policy goes up—or if you're already in your forties or fifties and want to

YOU'LL THANK YOURSELF LATER

There are hundreds of insurance companies and a plethora of products available. Only buy life insurance that you understand and that fits into your financial plan. Insurance is not an investment; it is protection of assets and income. Look elsewhere to invest.

QUICK **n** PAINLESS

What's a quick way to get inexpensive life insurance? Through your employer! See if life insurance, or disability policies, are offered by your company. This can be an easy way to get some basic coverage. As always, check the terms and costs, especially cancellation and price increase clauses.

continue an insurance policy—look into whole life or universal life policies.

3. Don't use an insurance policy as a pension plan. Use it to prevent a loss of income to your family if you die or to pay for your funeral costs if you're single without heirs. It can also be used as part of your estate.

Your expectations will shape your insurance decisions. Term policies are good for set periods of time, but not always for true lifetime coverage. A cash-value policy such as whole life may be a better choice if you want a long-term policy, despite the higher costs in the initial years over that of a term policy. Any cash surpluses can grow tax-deferred until you cash in. If the policy is held until death, there is no income taxation on the proceeds. As part of your estate planning, an intact cash-value policy can be used to pay off estate taxes without having to liquidate other assets. This is especially true if much of the estate is tied up in property or a business.

An insurance company, like any business, can fail and getting your funds from them can be time consuming. Well-rated companies will probably be around for awhile. How do you find out their rating? Simple. Go through an insurance-rating service such as:

- A. M. Best (A++ highest rating)
- Duff & Phelps (AAA)
- Moody's (AAA)
- Standard & Poor's (AAA)

Each insurance company offers its own products so don't assume one is the same as the other among companies. A policy with a higher premium may actually be the better deal in some cases. Quotesmith shows the ratings for all the companies whose policies it quotes.

Remember, job benefits change—and you might change jobs! Either way, any life insurance coverage you have through work may discontinue. If you take to heart the Nineties notion of changing jobs a dozen times or so in your lifetime, it's a good idea to maintain a separate life insurance policy—a term policy would be easiest—in addition to a group policy at work.

First Comment About Insurance Agents

Some agents—maybe a lot of agents—may influence you to buy a life insurance product either you don't need or that is excessive for your purposes. The commissions on life insurance can be hefty, thus the motivation to sell. The role of an independent agent is to educate you, as a consumer, and guide you toward appropriate coverage. If your agent isn't doing the job, start looking for someone else.

IT'S JUST A FLESH WOUND— DISABILITY INSURANCE

In some respects, disability insurance can be more crucial than life insurance. While a disabling injury or illness can reduce or eliminate your income, it can also leave you bedridden and running up the medical-expenses meter. Not only are you not bringing home the bacon—or eggplant for you non-carnivores—you may be consuming it at a possibly alarming rate.

YOU'LL THANK YOURSELF LATER

Don't let anyone talk you into a policy you don't need. Determine your needs and gather information on different policies before singing on the dotted line.

If your employer offers optional disability insurance, consider buying a policy. It may not be the most thorough coverage compared to a private policy, but it's probably more affordable—and the payment comes right out of your paycheck with no effort on your part.

The chances are higher that you'll suffer a disabling injury, rather than die, before the age of 65. This is true for both men and women, regardless of your occupation. You can work in a rare bookstore as an appraiser and never be exposed to anything more harmful than old book dust, but that doesn't mean you can't have a disabling accident elsewhere or contract a devastating illness.

(To check out some statistics on injury vs. dying, try the calculator at www.theguardian.com/disability/chance_of_disability.html or the table at www.alldigins.com/disable.html.)

Statistics, probabilities, and the study of chance being what they are, you have to give this some perspective. What are they when compared to a more common insurance-related event, such as your house burning down or being in a major automobile accident? The parameters we choose can make for some fuzzy comparisons. The chances are greater—forgive me, UFO believers—that you'll be struck by lightning than that you'll be abducted by aliens from Neptune. Does this mean you should move to Death Valley to avoid lightening storms? Nevertheless, you need to consider disability insurance as part of your financial plan.

Disability insurance may already be part of your life through:

- Employer-provided benefits
- Workers' Compensation
- Social Security

Employer-provided benefits vary, but you should take advantage of them and understand your policy. As with a personal disability policy, you'll want to know:

- The benefit period: how long will the benefits be paid?
- The elimination period: how long do you wait before the benefits start being paid?
- How disability is defined?

Long-term disability—usually through age 65—is better than a short-term policy that covers five years or less. Injuries and illness don't follow neat time frames, so you'll want to be covered in the event of a lengthy disability. On the other hand, a short-term illness or accident may keep you out of work for less time than it takes for the benefits to start being paid. This is all about risk management and your comfort level with risk.

The elimination period is like your automobile insurance deductible: The longer you wait for your disability benefits to kick in, the less expensive your premium.

Disability can be defined as:

- The inability to perform your normal occupation.
- The inability to perform any occupation for which you possess the required skills.
- The inability to work at any occupation.

The broader the definition of disability, the greater your coverage—and the higher the cost of the premium.

YOU'LL THANK YOURSELF LATER

Unless you've got a fabulous disability policy at work, check out individual coverage. No one is immune to injury and harm, much of which happens outside of work.

Nothing Ever Happens to Me

"It"—spills, falls, bicycle collisions—happens to everyone and the costs can be devastating. A personal disability policy is more expensive than a group policy through work. Your cost will be determined by:

- Your age and occupation
- The amount of benefit the policy provides
- The elimination period
- The benefit period
- The definition of disability
- Whether the policy is noncancelable or guaranteed renewable

A noncancelable policy gives you the right to renew as long as you keep the premiums current. The insurance company cannot raise the premiums beyond the stated amounts in the policy, although they will increase them as you get older. A guaranteed renewable policy is similar, except the premiums can be increased only if the insurer raises them for every policy in the same rating class. Either of these policies is preferable to one that can be cancelled by the insurance company because they've decided your hobby of extreme skateboarding down abandoned logging roads is getting out of hand.

By now you should be convinced that disability insurance should be considered for your "To Buy" list. Now you have to figure out how much coverage to buy.

A COMPLETE WASTE OF TIME

The 3 Worst Alternatives to Disability Insurance:

1. Bankruptcy.
2. Depending on your children to support you.
3. Living off government welfare.

Well, Maybe I Can Get By on $5,000 a Week

The amount of coverage you buy will depend, in part, on its tax status. If your employer provides disability coverage, you will usually be taxed on the benefits you receive. Benefits from policies you pay for personally with after-tax dollars are tax-free when disbursed. You can have a policy that pays 60 percent of your usual pre-tax income and not feel too much of a financial pinch if you're in the 28-percent tax bracket.

You will also need to factor in:

- Your decreased costs from not working (commuting, work-related clothing, tool maintenance)

- Increased personal care costs due to disability

- Any benefits paid by Workers' Compensation, Social Security, and employer-provided insurance

Remember, Workers' Compensation only covers work-related injuries. Social Security has limited benefits, a long elimination period, and only pays if you're barely breathing and little else. (For more information, send for the free booklet, "Consumer's Guide to Disability Insurance" by writing to: Health Insurance Association of America, 555 13th Ave. NW, Washington, DC 20004-1109.)

QUICK ⬛ PAINLESS

Are you in a high-risk profession or one that involves a lot of physical labor? Could you do your job if you were injured? Are you covered by Workers Compensation? If you answered yes, no, no, you need disability insurance.

A COMPLETE WASTE OF TIME

The 3 Worst Ways to
Buy Life Insurance:

1. Not comparing prod-
   ucts and going only by
   price.

2. Buying from a com-
   pany with a sub-
   par rating.

3. Buying more than you
   need.

TO BUY OR NOT TO BUY

Simply put, disability insurance is always considering if you can get an inexpensive policy through work. If
you're a self-employed individual in a risky profession—
e.g., a roofer, deep-sea explosives expert, or maybe a
divorce lawyer—you should certainly consider buying
your own disability coverage. It won't be cheap, but
what's the cost of being laid up for months on end if you
tumble off a roof? That said, how likely is it that you'll
take a tumble if you're a safety-conscious roofer?

Life insurance, especially term, gives you more bang
for the buck and takes care of your family if you're suddenly out of the picture. You should at least have an
inexpensive term policy to take care of any bills and
funeral expenses if your chute doesn't open the next
time you try parachuting off the side of the World Trade
Center towers.

Risk management and money management go hand-
in-hand. Sufficient insurance coverage will protect your
hard-earned assets at a reasonable cost. Think of it this
way: For the price of an insurance premium, you can
ensure that life will go on in reasonable comfort for you
and your family. That's an easy investment.

Getting Time and Money on Your Side

	The Old Way	**The Lazy Way**
Thinking you'll live to be 100 and not buying life insurance coverage vs. ascertaining the risks and buying coverage:	I told him the oysters didn't look that great, but did he listen to me?	If anything happens to me, the kids are covered.
Not increasing your insurance as your income and assets move up in value vs. assessing your insurance needs on a regular basis:	My policy is fine. I bought it out of one of those machines at the grocery store a few years ago.	Whoa, I got a raise and we bought the bungalow. Better check the ol' life insurance.
Buying the first policy a door-to-door sales-person sells you vs. doing your homework and comparing policies and costs:	Hmm, according to this, I'm paying $20 every two weeks plus double over holidays and they pay off only if I get electrocuted while turning on the TV.	You want how much? Let me check out Quotesmith.
Ignoring disability coverage vs. considering and purchasing it:	I'm a professional snake handler. What's going to happen to me?	I can sleep at night now—something I can't do working as an uninsured demolition contractor.

seven

Insurance to Keep Everything Else Simple

Do an Internet web search for just about any topic—sea sponges, Nordic cuisine, Lucrezia Borgia—and usually no fewer than 600,000 possible hits show up on the screen. Try that for insurance jokes (or insurance humor, gags, quips, funnies) and the much-touted information superhighway suddenly becomes a dirt road whose signs read, "URL not found." Insurance, it seems, is simply a humorless force in our lives, always lurking in the background, ready to help put our lives back together for the price of a yearly premium. It's something like having your stern uncle—the one that always comes through when you need him—on retainer. Insurance, however, won't say, "I told you so."

Insurance isn't a perfect institution. Settlements can sometimes be slow, we may resent the monthly payments if we never make a claim, and the policies are less than thrilling to read, which makes them perfect as insomnia aids. Without insurance, however, driving a car, owning a home, and paying for health care would be far more difficult. Good insurance coverage should require nothing more from you than an occasional review and periodic payments. As simple as that.

OF COURSE IT WAS AN ANTIQUE—HOMEOWNER'S INSURANCE

Our homes are usually more valuable than our cars, but many of us pay more attention to our automobile insurance than to our homeowner's or renter's coverage. True, we can't drive our homes at 75 miles an hour and chance running into a wayward colonial crossing over the center line, but our homes still demand our attention. Weather-related damage, fires, broken pipes, and accidents don't just happen in bad movies. Why not rest easy and keep yourself covered?

Homeowner's insurance can cover:

- Damage to the property itself
- Your home's contents
- Liability
- Flood and earthquake damage

The best coverage will cover the costs of replacing your home and its contents (replacement costs), rather than only a percentage of their value. What good is a policy that will only pay for, say, 50–80 percent of the replacement cost of your home after a fire? What do you do, rebuild without a kitchen?

And don't forget your possessions! Unless you're still living with the Goodwill furniture you had in college, go for replacement cost coverage.

IF YOU'RE SO
INCLINED

If you're buying a house in the near future, the bank or mortgage company will require homeowner's insurance. Start shopping around and familiarizing yourself with different companies while you look for a mortgage.

How do you keep track of what you have? Describing your prized antique chair to an insurance adjuster can be a chore. Grab your camera and start snapping away. A picture is worth a thousand words. In this case, it can be worth a thousand dollars! Keep a written description of each item with the photos.

Photograph your rugs, paintings, jewelry, anything of substantial value—the cats don't count, at least not as much to your insurance company as they do to you. If you prefer, use a video camera and make a real production out of it. You can even have some of your friends appear as masked burglars, only to have a celebrity look-alike commentator step in and espouse the prudence of filming an inventory of your house.

Rather keep your records digitally? Try Quicken, which has a Home Inventory section. This is as easy as this kind of record keeping gets. Store one paper copy somewhere secure, like a safe-deposit box. Your inventory won't do you much good if it's in the house and you have a major fire! Storing an additional copy on disk is also a good idea. Keep additional copies around your home for regular updating.

Did you inherit your great-aunt's jewelry collection? Or maybe the family silver? You want these to be covered, too. A standard homeowner's policy usually limits how much it will pay when special items such as antiques, silver, or coin collections are stolen or damaged. Talk to your agent about additional coverage—called riders or endorsements—on anything you own that might be in question. You've had that collection of Superman comics

YOU'LL THANK YOURSELF LATER

Replacement coverage is the ultimate in hassle-free insurance, and will keep pace with inflation and rising construction costs. Shop carefully! Many insurers are now capping this coverage at 120–125 percent of the face value of your policy. Make sure you accurately estimate the value of your home and its replacement cost. Inform your agent of any remodeling you've done that can affect your home's value.

since you were a kid and you don't want to lose them now!

A Slip of the Foot

In Bugs Bunny cartoons, after Elmer Fudd has slipped down an improbably long staircase, his nemesis rabbit's usual response is, "Eh, what's up, Doc?" When a neighbor or newspaper carrier slips down your steps, the only doc involved will be the one that attaches a cast to a mangled leg. This is where homeowner's insurance steps in to pick up any medical or legal costs involved in such mishaps.

How much coverage do you need? At a minimum, consider:

- $300,000 for liability
- $200,000–$300,000 for medical

Remember, it's easier to have higher coverage than to face a lawsuit involving your own funds because you didn't have adequate insurance! Along with insurance, civilization has also brought an avalanche of litigation. Good insurance will help keep your homeownership hassle-free; just don't expect it to do your maintenance for you.

Higher coverage may cost you more, but there are some ways to reduce your rates:

- Install smoke detectors and fire extinguishers.
- Install dead bolts on all exterior doors.
- If you own an old house, upgrade the plumbing and wiring—a good idea anyway. Insurance companies like new roofs, too.

■ When buying a home, proximity to a fire department and fire hydrant can affect your rates, as can the age of your house. Newer houses are less susceptible to fires and other hazards.

It's Still Your Home

Renting dispenses with many of the headaches of home-ownership. Call the landlord/lady when something breaks, and they're stuck with the repairs, not you. Painters paint and roofers roof and you don't have to do any of the work. It's something like having parents still taking care of everything for you, except that there's that nasty rent check due every month. It could be worse—your parents could be your landlords!

You may not own the place, but you can't escape all of your adult responsibilities. Renter's insurance won't cover damages to the building itself—that's the owner's problem, unless you caused them. It will cover your possessions and your own liability if someone is injured in your home or you cause damage to someone or their property.

How much coverage do you need? That's easy: you need the same liability that you would if you owned the property. Rentals don't have invisible protecto-rays that prevent people from slipping or injuring themselves. What about the contents? Insure them for a minimum of $20,000 replacement value. That will cover all the stuff you own but never added up, such as your:

■ Computer

■ Mountain bike

YOU'LL THANK YOURSELF LATER

Even if you have roommates (who may have their own policies) you should consider your own renter's insurance. Shared housing and insurance coverage can be a sticky issue, so carry your own policy. In some cases, all tenants can carry a single, joint policy, however.

- Jewelry
- Stereo equipment
- CDs
- Rock climbing equipment

Unless you've taken a nun's vow of poverty, you've probably accumulated a lot of goodies over the years, most likely more than you think. Americans are kind of genetically programmed to shop and feather their nests. Good insurance is a good investment—it may give you your best return yet if you ever need to file a claim!

I Felt the Earth Move Under My Feet

Home insurance policies cover the normal stuff: broken pipes, slipping people on slippery sidewalks, and tree limbs crashing through the roof at two in the morning. They do not cover the extraordinary—mainly earthquakes and major flooding. These require additional coverage—and more money from you!

Theoretically, we all live in flood zones, which must be news to residents of Utah's Great Salt Lake Desert. From a flood insurance standpoint, however, a flood can be caused by storms, melting snows, hurricanes, and dam and levee failures, among other things. The National Flood Insurance Program (NFIP) is the country's primary insurance program for residential flooding. It's administered by the Federal Emergency Management Agency (FEMA) and its policies are sold through thousands of independent insurance agencies across the country, including the aforementioned Utah.

QUICK 🄝 PAINLESS

Look at the history of the area where you're living. Does it have a history of floods? Earthquakes? Decide if you're comfortable with the odds and if the expense of the policy premiums justify the coverage.

Approximately 18,500 communities across the United States participate in the NFIP as a mandatory requirement for a homeowner obtaining one of the NFIP policies. Flood insurance is mandatory if:

1. You have a federally funded or insured mortgage, and

2. Your home is located in a special flood hazard area, a.k.a. a SFHA.

Of course, this begs the question why anyone would buy a home in a SFHA, but it beats living in a CBRS—a Coastal Barrier Resources System—where flood insurance is unavailable. Average policy cost, according to FEMA, is around $300 a year per $100,000 of coverage.

Earthquakes are another exception not covered by your standard homeowner's policy. According to the National Earthquake Information Center (NEIC) every one of the 50 states has had some earthquake activity at some point. Connecticut had its big one in 1791, for instance. North Dakota, another hotbed of seismic activity, had its biggest known shakedown in 1909.

For west coast residents, earthquake insurance is more pertinent than for our midwest or east coast neighbors. The 1994 Northridge earthquake near Los Angeles caused billions of dollars in damage, resulting in private insurers either pulling out of the market or restricting the scope of their policies. The state of California itself stepped in and formed the California Earthquake Authority in order to provide earthquake coverage for state residents.

YOU'LL THANK YOURSELF LATER

Every time there is major flooding in the U.S.—especially a repeat flood in an area that has been rebuilt at least once—there are calls to reexamine NFIP, which could result in higher rates at some point in the future. Consider this when buying flood-prone land.

Moving to another part of the country? Inquire with insurance agents regarding specific natural disasters—floods, earthquakes, excessive freezing—that you may need to insure against. This information may steer you to choosing one area over another.

Currently, private companies are testing the waters again and offering policies in California. Deductibles can run anywhere from 5 to 15 percent of a home's value. Thus, the deductible on a $300,000 house can run $15,000–$45,000! Living the fun-in-the-sun California lifestyle doesn't come cheap.

The easiest solution? Move! Head over to Nevada and you'll have waterfront property when the San Andreas fault decides to rearrange itself. Short of that, if you're living in a seismically active area, you should consider earthquake insurance. It's all a matter of risk and odds. In Washington state, for instance, every passing year brings us closer to a major quake, according to the seismologist du jour interviewed by the local news. Eventually, the predictions will be true—maybe next year, maybe in 20 years, or a century or two down the road.

With adequate flood or earthquake insurance you can relax, at least until the first rumbles come or you notice the river licking the top of its banks.

WHEN CARS COLLIDE—AUTOMOBILE INSURANCE

In America, we seem more concerned with automobile insurance than we are with just about any other type of coverage. After all, Detroit has made us a nation on wheels. Cars may be dumb and expensive, but we love them anyway. Unlike other loved ones—those who talk, argue, hug, bark, and shed—cars crumble, dent, bend, split, and rupture. Lamentably, mileage standards have mandated lighter weight cars, a boon for the plastics industry, but not if you're ever in an accident.

When you go shopping for automobile insurance, you don't want bargain-basement coverage. Car prices typically start between $15,000 and $20,000—that's a lot of plastic! Your car may be a rust bucket, but the one you hit may be a set of imported hot wheels. If you're uninsured or underinsured, the other driver's company will cover the cost and then be knocking at your door with the bill.

What kind of automobile coverage should you be looking for? You should consider:

- $100,000–$300,000 bodily injury

- $100,000 property damage

- $100,000–$300,000 uninsured/underinsured motorist

- $35,000 personal injury protection

- $50,000 uninsured/underinsured property damage

- $100 deductible for comprehensive, $500 deductible for collision (you pay these amounts in the case of an accident and your insurance company pays the rest)

These amounts look big, but they can get eaten up in a hurry if you or someone else is hospitalized after an accident. And don't think $100,000 for property damage is exaggerated. A high-end BMW can run well over $75,000! Total one of those and you'll be really glad you had $100,000 worth of property damage coverage.

You want to be able to get into your car and go, without worrying about accidents, damages, and injuries—or paying for any of them! You don't want to be the underinsured motorist who hits someone's first-

YOU'LL THANK YOURSELF LATER

Think about insurance costs before you buy a car. Consult with your insurance agent about the cost of coverage for any specific car you're considering buying. You don't want any surprises after you get it home!

new-car-ever-in-their-life, a car so new it still has paper license plates in the rear window.

What do the terms and numbers mean?

- $100,000–$300,000 bodily injury pays for injuries when you are at fault ($100,000 per person; $300,000 per accident).

- $100,000 in property damage—whether you hit a car or a house—also protects you when you're at fault.

- Uninsured or underinsured coverage covers you if another driver, who doesn't have adequate insurance or any at all, hits you and is at fault. This one is really important! If an uninsured driver hits you— and you don't have this kind of coverage—you, not your insurance company, get stuck trying to sue the other driver for damages.

- Personal injury protection (PIP) coughs up some money for medical bills for you and anyone covered by your policy, regardless of who is at fault for the accident. Your policy may also pay weekly disability payments to the policy holder in the event that he or she cannot work as a result of injuries. Coverage varies from state to state, so be sure to check your policy. Surprise your friends with your newfound knowledge of your insurance policies.

I Think I'll Walk

We pay dearly for our mobility, but that doesn't mean you can't cut the insurance costs down a bit. Discounts are often available for:

IF YOU'RE SO
INCLINED

Some people use public transportation and simply rent a car when they really need one. Examine your needs, this may work for you, especially if you live in a large city. If your credit card awards airline miles, then use it to rent a car—and fly somewhere later!

- Good driving records
- Multi-car households
- Car alarms
- Airbags
- Insuring your home with the same company as your auto insurance

There are also some lifestyle choices that will affect your auto insurance costs such as:

- Where you live—coverage costs more in downtown Manhattan than in Manhattan, Kansas.
- Being a safe driver and staying that way.
- Traffic tickets; if you do get one, consider contesting it.
- Good student discount; this can make a noticeable difference with your rates (and your parents).

You may also get a discount if you're 50 or 55 years of age. Unfortunately, you will pay a premium if you're under 25 years of age. If you're willing to take a higher deduction for collision—your '82 Datsun may not even be worth $500—you can get a lower cost policy. If your car is on life support and not worth reviving from an accident, you may want to drop your collision coverage altogether and lower your cost even more.

Check the cost of carrying comprehensive only—you can carry it alone without collision—but you can't carry collision without comprehensive. Comprehensive will cover you from falling tree branches and damages from nasty car burglars who go after your radio, in other words, damage not caused by a collision. If you have to

keep your vintage clunker going for awhile, it may be worth holding onto your comprehensive coverage.

Bottom line? A one car accident—with inadequate insurance by the wrong party—and you can be paying bills for years. The easy way out is to get adequate coverage—or take the bus! This is one place you don't want to skimp.

For more information, try http://www.moneyclub.com and look at their insurance links. They even have links for the coverage mandated in individual states. If you're thinking of moving, now you'll know what you'll be getting into insurance-wise!

NEVER FELT BETTER IN MY LIFE— HEALTH INSURANCE

Every once in awhile, a representative of a group like Vegetarian Physicians on Crusade to Control Your Life and Save Cows will announce, in a press release, your premature and painful death if you even think about eating another cheeseburger. About the same time, you'll read an article about a 99-year-old former asbestos worker who attributes his long life to cigars, cheap whiskey, and nightly T-bone steak dinners. Mr. Asbestos will bring cheers from carnivores sprawled on couches and watching TV all around the country. No matter which way you live, there are no guarantees you won't have some health problems.

Health issues and medical bills can find any of us unprepared. Simply put, you need health insurance—and

QUICK **n** PAINLESS

Does your teen-age son or daughter lobby you for a car of their very own? Get a price for the additional coverage from your agent, and warn your eager new driver that the bill will come with the car. That stops the harassment every time! Better yet, mandate that you split the cost.

don't hold your breath waiting for it to be government-issued. (Canada offers it, so moving north is always an option.)

Many employers offer some form of health care coverage. Individual policies can be expensive and have sizable deductibles. If you're self-employed and single, there aren't too many easy ways around this one.

What to do? Some people, especially if they have a family, position themselves in jobs with full benefits, insufferable supervisors notwithstanding. Others seek their own coverage. The available plans are diverse and need to be addressed individually. A couple to look at as examples are:

YOU'LL THANK YOURSELF LATER

Rolling the dice every morning hoping you stay well for another day isn't the best strategy. Keep your medical bills manageable, and at the very least, enroll in a basic medical plan.

- Kaiser Permanente, a large health maintenance organization, offers (mid-1998) some plans for individuals starting at under $100 a month. Go to http://www.kaiserpermanente.org/healthplans/individuals/htm and check out the rates for various states.

- Blue Cross of California has similar rates (http://www.surenet-insurance.com/BlueCross.htm). Click onto http://www.healthinsure.com for the multi-state plans they offer.

What's the easiest way to get a quote? Go to Quotesmith, of course. Quotesmith (http://www.quotesmith.com or 800-556-9393) provides quotes from 350 insurance companies across the country.

As with any insurance product, quotes are one thing, equivalent policies are another. Be sure you're

comparing apples with apples with your health care quotes, or, deductibles with deductibles, as it were. After you have your quotes, then talk with two or three knowledgeable agents for all the particulars. You may get quoted a low price online only to find that it's only good for the first year or that it doesn't quite apply to your situation. An independent agent—to whom you're offering the possibility of a sale—will throw out questions you may not have considered. At that point, you can properly evaluate your choices.

Health insurance coverage is part of overall financial planning. Your investments can be going gangbusters, your retirement account coming along nicely, the college funds started doing well . . . and then you have health problems. Everything you've saved can disappear in a heartbeat, especially if you have trouble with your heartbeat! Once you've established your health insurance, maintaining it is simply a matter of sending in your regular payments or co-payments. It will be as automatic as a mortgage or rent payment.

DOING WHEELIES AT THE NURSING HOME—LONG TERM CARE

Long term care (LTC) is an evolving insurance product that left something to be desired when it was first introduced some years back. Although it covers ages 18–99, only those readers of this book who are old enough to remember the *Howdy Doody Show* as cutting-edge television may find LTC worth considering.

As a population, we are living longer than our ancestors. Reaching age 65 is common these days and more and more of us are living well into our eighties. Some geneticists view 150 as doable. Bully for them. They can go celebrate their 95-year-old granddaughter's birthday party in the intensive care ward. The point is, as we age, we slowly disassemble, regardless of how much yoga, jogging, and deep breathing we do. If we live long enough, we may find ourselves in an assisted living situation, whether it's occasional help at home or a full blown nursing home.

Sometimes age has nothing to do with it. A large percentage of individuals needing LTC are under 65, but suffer from AIDS, muscular sclerosis, muscular dystrophy, or post-accident trauma. Various studies, however, indicate if you make it to 65, there's a decent chance you will require some form of nursing home care from anywhere from a period less than 30 days to more than three years. This is particularly true for women, who make up a disproportionate percentage of the LTC population.

Long-term care is like any insurance policy: it's not an investment, it's an expense. It's the price you pay to protect your other investments. The price of one month in a nursing home—currently averaging over $3,000 and climbing—can cover the cost of minimal coverage depending on your age. Don't expect Medicare or Medicaid to pick up the tab, should you end up needing care. Medicaid won't kick in until you've spent your own money and have reached federal poverty levels.

The younger you are, the cheaper the LTC premiums. The longer you wait, the more you pay. This is the real party pooper of insurance policies. It's not enough we have to cover our cars, homes, life, and immediate

IF YOU'RE SO
INCLINED

Think you'll never get old? Take a look at your older relatives and your family history. This won't absolutely determine how you will age, but it may give you some incentive to consider long-term care insurance.

health, now we have to think about how we may end up spending some of those retirement years we're also saving toward.

Long-term care encompasses a number of "ifs" such as:

- If I can afford it, should I go ahead and get it just in case I need it?

- Statistics suggest I may need some nursing care. What if it isn't until the last six months of my life anyway? Why pay all of these premiums for my final days? I can pay for that out of my own money.

- If I end up needing it for any extended length of time, the premiums are cheap.

- If I wait too long, maybe I won't qualify for a policy.

Two free booklets help explain the ins and outs of LTC:

- "A Shopper's Guide to Long-Term Care Insurance," is available by writing to:

  National Association of Insurance Commissioners
  120 W. 12th Street
  Suite 1100
  Kansas City, MO 64105-1925

- The American Association of Retired Persons (www. aarp.org) offers "Before You Buy: A Guide to Long-Term Insurance" (D 12893) available by writing to:

  AARP Fulfillment
  601 E Street NW
  Washington, DC 20049

Also available on the Internet are two good sites for immediate information:

- www.mr-longtermcare.com
- www.eldernet.com

When considering a LTC policy, compare:

- Benefit amounts
- Elimination periods
- Benefit periods
- Inflation protection riders
- Guaranteed renewable feature

Buying an LTC policy at age 50 doesn't mean you're suddenly really old and decrepid and need to go shopping for a town house in your local retirement village. Like any insurance, it's a question of managing risk and protecting your assets. It's certainly worth investigating to see how it fits into your overall financial future.

BUT IT ISN'T RAINING— AN UMBRELLA POLICY

An umbrella policy offers terrific coverage at a bargain price, maybe $150–$200 for a million-dollar policy (prices vary, of course). An umbrella offers extra liability coverage for those pesky lawsuits that exceed the limits of your automobile or home insurance policies. It is highly unlikely that an insurance company would sell you an umbrella policy without your having underlying home and auto liability policies. If they were willing to do that, every wise guy consumer would just buy umbrella policies and nothing else!

QUICK n PAINLESS

Is your life improving? Are your assets increasing? Look into an umbrella policy; they're a good deal for the money.

Just think of an umbrella policy as a cheap protect-your-wealth-policy. It's one of your best insurance investments as you move up in the world.

ANOTHER WORD ABOUT AGENTS

In the minds of perhaps not a few people, insurance agents, especially life insurance agents, have all spawned from the same genetic pool that has produced late-night infomercial personal injury attorneys and carnival sideshow hustlers. Such reputations don't materialize without some justification. Nevertheless, just because you can scan the Internet for information and price quotes, or read financial advice books, doesn't mean you know enough to ask all the right questions.

A knowledgeable, ethical insurance agent can guide you through the insurance maze. Get some recommendations from your friends and colleagues and interview two or three agents. If they can't offer you any better service or prices than you can get through Quotesmith, then pursue your insurance through the latter.

AREN'T WE DONE YET?

There's always another insurance policy waiting just around the corner: mortgage insurance, credit card insurance—it pays off your credit card balance if you become permanently disabled or die—pet insurance, and malpractice for various professions. The insurance train just keeps rolling without a caboose in sight!

Before you spend any of those hard-earned dollars on insurance you never thought about buying, here are a few rules to help you through this:

1. Don't just shop for the lowest price. You're looking for quality coverage without surprises.

2. Remember why you're buying your policies: you want to be made whole again after a major loss, to be brought back as close as possible to your former condition or state.

3. Make the agent do the work! He or she is the expert and should be asking you the questions about your needs and your specific situation. If he or she doesn't, find someone else or use Quotesmith.

4. Don't buy anything you don't understand! A good agent will explain a policy to your satisfaction.

5. Keep all copies of your policy and correspondence with your insurance company.

6. If you buy from an agent, be certain that he or she is licensed. You can check your agent's status with your state Deptartment of Insurance.

7. Don't let your premiums lapse! You could lose your coverage and, in the case of cash-value life insurance, your cash investment.

8. Don't buy policies whose fees and coverage don't make any sense to you, like overlapping medical or credit card insurance. Always compare with your existing coverage and the actual utility of the policies.

9. Check Quotesmith for your insurance company's A.M. Best and Weiss ratings (the higher, the better).

YOU'LL THANK YOURSELF LATER

Price isn't everything! Inadequate coverage at a bargain price is no bargain. Be sure your policy gives you the protection you need to avoid any out-of-pocket costs to you later.

THE LAZY WAY

A big, unrealized part of your adult world is facing up to your insurance needs—the same ones mom and dad took care of while you grew up in blissful ignorance of deductibles, cash-value, and comprehensive and collision! The bottom line is that we're clumsy bipeds who, however unintentionally, damage property, have our property damaged, get sick, and eventually pass on. If there's an afterlife, we'll probably need insurance there, too. At the very least, in this life you should consider having:

- Insurance on your car(s) with a reasonable collision deductible
- Insurance on your dwelling, for liability as well as damage and theft
- Basic medical insurance
- Term life coverage—especially if you have dependents

Two policies to consider having:

- Disability insurance, especially if you're self-employed
- An umbrella policy to protect your assets if you're sued beyond the coverage of your other policies

Getting Time and Money on Your Side

	The Old Way	**The Lazy Way**
Ignoring the need for renter's insurance in a house with five roommates vs. buying a policy:	Sorry, your stuff was ripped off man, I like, don't believe in locking doors, you know? It's spiritually restrictive.	Hello, J&J Insurance? I've want to put in a claim.
Living in San Francisco and canceling your earthquake insurance vs. keeping the policy current:	You call that an earthquake? Bah, 6.3 tops. This is just cosmetic damage.	Looks like we'll be remodeling and can actually afford most of it.
Not investigating an umbrella policy vs. buying one:	Yeah, I got an umbrella policy: when it's raining, I use my umbrella.	For the cost of a couple of cheap lunches each month, I know I'm covered if anything really serious happens.
Ignoring uninsured/ underinsured driver coverage vs. taking out a $100,000–300,000 policy:	But she hit me! How am I going to collect anything from a graduate student?	My insurance company took care of everything.

Where There's a Will, There's a Lazy Way

Every once in awhile, you read about an individual—all right, it's usually a guy—who wants to be buried in his car. This inordinate attachment is hard to understand for the majority of drivers who might like their cars, but mostly use them to keep the rain off while getting from point A to point B. The only reason some individuals—guys—don't get buried in their twin-engine Cessnas is because they would have to buy a quadruple cemetery plot.

Estate planning and writing a will is even further from our minds than retirement planning, especially when we're in our twenties, unmarried, without dependents, and driving around in a cranky Ford Tempo. But no one stays young forever, except for certain comic strip characters. Along the way, most of us marry once or twice, bring a few new consumers into the world, and accumulate some wealth. Part of financial planning includes intelligently preserving your assets and dispersing them and your wealth to your heirs and beneficiaries as

Before you write a will or a trust, find out which is favored in your state of residence. Revocable trusts are not as popular as a standard will in the state of Washington, for example, which has a less cumbersome probate process than other states.

you see fit—and avoiding a tax hit. A clear plan and a legal will should do the trick automatically.

LEAVING IT ALL BEHIND

Maybe the Vikings had it right. They pushed their dear—and not so dear—departed out on a floating funeral pyre with a few goodies to take along to the next world and then split up whatever was left. Plus, they got to wear those ultra cool helmets with the horns sticking out the sides. These days, irksome laws—EPA regulations, city, county and state health regulations, and the fire marshal—disallow floating infernos and probate distributes the goods if we don't leave a will. Civilization isn't always much fun, although if you live in Wisconsin, you can wear a hat shaped like a giant wedge of cheese and not be considered peculiar.

The whole point of estate planning, even if you don't have a huge estate, is to:

- Keep your wealth and property intact for your family and beneficiaries.
- Lower your probate costs and estate taxes.
- Establish trusts to curtail these expenses.
- Name your beneficiaries.
- Name a guardian for your children.
- Assign a durable power of attorney.
- Establish your health care directives.
- State your final wishes regarding your funeral.

Not exactly the cheeriest stuff to think about, but it's far easier to do your estate planning early when you're clear-headed and in good health. Lying in a hospital bed after a motorcycle accident is not the best time to decide which beneficiaries are going to be getting the goods or who is going to raise your minor children if you're suddenly out of the picture. Even with current-day alternatives to the traditional family, the usual assumption is that two parents will be around to raise the kids until adulthood. If you're gone, estate planning will at least ease the financial burden on your surviving spouse.

The main document you'll need is a valid will. A will must:

- Be written.
- Be dated.
- Be signed and witnessed according to the law.
- Have at least one substantive clause.

Wills written on the backs of envelopes and witnessed by bartenders are valid in old westerns, but are not so easily accepted off screen. According to a study by the American College of Trust and Estate Counsel of will requirements in the 50 states and District of Columbia, as of December 1996, 28 states allowed holographic wills. Some required 2–3 witnesses to attest to the validity of the handwriting. Stick with a printed version, even if you're a calligrapher!

What will pass as a will? Well, you can write your own as long as it has:

- A date.
- A signature.
- At least two signed witnesses.

■ A substantive clause. For instance, a clause that leaves property to someone or appoints a guardian. (A clause that reads, "Nerds Rule!," doesn't count.)

Stationery or office supply store wills—which don't always make sufficient allowances for individual situations—aren't the best choice. The easy way out is to hit the software shelves. A highly lauded software program—Willmaker 6.0 by Nolo Press—is available in both Windows and Macintosh versions on CD-ROM. This program will help you:

■ Create a will

■ Write a living will (health care directive)

■ Establish your final arrangements (funeral preferences, etc.)

The program is simple: answer some questions and fill in the blanks. Willmaker leads you through the process painlessly and thoroughly. To order, go to http://www.nolo.com/item/wdg.html and follow the directions.

It can benefit you to have even a simple will reviewed by an estate attorney. It is an absolute necessity for more complicated estates.

Can I Get a Witness?

Two witnesses are required to sign your will—and they should not be your beneficiaries! It can look a little fishy if one witness to your freshly printed will—the one that disinherits the kids and leaves the mansion and $10 million in cash to the housekeeper—just happens to be the new housekeeper. It looks worse if the second witness is her fiancé. Three witnesses are required in Vermont; they may want to be extra sure you're not addled by maple syrup on the brain.

It's a good idea to have the signatures notarized. If not, the witnesses can sign a separate notarized statement later swearing that the will is valid. This way they don't have to be chased down during probate, the court process that validates the will and deals with the estate. More on probate later—you want to avoid it as much as possible!

You don't want to write a will? Fine. The courts will decide what to do with your property. If you're single and childless, your parents will get all of your stuff. Do you really want them going through all of your belongings? A basic will is simple—just do it!

Conflict Resolution

Once you start building up your wealth, a will and other documentation become more important. After you're gone, you have no control over your estate and how it's distributed. Courts don't favor psychics and spirit channelers trying to deliver your postmortem message stating, for instance, that you really don't want the twins to get hold of your IRA account.

Make your wishes clear when they're still clear to you. Talk them over with your family and other beneficiaries. If your son and daughter both want your '63 Corvette, get it settled while you're still around to discuss it. Otherwise, the one who gets it will drive by the other's house every day tooting the horn, a reminder of who you

YOU'LL THANK YOURSELF LATER

Be sure your executor and any guardians for your children know where to find a copy of your will or trust. You may want to leave a sealed copy with your executor.

If you want to disinherit any of your children, you must specifically state this in your will. Otherwise, the court can assume it was an omission and can award part of your estate to that child anyway.

liked best. You want your departure to be as stress-free as possible for your family. If anyone gives you any grief over your wishes, just offer to leave everything to the Salvation Army (not a bad idea anyway). You'd be surprised how reasonable everyone becomes! If anyone really gives you a hard time, just put a "no-contest" clause in your will. This states that anyone who challenges your will gets nothing if the challenge is unsuccessful.

Writing and updating a will helps keep your life simple. Review it every few years, especially if you have a big change of assets. As you get older, you won't have to think twice about a fair and designated distribution of your estate.

A LITTLE ADULT SUPERVISION

Kids often believe they can get along just fine without any supervising adults or parents hanging around. Just leave us some money and the number for the pizza guy, we'll be fine, they plead. As parents, there are times you're tempted to take them up on their offer and move to your own apartment, like for about 5 or 10 years. Still, if anything happens to you and your spouse—and your kids run out of money for the pizza guy—you'll need to have a guardian lined up to look after them. You'll also need someone, perhaps a different person, to look after the estate you leave to your kids and handle the finances.

As parents, the guardian you choose:

- Does not have to be a relative.

- Must be someone upon whom you both agree and someone who readily accepts the responsibility.

- Should be willing, if they decline to do so themselves, to accept someone else controlling the estate funds.

Choosing a guardian can be a big task. Take your time, discuss it between yourselves, and make your decision. As your children get older, you may decide on a different guardian. You'll score big points with your kids if you pick a pizza lover.

While you're thinking about guardians, you should also consider choosing:

- An executor.

- A trustee.

Your executor—if you don't choose one, the court will—files the necessary papers in probate court, proves that your will is valid, assembles a list of relatives, creditors, and beneficiaries to be contacted, and manages your assets during the probate process. They're a lot easier to manage if they can be found, so make your list and keep it in a readily accessible place, or better yet, with the actual executor (see "Open If I Kick Off" envelope on page 141).

A trustee manages any money or funds that you want put into a trust and then distributed to your beneficiaries. This normally is done for minor children, but you can specify this arrangement for adults or charities, as well. Professional trustees or bankers are the way to

YOU'LL THANK YOURSELF LATER

If you have a substantial estate, it might be easiest to hire an executor and trustee. Legal firms and banks can help you out and avoid family wrangling. You won't owe explanations to anyone who feels they should have gotten chosen.

go, especially if you have large trusts. Make your wishes clear—as you would any other provision in your will—and keep close relatives out of it. You don't want decisions about trusts to become personal conflicts with family members after you're gone. Discuss your decisions with those adult family members who will be affected by them so you can deal with any disagreements or turmoil while you're still around to do so.

Both executors and trustees are there to make your life easier. They ensure that your wishes, as expressed in your will and trusts, are followed through, and you don't have to worry about your collection of velvet paintings falling into the wrong hands.

GIVING IT ALL AWAY

If you're married, and you have no signed agreement to the contrary, your spouse automatically receives a percentage of your estate. In community property states, you each get half, but you're free to do whatever you want with your half. Other states give the surviving spouse one quarter to one half of your estate, regardless of the will. You can write your minor children out of your will—which would say something about your offspring and your relationship with them—although some states require that some amount of property be set aside for them if there is no surviving spouse, regardless of the decrees in your will. This is not true in Louisiana (they still follow some French legal traditions down there as well as mega-calorie meals). It is quite likely that any attempt to

YOU'LL THANK YOURSELF LATER

Be sure to name a back-up executor, trustee, and guardian in case your first choices cannot carry out these functions.

completely disinherit minor children would be met with a court challenge.

Living in sin? Sorry, neither of you has any legal right to the other's stuff unless:

- You specifically name your partner as a beneficiary in your will.
- You had joint ownership of property with a right of survivorship giving the property to the surviving partner.

There are some problems with joint ownership with a right of survivorship that you should be aware of. If one party is sued, a lien can be put against the entire property and sold to satisfy the lawsuit, even if you, as the joint owner or survivor, had nothing to do with the lawsuit! The simplest way around this is to maintain sole ownership and pass the property through your will, but this may not be feasible in some circumstances. This is one of those "consult your attorney" situations before establishing ownership.

Second (or third or fourth . . .) marriages can really complicate things. After a divorce, it's unlikely an ex-spouse could make any claims on, say, your later earnings beyond agreed upon support payments, but divorce attorneys are always ready to track across a new hunting ground. There's little that pleases an attorney more than being personally responsible for a precedent-setting case. And then there are kids—yours, hers, his, ours. Sit down with a couple of cocktails some evening—or maybe two evenings—and sort it all out. It's far simpler

A COMPLETE WASTE OF TIME

The 3 Most Careless Estate Planning Errors:

1. Not leaving a signed, updated will.

2. Ignoring expected estate tax costs.

3. Not assigning a durable power of attorney.

to do this decision making far in advance of needing it. Not that you can ever predict a time frame. Critically misread a text on harvesting wild forest mushrooms and that night's dinner salad may be your last.

NOT EXACTLY A LAWYER

Durable power of attorney gives another person, usually a spouse, legal authority to act in your behalf. Not a bad idea if you're set to spend the evening at the opera with boorish in-laws and you want someone to sit in for you. You set the rules. Your agent—the person to whom you bestow this authority—can have full power or limited power of attorney.

Once you've signed the document on the dotted line—and it's witnessed by a public notary—the power goes into effect. You can stipulate, however, that your agent cannot step in unless you're incapacitated, which is the time this power is normally used. Power of attorney ends with your death.

As if one power of attorney wasn't enough, you really need a second one, as well, this time a durable power of attorney for health care. This agent can make decisions regarding your medical care if you're incapacitated. No, they can't decide to have exploratory surgery done to you or order a face lift if you're in a coma, but you had better be nice to them just the same while you're in a non-coma state.

A durable power of attorney for health care coordinates his or her decisions with your wishes as expressed in a living will.

A what?

A living will is a notarized document that outlines the medical treatments you expect your doctors to perform—or withhold—should you become incapacitated. Many people view living wills as dictates to deny excessive measures to save a life or even provide water or nutrients to prolong a life. This is often true, but you can state just the opposite—you may want every possible measure taken to save you. Hey, you paid all those health care insurance premiums, maybe you just want your money's worth. Your agent will step in and be sure your wishes are followed should your physicians waver.

A living will is another means of simplifying life in a civilized world full of antibiotics and advanced life-prolonging medicine. The last thing you want is to be lying semi-comatose in a hospital room, unable to express your wishes to a physician to shut the machines off and call it a day. Take action now and the doctor's actions should be automatic. This also removes the burden of decision from your spouse or children, who may not be aware of or agree with your wishes. Take care of it beforehand and keep them from having to make an emotionally charged decision that no one may be happy with.

NO DEBATE—AVOID PROBATE!

Probate validates your will in a court of law. Basically, it's a kind of judicial snooping to be sure your estate is dispersed properly, your final bills are paid, and your relatives and creditors are notified that you won't be around

YOU'LL THANK YOURSELF LATER

Be sure your doctor understands your wishes should you become incapacitated. Get some medical opinions so you can better form your own. You may have some religious issues to clarify, as well, but do so while you're in good health.

for next Thanksgiving's dinner nor be personally sending any more checks to MasterCard. Probate can tie up your estate for a year or more and gets expensive—around five percent of your estate's value in some states!

Some states do allow a simplified probate process for small estates, but your best bet is to keep as many assets as possible out of the probate process. You can do this— it isn't burdensome and it's completely legal!

How do you keep property out of probate? Easy, just decrease the size of your estate! You can do this by:

- Setting up payable-on-death bank accounts.
- Establishing brokerage beneficiary brokerage accounts.
- Establishing joint ownership of property with a right of survivorship.
- Setting up various trusts.
- Giving individual cash or cash equivalent gifts of up to $10,000.
- Directly paying someone's medical or tuition bills.

These are not complicated strategies, but they must be set up properly! When you establish a trust, you transfer the ownership of various assets to the trust. Since probate deals with people—and not trusts, which are separate entities—a trust can thumb its nose at probate court.

You could write an entire book about estate planning and reducing probate. In fact, someone has! Go to http://www.nolo.com and look for the book, *Plan Your Estate* by Dennis Clifford and Cora Jordan, two estate planning attorneys. The information is good in all states except Louisiana. Apparently they just do things a little differently down in Cajun country.

The best time to start your estate planning is before your estate gets too complicated. The sooner the better! Federal estate taxes start at 37 percent on up to 55 percent—and some states charge their own estate tax! Currently, a $625,000 estate is exempt from estate taxes. This figure will hit $1,000,000 in 2006. With house prices appreciating and heavy 401(k) savings, a million-dollar estate is not out of the question for many people. Throw in a dose of inflation, and you may die wealthy whether you meant to or not.

Future Estate Tax Exemptions

1998: $625,000

1999:   650,000

2000:   675,000

2002:   700,000

2004:   850,000

2005:   950,000

2006:   1,000,000

You don't want to die a millionaire only to have Uncle Sam step in, rubbing his hands together, and saying to no one in particular, "My, my, looks we got our- selves a big, fat estate here, ripe for the pickin'."

YOU'LL THANK YOURSELF LATER

Be sure to review your will and trusts periodically as your circumstances change. You may want to add or remove beneficiaries, for example.

Grab a snack and boot up your PC or Mac. A few helpful sites include:

- http://www.laweasy.com
- http://www.nolo.com
- http://www.mtpalermo.com
- http://www.valueplan.com
- Go to your search engine and do a search on "probate," "wills," or "estate planning."

Like any other source of information, just because someone writes it with authority—and in this case, distributes it on the Internet—doesn't mean you shouldn't read it with a skeptical eye. In addition, be sure to:

- Always read multiple sources of information.
- Note that tax laws change.
- Review your plans regularly, especially as your wealth and estate change.
- Engage an attorney specializing in estate planning; they are the only ones who stay on top of this stuff!

A VOODOO CEREMONY WOULD BE NICE

Does the idea of a church ceremony give you a severe case of the heebie jeebies? Cremation turn you cold? Do you picture yourself being interred in a huge mausoleum after a high mass by the local bishop? Whatever your preference, make your wishes known in a separate document. (You can't put this in a will, which typically isn't read until after your funeral anyway.)

Include with this document—the "Open If I Kick Off" document—a list of your:

- Bank accounts
- Brokerage accounts
- Retirement, pension, and profit sharing accounts
- Insurance policies
- Names of your accountant and attorney
- Property holdings
- Outstanding loans
- Money owed to you
- Savings bonds and stock certificates
- Credit card accounts
- Location of will, trust agreements, durable power of attorney agreement, birth certificate, partnership agreements, property deeds, other pertinent documents and safe-deposit box key
- Relatives and friends to be contacted
- Location of accounts and account statements
- A deed to your cemetery plot

If you want to go one step further, write down all account numbers and any beneficiaries of those accounts. List all insurance policy numbers and expiration dates. If your children are adopted—and you never quite got around to telling them—indicate where the adoption papers are located.

If you would prefer a ready-made fill-in-the-blanks format, try *The Beneficiary Book* by Martin Kuritz. Software also available.

YOU'LL THANK YOURSELF LATER

A listing of all your assets, accounts, and location of important papers and documents will greatly simplify the execution of your estate. A little time on your part now will make it easier for your family or executor later.

Put these papers in an envelope and mark it, "Open If I Kick Off." Put it on your refrigerator—use smiley face magnets for a slightly incongruous juxtaposition—and update the contents periodically. Why the refrigerator? So it can be found immediately in case your first day of deep-sea spelunking doesn't go quite as planned. This is absolutely the easiest way to do this; let it become part of your everyday life. I've marked ours with a skull and crossbones and everyone knows where it is.

If the refrigerator bothers you, leave updated copies with a close relative and the executor of your estate. Just be sure it's someone who lives close by and is assured to be notified if anything happens to you.

GETTING BETTER? OKAY, BUT YOU'RE STILL GETTING OLDER

In theory, a regularly maintained physical structure—a house, high rise, popcorn wagon—can last indefinitely. Keep it sealed against the elements and replace any worn components, and the family homestead can still be around hundreds and hundreds of years from now, albeit with a more hip color scheme. Unfortunately, the same can't be said for living, breathing life forms.

No matter how many replacement body parts are available in the future, we're going to wear out and pass on. Some of us may have very expensive maintenance costs in our later years. That's where long-term-care insurance, or LTC, comes into the picture.

It's worth repeating the importance of LTC (covered in Chapter 7) from an estate-planning viewpoint. Statistics based on the existing elderly (turning 65 in

1990) suggest a good percentage of them will spend some time in a nursing home after turning 65. Age aside, unexpected illness or accidents can also incur LTC.

Studies—and the statistics they produce—can be a little wormy. People turning 65 in 1990 didn't have the same lives as those born in the 1950s. They had less awareness of the health effects of smoking, for instance, or problems with exposure to toxic substances on job sites. Seat belts weren't mandated until the 1960's and no one thought twice about lying out in the sun, slathered with baby oil.

Boomers, on the other hand, have jogged an untold number of miles, almost guaranteeing future joint damage. Certain recreational practices have taken their toll and will continue to do so. And who knows where all this espresso consumption will lead.

Will their need (or that of people now in their twenties) for LTC be radically different than current statistics indicate for older Americans? Do you want your accumulated wealth to go toward assisted living care or nursing home fees for you and your spouse? Currently, at $3,000–$4,000 a month, it can eat away at that 401(k) in a hurry. And who knows what future costs will be.

Long-term care can provide effective health coverage for a reasonable cost—if you buy a policy early enough. It's a lot cheaper to buy a policy at age 50 than age 75! The purpose of LTC isn't simply to provide funds to pay the nursing home, or assisted care at home, but to keep your estate intact for your family.

It's easy to say, "Hey, I'm healthy as a horse. I'm never going to end up in a home." Well, Roy Rogers' horse,

YOU'LL THANK YOURSELF LATER

Remember what insurance is for: to make things whole again after an accident or unexpected occurrence, such as a theft or death. Look at the benefits at least as much as the costs.

Trigger, was pretty healthy, too, but now he's stuffed and standing in the Roy Rogers museum. This is about risk management and keeping your estate intact, not about beating the odds, which you may well do, but do you want to chance it?

Re-read the section on LTC in Chapter 7 and then get some quotes on a policy. You want a policy with an inflation clause? What good does it do to pay $120 a day coverage when you're 50, but find out it's $300 a day when you're 85?

DIE BROKE

It's easy to die with little or no money. The trick is to do it intentionally. An article in *Worth* magazine (July/August 1995, "Die Broke") points out the advantages of spending your money now while carefully ensuring that you have sufficient funds into your old age. Why not enjoy—judiciously—everything you've worked for, ask the article's authors Stephen Pollan and Mark Levine, instead of leaving a sizable estate to your kids?

Baby boomers are looking at a potentially huge pile of money from their more frugal parents' estates. Some, including these two authors, question whether these inheritances are such a good idea. Better that the heirs stand on their own, the authors suggest, rather than expect a lot of money later to bail them out of their financial problems.

Are these guys heretics? It goes against all of our traditional notions of saving and retiring: work, save, work some more, retire, live modestly, die and leave everything to the kids. Levine and Pollan figure if you earned the money, you should enjoy it and take care of yourself. And ignore your kids? Nope, but give them a hand along the way when:

- They can really use it.
- You'll be around to enjoy the giving.
- You can see what your kids make of your generosity.

This is an easy philosophy to follow, but you've got to secure a few things for yourself first, such as:

- A continual source of income (authors suggest annuities, but there are other choices)
- Long-term-care insurance
- Disability insurance
- Major medical insurance
- Term life insurance

That looks like a lot of insurance, but other than the long-term care, it really isn't any greater than what is normally recommended.

Dying broke may not be for everyone, but a modified version is worth considering. Think about how much you'll need when you retire. A couple of million? Five million? What for? By that time, your home should be paid for, you won't have any kids to put through school, and if they haven't made it on their own by now, why feel compelled to save them with a big inheritance?

Your kids can really use the money earlier on: to buy the first house, to help with college tuition, maybe to start a business. Give them a hand then and figure your job is done. Then take yourself to lunch—in Paris! Go to

Remember, it's your money and your estate. Your first concern should be spending and distributing it as you see fit, not to support wayward relatives or children who may not be deserving of your largess. Enjoy yourself, you've earned it!

The Lazy Way

QUICK n PAINLESS

Review your estate plans
once a year. Pick an annual event—New Year's, tax
day, etc.—to do your
review. Doing it on your
birthday might be a little
dreary, however.

New Orleans for a cup of coffee. Road trip? Sure, do it in your new Mercedes. The point is, after a certain dollar amount—if you follow the principles in this book—you'll have more than you'll ever need. Don't go nuts accumulating tons of money without enjoying it.

THE LAZY WAY

You need a will. A neat, printed, witnessed, signed will. It doesn't have to be complicated if you have a modest net worth. Kids? You'll need to name a guardian. Name a backup as well in case your first choice can't take on the responsibility.

While you're still alive and kicking, make your wishes known to everyone concerned. Discuss them with your family, beneficiaries, lawyer, and physician. And don't think you can skip this because you're 22 and feel indestructible! One good tumble off that snowboard and it could be the land of the brain-dead for you. Write a living will if you want the plug pulled.

Is your desk piled high with papers, CDs, floppy disks, and computer books? That's your business, but leave a list of the important information—your accounts, insurance, debts, property—where it can easily be found (presumably not on your desk).

Finally, once you get this out of the way, forget about it! Review your plans regularly and, as your circumstances or wishes change, go back and alter all the pertinent documents. Set up your trusts so you can stay out of the evil probate court and go ahead and enjoy your money—you've earned it!

Getting Time and Money on Your Side

	The Old Way	The Lazy Way
Ignoring the need for a will vs. writing one regardless of your age:	While lying in a coma after a severe break dancing accident, but still able to hear voices, you listen as your siblings divide up your goods.	Whew! I'm glad I wrote a will. The last thing I want is for my sisters to get my mini-skirt collection.
Naming a guardian for your teen-age children without discussing your choice with them vs. hearing their wishes:	Oh, no, not Aunt Margaret and her tofu casseroles!	Yea!, Aunt Hilda, the peanut butter cookie queen!
Forgetting to establish a health care directive vs. establishing one and a durable power of attorney for health care, as well:	Amazing what medical science can do. We've kept Jimbo here on life support since 1988.	Look, I said to pull the plug if I wasn't going to come out of a comma, not when I'm going in for a routine physical.
Not discussing your wishes with potential beneficiaries vs. stating your intentions and getting feedback from all involved:	We'll fight the will in court until there's nothing left in the estate if we have to.	OK, have we got this straight? Mary gets your grandmother's diamond broach and Jack gets your mother's ballroom gowns.

Forget the Rocking Chair

Baby boomers have entered their fifties and their kids are getting really tired of reading about it. Fifty? When boomers were in college, the idea of being 50 was about as likely as their parents buying Japanese cars and eating pesto. Well, actually that has happened. Not only that, but Hondas and Toyotas are being manufactured in the Midwest and a salsa is on everyone's grocery list. Talk about your cultural/generational shenanigans.

Many of our parents and grandparents had different lives. Meat and potato diehards—thanks to dad's appetite demands, usually—they often stuck with one career and even one employer for years. Rising economic tides after World War II brought steady money so Mom could stay at home with all of her little darlings. These generations weren't, as a rule, great risk takers in the stock market, but many could depend on an acceptable retirement between a company or union pension, savings, and Social Security.

In this leaner, just-in-time era, more and more of us—boomers, Xers, boomerangers, and all other variations on generations—have responsibility for our own retirement well-being. Many companies have gotten away from traditional pension plans and now require employee participation to direct the allocation of funds in other voluntary plans, such as the 401(k). Do you want your money in this mutual fund or that one? What about putting it into the company stock? How much do you want to keep in a money market?

Like '64 Pontiac GTOs running on eight cylinders and spewing leaded gas fumes, we may never be able to return to the days of staid retirement programs that our parents and their parents knew. Don't worry, with some simple, basic planning, you'll retire in style.

FIRST THINGS FIRST

Once upon a time, retirement consisted of:

- A gold watch or the equivalent
- A goofy going-away party (at least if you were in management)
- Moving to Arizona and playing 100 rounds of golf a week on a grass golf course, actions completely at odds with a desert climate (official state motto: The Twilight Zone State)

Few boomers, or any generations following them, will be heading for the Southwest with T-shirts reading, "I'm a Big Snowbird" and "I'm with the Big Snowbird," unless snowbirding becomes retro-hip 20 years from now. They fully expect to be skiing, backpacking, mountain biking, and traveling overseas. Many anticipate working at least part time, opening a small business or assuming the nebulous title of consultant. Working income (there may be a lot of sixty-something consultants running around) aside, your retirement years will be funded by:

- Your savings
- Social Security
- Your retirement funds

Your savings will be all the taxable accounts you'll have put together over the years—not the easiest way to put away retirement dollars. Social Security? I don't think it will be bankrupt as some pessimists predict, but the pay-out terms may change by the time you start drawing out of it. No one knows. For instance, the minimum retirement age to receive full benefits might be raised.

Your real retirement income will come from your own planning. You've already started laying the groundwork by:

- Writing up a financial statement.
- Shaving your debt, especially debt from discretionary spending; this money can be better spent by investing, particularly for your retirement.
- You figured out your goals, and one of them was retirement; now you can see how to accomplish it.
- Your estate planning is in order, or at least in process, and you're beefing up your emergency fund.

YOU'LL THANK YOURSELF LATER

Be conservative regarding your retirement income. Figure a minimum payment from Social Security and be pleasantly surprised if you get more.

What's next? Pumping those tax-deferred dollars into a retirement plan. The toughest part? Taking the first step. Get beyond that, and saving for retirement will become part of your everyday routine.

SO MANY PLANS, JUST ENOUGH TIME

Your first investment dollars should go into a retirement fund, plain and simple. Why? Because the longer the money can ferment and multiply in a tax-deferred account, the frothier the return when you need it later. We're all living longer than ever now (a mixed blessing), easily into our eighties. What are you going to live on if you stop working in your late sixties or early seventies? What if you want to work, but are no longer able due to health or family circumstances? Start early, invest consistently, and you can ignore these questions.

How much difference can time make? A lot. There have been some examples floating around in financial advice articles lately comparing two women—it's always women, which may be a hint, gentlemen—who start socking away retirement money. In one example (by Ken Kurson, *Worth* magazine), with which I'll take some literary license, a woman we'll call Prudent Peggy puts $1,000 a year away for 10 years and then stops, changes her name to Isadora, and runs off to Paris to write really bad poetry that even the French can't understand. Meanwhile, her money is earning 10 percent interest, compounded annually. Compound interest—interest paid on principal and the interest itself—is more

YOU'LL THANK YOURSELF LATER

Put time on your side! The sooner you start putting money away the longer it has time to multiply. Missing out on even 10 years—starting in your thirties instead of your twenties—-can have a huge impact!

awesome than extreme snowboarding in the Himalayas, as this example will show.

Peggy's friend, Not-So-Prudent Natalie, doesn't start her retirement account until 10 years after Peggy, that is, when Peggy stops contributing. She puts away $1,000 a year for twenty years. Thirty years after Peggy, now Isadora, started her account, her $10,000 is worth $170,000 while Natalie's $20,000 is worth $134,000. Natalie will never catch up with Peggy/Isadora. In another 10 years, Peggy will have $280,000. Natalie would have to put away $1,500 a year for 30 years to equal Peggy's 10 years of contributions of $1,000 a year.

A thousand dollars a year is doable for just about everyone; think what two or three thousand will yield! The key is consistent contributions and leaving the money alone. The really dramatic results come in later years when the numbers jump and your money starts cloning itself. On top of that, the dollar you invest now is the same as 72 cents after taxes (28 percent tax bracket). Sure, you'll pay the taxes later, but meanwhile, for the years your account is open, you'll be getting tax-deferred returns. Despite the size and scope of the United States Tax Code, the IRS doesn't offer too much good cheer to taxpayers. Tax-deferred retirement accounts are their version of Christmas eggnog, so drink heartily and then go back for seconds.

WARNING: BAD IDEAS AHEAD

Before we get into choices among retirement vehicles, we should mention some questionable retirement ideas such as:

IF YOU'RE SO
INCLINED

Run some calculations with different retirement contributions over varying lengths of time. This will give you an idea what your minimum contributions should be to a retirement account.

Putting away a hundred dollars a month shouldn't call for much sacrifice. It's a little more than $3 a day—and that can be worth thousands years down the road.

- Accessing the equity in your home
- Expecting an inheritance
- Depending on the sale of your business

There Are Liquids and There Are Solids

Your home is your home first and an investment second! Even if you own it free and clear by the time you retire and plan on selling it, then what? You have to live somewhere and renting or buying again, even a cheaper house, costs money. House prices in your area may be depressed or they may stagnate when you decide to sell. Think of the profit from selling your house as an easy bonus, but not retirement funding!

Depending on an inheritance, even if it looks to be a substantial one, is not a retirement strategy! It could be easy money or no money at all. Intentions change, the deceased may write you out of the will, before they cease, that is. Poor estate planning can result in huge taxes that can eat away at any money or property you thought you would be receiving. Forget about inheritances and be pleasantly surprised if you receive one, as long as it's not Dad's collection of mounted sea bass and bowling trophies.

A business, like a house, is not very liquid; it can't be easily converted into cash. You could be going gangbusters now and be in a shambles when you reach retirement. Increased competition could prevent you from charging the price you expected to receive. Despite your best intentions and efforts, the business may not be the hot asset you think it will be so many years down the road. There's nothing to this one. Run the business well, but keep a retirement account going, too!

HOW MUCH IS ENOUGH?

It's been said you can never be too rich or too thin, which summons up visions of an undernourished millionaire trading equities 18 hours a day, eyes glued to six computer screens, monitoring currency trades all over the world. Unless you envision a retirement in a guarded executive mansion in Florida, complete with the requisite yacht and Rolls-Royce, your financial needs may be a bit more modest.

How much will you need? How much do you need now? Do you expect any changes when you retire?

Well, you can expect some big changes when you retire:

- Your home will probably be paid off.
- Children's college costs should be finished.
- You will want to be able to live comfortably without earning a salary.
- You may want to spend more on travel or recreational activity than you did during your working years.
- There's a good possibility you'll live well into your eighties.

Financial advisors recommend figuring on anywhere from 60–80 percent of your preretirement income to maintain the lifestyle you've become accustomed to, or

YOU'LL THANK YOURSELF LATER

Don't get weird with your retirement investments! They have to be aggressive enough to grow so they'll provide for you, but not so risky that you can lose money! This isn't the place for undercapitalized, flighty $2 stocks.

IF YOU'RE SO
INCLINED

Investigate several of the Internet calculators for your retirement plans. Calculators have different assumptions built in and you must take these into account when using them.

more if you want to become accustomed to a different life. The amount of savings you will need—and the amount of money you will have to put away now—depend on a number of factors, such as:

- Your current salary and expenses
- Your tax rate and anticipated rate of inflation
- Any expected decrease in your living expenses
- The number of years until your retirement
- The size of your taxable and tax-deferred accounts
- The rate of return on your investments

There's a certain amount of guesswork involved. What if inflation is seven percent instead of four percent? You may retire during extraordinarily prosperous times and get an unexpected rate of return on your investments. The simple way to pencil out various scenarios is to use one of the retirement calculators available on the Internet including:

- www.troweprice.com/retirement/retire.html
- www.quicken.com/retirement/planner
- http://majestic.vanguard.com/RRC/DA

These calculators allow you to figure a variety of values—inflation, taxes, returns—effortlessly and quickly.

Retirement planning material is also available from many employers via 401(k) plan administrators, which leads us to fun places to easily squirrel your retirement money away.

HAVE WE GOT A PLAN FOR YOU

There are plenty of real plans you can depend on for retirement and they're yours for the taking.

- 401(k)
- IRA (several types)
- Keogh
- Pension funds
- Annuities

With this many retirement vehicles to choose from, you should be well covered when you decide to say good-bye to corporate America and go bass fishing and build up your own collection of mounted fish—just like Dad.

NO, 401(K) IS NOT A BREAKFAST CEREAL

Actually, 401(k), which is a tax-deferred, personal pension plan for employees, refers to a section of the IRS code. This is one section of the code you can really warm up to, unlike, say, depreciation schedules for lima bean farmers. The 401(k), established in 1981, has become the retirement plan of choice for many working Americans. You make your contributions and choose among various mutual funds and company stock, if available, to invest your money.

Why is the 401(k) so hot?

- Your contributions and earnings are tax-deferred and can be automatically deducted from your salary.

YOU'LL THANK YOURSELF LATER

Assume that longevity will be on your side. You don't want to underfund your retirement and spend all of your money because you didn't think you'd make it to the age of 90.

YOU'LL THANK YOURSELF LATER

Make the largest contributions you can afford to your retirement account. You're going to be living off this some years down the road so don't cut yourself short.

■ You decide on the amount of your contribution.

■ Many employers will match a percentage of your contribution.

■ You decide how your money is invested within the funds offered by the plan.

■ You can personally contribute up to $10,000 a year; with employer matching funds, the total can be $30,000 or 25 percent of your salary, whichever is less.

■ Your contributions are protected by the Employee Retirement Income Security Act (ERISA) and are invested within a trust account.

■ If necessary, you can borrow from your 401(k).

What more could you ask for? A 401(k) is available through work, you can pay for it with pre-tax dollars through payroll deductions, and your employer may match part of your contributions. Even small contributions add up, so don't feel like your not measuring up because you can't make the maximum contribution. A lot of Americans—some figures claim up to 50% of eligible workers—don't participate in retirement plans at all! Fill out the paperwork and you'll never look back.

Contributing to a 401(k) is an effortless activity: you just use payroll deduction. The company bookkeeper hits the keyboard and your monthly contribution sprints off through cyberspace until it puts on the brakes and hops into your retirement account. You never see the money, so there's no chance of your spending it on a weekend at a bed-and-breakfast in the Berkshires. It's safely put away as it should be.

Regular contributions allow you to take advantage of a much-touted principle of investing: dollar-cost averaging. Also called the constant dollar plan, the *Dictionary of Finance and Investment Terms* defines it as: " . . . method of accumulating assets by investing a fixed amount of dollars in securities at set intervals. The investor buys more shares when the price is low and fewer shares when the price is high; the overall price is lower than it would be if a constant number of shares were bought at set intervals."

In other words, since the market goes up over the long term, you'll buy more shares each month or contribution period at a low price and fewer shares at higher prices when you dollar-cost average, which usually results in a lower average cost per share. By contributing the same amount each month to your 401(k), you take advantage of low-cost investing while building up the value of your account.

You Can Take This Job and . . .

A 401(k) is like modern Americans—it's highly mobile. If you change employers, you can rollover—this is the movement of funds from one investment to another—your account into either:

- A new 401(k)

- A rollover or conduit Individual Retirement Account (IRA)

A COMPLETE WASTE OF TIME

The 3 Worst Approaches to Take with a 401(k):

1. Not contributing at least up to your employer's match.

2. Investing too conservatively.

3. Constantly switching among funds.

You can take all of your contributions, but you may not be able to rollover your employer's matching contributions. This will depend on the terms of your vesting schedule—the rules by which an employee earns the right to own these employer contributions. Vesting is generally determined by your length of employment. Be sure to check your company's requirements.

As automatic and advantageous the 401(k) appears to be as a retirement strategy, there are some caveats associated with it.

- You must decide the investment choices for your account; your employer is constrained from providing anymore than basic information on the investments available within the account.
- Your money is secure within a trust, but the account can still lose value depending on your investment decisions and market conditions.
- Your company's 401(k) program may only offer limited investment options.
- Borrowing against your 401(k) can be problematic if you have trouble paying the money back.

Pick Your Poison

401(k) plans normally offer a range of investment choices including:

- Company stock
- Fixed-income instruments
- Mutual funds—both bonds and stocks

Your choices within that range are far more limited than the market at large, which offers thousands of

YOU'LL THANK YOURSELF LATER

If you plan to roll over your 401(k) money into an IRA or another employer's plan, make sure the money is transferred directly to the new custodian. If you receive the money yourself, even with the intention of rolling it over, your employer is required by law to deduct 20 percent for income taxes.

mutual funds. The Boeing Company (mid-1998), for example, offers an unusually large choice of several index funds, a bond market index fund, small companies fund, science and technology fund, value fund, and growth fund. The funds available in your 401(k) may not always be the best performers available. Consequently, you'll have to monitor them regularly through your monthly statements and consider moving your money into different selections within your 401(k) for a better return.

How do you pick? Asset allocation (see chapter 11) is the not-so-difficult notion of spreading your risk by not putting all your money eggs in one investment basket. Different segments of the market—large company stocks, foreign stock, bonds, etc.—perform differently at different times. No single segment is the top performer at all times. By spreading your risk among different parts of the market, you have a better chance for consistent growth than by sticking with only one type of investment. It's like your diet: Eating pasta Alfredo three times a day will take care of your carbohydrate and fat needs, more than take care of them, actually. But you'll be short on protein, vitamins, roughage, all the other nutrients needed to grow strong instead of portly and ravaged with scurvy.

Like your diet, your asset allocation will change with age. Try and eat like you did as a teenager when you're past 40 and you'll be looking at weekly Weight Watcher meetings. Put your money into low-yielding bonds when you're 25—and keep it there until you retire—and the

QUICK ⬛ PAINLESS

A diversified portfolio, regularly contributed to, gives you a straight shot to an easy retirement. Contribute monthly and reap the rewards later.

windfall you were expecting will turn into one huge shortfall. Stocks, in the long run, which is the time frame we're talking about with a retirement account, will outperform both bonds and cash, despite their periodic volatility. The younger you are, as a rule, the heavier you want to be invested in stocks. You'll have plenty years in front of you to make up for any losses that can occur.

I Want My Money

You can start 401(k) withdrawals at the age of $59\frac{1}{2}$, but no later than age $70\frac{1}{2}$, although you can delay beginning withdrawals past age $70\frac{1}{2}$ if you are still working for the employer with whom you have the plan. These withdrawals are subject to taxes. After all, the tax on contributions and earnings has been allowed to grow tax-deferred. Check your plan's loan eligibility requirements should you need to borrow from your 401(k). Repayment, including interest on the amount borrowed, will be done through payroll deduction. Even though you're borrowing from and repaying yourself, you're also losing out on growth within the account. Think twice before shaking money out of your 401(k) piggy bank.

A Couple of More Numbers

A 403(b) is similar to a 401(k) except it's set up for employees of schools, nonprofit organizations, and hospitals.

A SIMPLE-401(k), or Savings Incentive Match Plan for Employees, is available to businesses with fewer than 100 employees. It's a somewhat scaled down version of a regular 401(k) in that:

- An employee must earn at least $5,000 in compensation; the plan limited to $6,000 in employee contributions.

- Employer matching, which cannot exceed $6,000, is limited to three percent of the employee's salary.

- Alternatively, an employer can contribute two percent of each eligible employee's salary—up to $160,000, adjusted for inflation—into the 401(k) regardless of whether the employee makes any contributions; in other words, the employer will fund the account up to $3,200 whether you do or not.

- Eligibility requires the employee to be at least 21 years of age and employed for one year with the company.

- The employer contributions are fully vested at all times.

A SIMPLE-401(k) is a less complex version of a standard 401(k). As with any 401(k), it must offer at least three investment alternatives (usually a stock, bond, and money market fund) with different degrees of risk and possible returns. As with any employer retirement plan, you should beware of:

- High management fees (well-managed no-load funds should charge under one percent)

- Investments in real estate, art, gems, or too much in the company's own stock.

- Possible abuse of the fund by company management.

QUICK 🪙 *PAINLESS*

Matching employer contributions give you an immediate return on your money. Twenty-five cents on the dollar gives you a 25 percent return during the year of contribution, a big advantage over other retirement plans.

If a retirement plan is important to you, then use it as a criterion for your employment. All things being equal, consider an employer who offers a 401(k) or other program.

There are always precautions to take when investing your money, but don't let them stop you from taking that first step and starting your retirement account. Your own sense of prudence will see you through. You don't like your employer's 401(k)? Fine, you have other options—exercise them! And what if your employer doesn't offer a 401(k) program or other retirement account? In that case, there's an IRA for just about everyone.

GIVE ME AN "I," GIVE ME AN "R," GIVE ME . . .

Individual Retirement Accounts (IRAs) are the original retirement accounts for taxpayers large and small. They're simple. The maximum contribution you can make is $2,000 per year. No employer contributions here, you're on your own.

Once upon a time, anyone could put $2,000 in an IRA, all of it deductible and tax deferred. This was a gift from Congress, but what the government giveth the government can take away, and take away they did. Well, let's just say they remodeled it.

You can still contribute $2,000 to an IRA, but it may not be deductible. It depends on your AGI, which has nothing to do with your aura or personality test results. AGI—currently line 32 of your 1040 tax form—stands for adjusted gross income. The current rules for IRAs state:

- Anyone can open a nondeductible IRA, that is, their $2,000 contribution is not tax-deferred, but the earnings are until withdrawal.

- If neither you or, if married, your spouse, is covered by an employer-sponsored retirement plan, either of you can open a fully deductible IRA regardless of your income.

- If either you or your spouse is covered by a retirement program, you can still open an IRA if your income is $50,000 or less (partial deduction for incomes up to $60,000).

- A single individual, covered by a plan, can open a deductible IRA with an income of $30,000 or less (partial deduction for income up to $40,000).

- A spouse who is not an active participant in an employer-sponsored retirement account can make a deductible IRA contribution, up to $2,000, even if the other spouse is covered at work if the couple's income is under $150,000 (partial deduction for income up to $160,000).

These income limits are increasing between now and the year 2007.

There isn't much point in contributing to a non-deductible IRA unless you've exhausted all other retirement programs—a dilemma a lot of people wouldn't mind having. If you have an existing IRA that is no longer deductible, but you still contribute money from time to time, be certain to keep your records of these contributions! You don't want to get taxed on them twice.

QUICK ⏺ PAINLESS

Even if you can't make the maximum $2,000 IRA contribution, consider opening an account anyway. Every penny counts when you're planning your retirement.

Mutated IRA Clones

A few new IRA organisms have been whipped up in the government labs over the years, including the:

- Education IRA
- Conduit IRA
- First-Time Homebuyer Distributions rules
- SIMPLE-IRA
- Roth IRA

No wonder accountants love the IRS! Talk about job security. To put it simply:

An Education IRA allows for nondeductible contributions—a whopping $500 a year—to be put into an IRA account to cover qualified higher education costs. The earnings can be taken out tax-free when needed for college. You might even earn enough to buy books for a few semesters.

A conduit IRA has to do with rolling over, or moving, tax-exempt money from one employer's retirement plan to another.

The first-time buyer clause allows for up to $10,000 to be taken out of an IRA without penalty for the purchase of a principal residence for a first-time homebuyer.

The SIMPLE-IRA (Savings Incentive Match Plan for Employees-IRA) accepts contributions from employees and employers with a 1997 limit of $6,000 per employee contribution; it's a simpler version of a 401(k) set up for small businesses.

Other than the Roth IRA or possibly the SIMPLE, you probably won't run into any of these accounts.

The New Kid on the Block: Roth

By my own estimation, approximately 4,000,000 pages—give or take few hundred thousand—of text in the form of books, magazine articles, and website postings have been written about section 408(a) of the tax code. This section, better known as the Roth IRA (named after Senator Bill Roth of Delaware) is a new and intriguing addition to the IRA family. Available in 1998, the Roth IRA has already undergone some technical corrections—something like regular software updates after a new product is foisted on the public—and will undoubtedly be adjusted further.

The biggest difference between the Roth IRA and every other retirement plan is this: Contributions are made in after-tax dollars, but the distributions—the money you take out in retirement—are tax-free! Let this sink in a minute, because it apparently has not done so with the Congress. Pay your tax on $2,000 now, providing your earned income is at least that high, and pay no tax on potentially thousands of dollars years down the road. In my opinion, there's no way this program will last in its present form. Future legislators—who will have dartboards with Senator Roth's image on them—looking at budget shortfalls, will start zeroing in on these funds as a source of new taxes while trying to explain to voters why they're yanking this program.

IF YOU'RE SO INCLINED

Your situation may call for a combination of plans: a 401(k), an IRA, maybe a Roth IRA, as well. Lay out all the options and decide which ones you can fully fund and take advantage of.

Here are the basics of the Roth IRA:

- Individuals with incomes up to $95,000 can contribute $2,000 to a Roth IRA; allowable contributions decrease with an income up to $110,000.

- For married couples, the income range, with contributions decreasing, is $150,000 to $160,000.

- Withdrawals can start at age $59\frac{1}{2}$ for all accounts active for at least five years; exceptions are made if you become disabled or remove up to $10,000 for a first home purchase.

- There is no age limit for beginning withdrawals, unlike other programs which must begin by age $70\frac{1}{2}$.

- You can convert your existing IRA to a Roth IRA, but must pay income tax on the amount being converted.

A Simple Idea, a Complicated Strategy

Although determining whether you should pick a Roth over other retirement plans depends to a great extent on your age, health, tax brackets, and other factors specific to your situation, there are some factors that most experts agree on:

- If you're in a low tax bracket now and expect to be in a higher one at retirement, the Roth is a good idea for you. You're paying a cheap tax rate for later tax-free earnings.

- A Roth IRA can still grow and compound after age $70\frac{1}{2}$, a valuable feature for increasing your retirement income or estate value.

QUICK 🔘 PAINLESS

A Roth IRA doesn't require a lot of consideration. If it's a choice among a Roth, a non-deductible IRA, or a taxed investment account, go with the Roth. It makes the most sense in this situation.

- Since earnings are tax-free, the Roth can be a tremendous vehicle for passing money through an estate; by naming a beneficiary, the account can pass directly and skip probate and continue to earn and distribute funds for the lifetime of the beneficiary.

- The conversion of an existing IRA to a Roth IRA works if you pay the taxes from funds outside of your IRA.

- A Roth started at an early age offers the most advantageous use of the program as it allows for a greater build-up of tax-free funds.

- A Roth removes the complexities-involved with other IRAs, such as age requirements, minimum withdrawals, etc.

State treasuries might come snooping around, too. Not all states conform to federal tax changes; some don't have any income tax. Others are considering, or have pending, legislation on Roth IRAs and the IRA conversions.

The conversions work if you don't raid your IRA to pay the income tax due. There are other considerations, including:

- Your current age and number of years to retirement (you want to recover the conversion costs before starting withdrawals).

- Present tax bracket and anticipated tax bracket during retirement.

- The amount of money you're converting.

- Life expectancy.

IF YOU'RE SO
INCLINED

If you contribute to a Roth, you cannot contribute to any other IRA account (although SEP-IRAs and SIMPLE-IRAs are okay). This is true with all other IRAs, as well; your total contribution(s) per year cannot exceed $2,000.

In a sense, converting an existing IRA to a Roth IRA while paying the taxes from outside the IRA is like opening the door and throwing a huge pile of cash at it. It enables you to have this whole wad of money and securities continue to grow undisturbed and then be tax-free when distributed.

The Roth IRA makes a lot of sense as an alternative to a non-deductible IRA, an annuity, and in some cases even a deductible IRA. If you've already maxed out your 401(k) with its employer matching contributions, then by all means open a Roth. If you're young and in a low tax bracket, you should definitely open a Roth IRA. The future is uncertain, however:

- Will Congress change the tax laws to diminish the advantages of Roths?
- How can you predict your tax rate years and years down the road?
- If you convert now and pay the taxes on the present value of your IRA, the market could sink shortly thereafter and you will have paid taxes on inflated fund values without having anyway to recover the cost.

Funding a Roth IRA is easy. You don't have to put in $2,000 when you open the account. Open your Roth with a smaller amount of money and add to it throughout the year either with a automatic payroll or checking account deduction, if your Roth provider will accept such payments. Or treat your Roth contributions like any other monthly bill and mail it along with the others. You have until April 15, 1999, to fund your 1998 Roth IRA.

For further information, go to:

- www.troweprice.com
- www.rothira.com

I WORK FOR EVERYBODY— I'M SELF-EMPLOYED

If you're self-employed, you can add one more task to your list of things to do: Start and fund your own retirement. Do this right after you've filled out the payroll sheets, ordered the supplies, spent two hours on the phone with your suppliers, and swabbed out the bathroom 12 hours after you came to work. No corporate hack is going to tell you what to do in some oppressive high rise office with paid vacations and full medical benefits.

Self-employed individuals and their employees have three specific choices cater-made to their situations:

- Keogh plans
- SEP-IRA (Simplified Employee Pension-Individual Retirement Account or SEPs)
- SIMPLE-IRA (Savings Incentive Match Plan for Employees-Individual Retirement Account)

You can use a Keogh or a SEP-IRA if you're self-employed without employees, too. They are terrific retirement tools as well as tax shelters! A Keogh allows you, as the big cheese of the company, to sock away up

YOU'LL THANK YOURSELF LATER

If you're self-employed, you have no one you can depend on for retirement funding but yourself. Take every advantage you can of available retirement programs.

to 20 percent of your self-employment income to a maximum of $30,000. Put that much away for a few years when you're in your twenties and you'll be shopping for Corvettes when you reach 65.

There are a couple of catches to this Keogh fantasy if you're an employer, however:

- You have to choose between two flavors of Keoghs: the Profit Sharing plan or the Money Purchase plan.

- You must pay the same percentage of an employee's salary into their Keogh as you pay into yours.

- All qualified employees must be covered.

- The set-up and paperwork requirements for a Keogh plan can be a real pain, even if you're the only participant.

As an employee, it's your employer who pays the tab and decides the percentage (you may want to use this as a point of negotiation when considering a job offer). The contributions are all tax-deferred, that is, no tax until you withdraw. This is true for the earnings, as well. Keoghs are for employees of unincorporated businesses or the self-employed—sole proprietorships—just one guy running the place or partnerships.

The paperwork for filing and establishing a Keogh is a nuisance, but it's an easy way to put away a lot of money if you're self-employed—far more than an IRA or a SEP-IRA will allow. And, you can still invest in an IRA even if you max out your Keogh contributions! As an employer or employee, these plans are well worth considering.

Being Hep with a SEP

If you want an easier alternative to a Keogh, and one that makes more sense if your contributions aren't exactly in the $30,000 maximum range, consider a SEP-IRA. These plans have no yearly reporting requirements—just a mention on your 1040—and can be set up is hands down simpler than a Keogh.

As an employer, you can tuck away a little over 13 percent—okay, 13.0435 percent—of your self-employment net income into one of these accounts, all tax deferred, up to a maximum of $24,000. For qualified employees, your contribution is limited to the smaller of $24,000, or 15 percent of their compensation. Employee qualifications (rules on minimum age and salary as well as length of employment) can all be spelled out on IRS Form 5305 SEP.

SEPs are a painless retirement program for just about everyone involved. The money is put directly into IRA accounts over which the participants—that's you, hopefully—have a choice about investments. If you're really a saver, you can contribute to an IRA account outside of the SEP, as well!

Even though early retirement contributions are a great idea, be sure you can afford them! You don't want to start your contributions and then find that you need the money for an emergency. Look over your budget sheets and figure out what you can afford. It doesn't have to be the maximum! Anything to get the retirement ball rolling—even $75 a month—will start adding up sooner than you think!

QUICK n' PAINLESS

Self-employed? Take the easy way out and talk with your accountant before you set up a plan! The one available to you may not be the best for your situation. Once your money is in the plan, it's tough to get it out without incurring tax penalties. The fee you pay could save you a lot of headaches!

Simply SIMPLE

A SIMPLE-IRA, or Savings Incentive Match Plan for Employees-IRA, was established for calendar year 1997. It's aimed at sole proprietors or businesses with fewer than 100 employees. The contributions by both the employee and employer are similar to the SIMPLE-401(k):

- Each can contribute up to $6,000.

- The employer can choose to contribute two percent of each eligible employee's salary—up to $3,200— regardless if the employee contributes or not.

- Each company may have different eligibility and vestment rules.

IF YOU UNDERSTAND YOUR INSURANCE POLICY . . .

An annuity is an insurance product that offers some tax benefits—the interest is tax-deferred—but this isn't a good enough reason for investing in them. There are a number of different annuity products available, but they should only be considered after you've fully contributed to an IRA account or an employer-sponsored plan.

Annuities can have expensive fees depending on the type of account. Scott Burns, writing in *Worth Online*, claims the average annuity cost is 2.09 percent—more than most mutual funds! And, unless you're in the insur- ance business, they are not all that simple to understand and evaluate. It isn't easy to find a financial writer who is a cheerleader for these products. Annuities might make sense if you have:

- Maxed out your 401(k) or other employer-sponsored retirement program.

- Made your $2,000 annual contribution to a deductible IRA or a Roth IRA.

- Put aside an emergency fund and have money invested for other intermediate-term goals.

- Additional money to put away for retirement.

- No need for the money for 20 years.

For further information, go to www.annuity.com.

THE LAZY WAY

Retirement strategies are simple: invest early, invest consistently, and take advantage of any employer matching contributions. Time will take even your modest contributions and multiply them several times over if you give them the opportunity to do so. Automatic payroll deductions offer a painless approach to securing your financial future. It lets your funds grow in the background while you take care of more mundane concerns, like doing the laundry and cleaning up after the puppy.

Your choice is easy: take advantage of the best-suited retirement account available to you and put in as much money as you can afford. The other choices you make today—how and where your money is spent, whether you save a little or save a lot—will determine if you take off for Mexico three months of the year when you're 70 or if you're toughing it out on Social Security and savings. Funding a retirement program, even if you start modestly, puts Mazatlan a little closer every passing year.

QUICK n PAINLESS

The biggest obstacle to retirement planning is taking the first step and opening a retirement account. Make it your goal to start an account—or gather information—this week.

Getting Time and Money on Your Side

	The Old Way	The Lazy Way
Figuring your retirement finances will somehow take care of themselves vs. early, active planning:	I wanted to retire to a warm climate. I didn't expect to be camping in the woods.	Man, look at the size of my 401(k). Starting at 25 made all the difference in the world.
Making irregular contributions to your retirement account vs. the maximum contributions on a regular basis:	This thing is really growing. Ten years ago I only had $670, now it's close to $4,000!	Millionaire Row, here we come.
Depending on an inheritance vs. doing your own planning and saving:	And to my son Dave, I leave $75 with the hope that he will spend it with care.	We've got more than we'll ever need. What did you say about your brother Dave wanting a loan?
Believing Social Security will see you through retirement vs. your own funds:	Whoo, hoo! Our check came. We can go out and split a pizza.	Hey, our government entertainment check came today.
Not figuring a life span into your eighties vs. knowing you may live a long life:	Let's see, my last penny will be gone when I'm precisely 77.938 years old.	We won't spend all this if we live to be 100.

ten

Mutual Fund Basics: The Lazy Investor's Best Friend

In 1928, the Pioneer Fund—one of the forerunners of the modern-day mutual fund industry—opened its doors and introduced its investors to this newfangled investment idea of pooling their money with other investors to buy stocks. Talk about timing! One year later, the term Black Thursday entered the financial world's lexicon as panic selling got out of control and prices were down 20%. The following Tuesday, 16,410,030 shares were sold on the New York Stock Exchange—a record for the time. Things didn't get any better as the world settled in for the Great Depression, soup lines, and diversionary Shirley Temple movies. This wasn't the most auspicious time to start the mutual fund industry.

Yet, the Pioneer Funds ended the year 1997 with over $21 billion in its coffers. A $2,000 investment compounding at an 11-percent return over this 70-year period would be worth

close to $3 million today (okay, $2,976,030 if you really want to know). The mutual fund industry itself has grown to more than 7,000 different funds, and hit the $5 trillion mark in 1998. There are more funds than there are stocks listed on the New York Stock Exchange.

For many investors, mutual funds offer an easy way to invest in a broader array of stocks and bonds than almost any single investor could individually afford— Warren Buffett, billionaire Nebraskan—doesn't count. Send the fund a check, or arrange an automatic investment via a monthly withdrawal from your checking account, and let professional money managers do the picking and choosing for a yearly fee. There are as many types of funds as there are equities, although none that invest in stuffed toys like Beanie Babies, at least not yet.

After retirement plans, mutual funds may be the greatest invention ever for the lazy investor. Why?

- Easy management and diversification: mutual funds buy a broader range of stocks and bonds, thus, limiting risk, than you're ever likely to do on your own.

- It's tough to beat the market and full-time fund managers on your own. Well-managed funds, especially index funds, offer solid returns without the hassles of picking your stocks individually.

- A low-cost fund keeps your transaction costs to a minimum vs. commissions from trading individual stocks and bonds.

We'll sort through the terminology and the numbers so your decision-making is easier yet.

EVERYBODY INTO THE POOL

Recently, a group of Westerville, Ohio, machine shop workers won a multistate Powerball lottery to the tune of $295.7 million. They had pooled their money, purchased 130 tickets, including the winning number, and then decided to take a lump sum payment—as opposed to a 20-year payout—of $161.5 million before taxes. Mutual funds use pools of money too, with admittedly less spectacular results. Still, the principle is the same:

- Individuals invest their money with one of thousands of mutual funds, operated by an investment company, forming a large pool of cash.

- The investment company purchases stocks, bonds, options, commodities, or money market securities, depending on the kind of fund it is.

- Each investor shares proportionately in the gains or losses of the fund.

In other words, for a lazy portfolio, much of the work is already done for you. There's a reason mutual funds are so popular: They work! Even seasoned investors and pension fund managers advocate mutual funds for individual investors.

In the case of the machinists, who had been buying tickets for several years with regular monthly pools, the added feature of the random selection of numbers allowing only one winner skews our mutual fund analogy. When you buy into a mutual fund, the value of your shares is determined by market conditions, not the luck of the draw—even though it may seem that way

YOU'LL THANK YOURSELF LATER

Trading in and out of mutual funds is just as unprofitable as trading in and out of stocks. Pick carefully and let the returns do their work.

sometimes! Like the machinists, you can easily invest in mutual funds each month, you just won't have to do it with $20 bills after cashing your paycheck. Many mutual funds offer automatic investing via monthly withdrawals from your bank account. No muss, no fuss, and no hassle.

Mutual funds will take your pooled money and offer:

- Professional management. Someone else does the research, the trading, and keeps any cash in a money market mutual fund.

- Diversification and lowered risk. By buying a broad range of the market, a fund spreads the risk and can better absorb the losses from individual securities.

- Availability for small monthly investments, which is especially convenient when done through automatic withdrawals.

- One consolidated, monthly statement. If you're buying into more than one fund, consider going through a discount broker, who will list all transactions on one statement.

- Liquidity. Although as a long-term investor you don't want to sell your holdings, you can, if necessary, sell at any time at the current, end-of-day net asset value.

FUNDS AND MORE FUNDS

The mutual fund industry is a huge financial smorgasbord offering everything from speculative high-tech companies to the bluest blue chips (these are the large,

YOU'LL THANK YOURSELF LATER

Determining your investment style will help you settle on a fund selection. Are you cautious? Involved on a daily basis? Looking for dividend returns or growth? There's a mutual fund for every type of investor.

established companies like IBM). There's a fund for everyone including:

- Index funds
- Stock Funds, ranging from conservative to aggressive
- Bond funds of all types
- Sector, or specialized, funds that invest in a particular segment of the market
- International funds
- Fund of funds (this buys other funds)

Mutual funds charge fees for all the hunting and gathering of stocks and bonds that they do for you. This brings us to the two major divisions of mutual funds, from an expense standpoint:

- Load funds
- No-load funds

The term load refers to a sales charge or commission (the front-end load), which can run anywhere from approximately two to eight percent. Load funds are typically sold through brokers, hence the fees. Just to get your load cost back, the fund will have to earn in excess of the sales charge the first year. How come? Say you invest $2,000 at a five-percent load. That's $100 in fees, leaving you with $1,900 invested. Your fund has to earn at least 5.263 percent for you to break even. Sometimes there are even redemption or back-end fees when you sell your shares.

IF YOU'RE SO

INCLINED

Mutual funds are an excellent way to invest in international stocks. Many advisors recommend owning some international investments to balance out a portfolio. They believe that foreign markets may grow faster in the coming years than the U.S. stock market, current slowdowns notwithstanding.

No-Load, No Fees—Almost

As you may have guessed, a no-load mutual fund doesn't have any sales charges attached to it. These funds are typically sold directly by the fund company itself. Open up *The Wall Street Journal* or any investment magazine and you'll see ads galore for no-load funds, touting their returns and ratings. Charles Schwab, Inc., the discount brokerage firm, ever vigilant for new products, began offering hundreds of no-load, no-transaction fee mutual funds, through its OneSource program. This is a terrific idea and makes mutual fund investing as easy as it gets: one phone call, or Internet connection, for over 850 funds, instead of having to deal with individual companies. Throw in an AIP (automatic investment plan) and you can automatically buy funds every month without fees and without thinking about it. You can contact Schwab at www.schwab.com or 800-435-4000.

Carry this one step further, as you should with any mutual fund investment, and reinvest all your dividends by buying more shares of the fund. Reinvestment is the equivalent of compounding interest: In later years, the appreciated value can be astounding. For the lazy investor, your portfolio will almost take on a life of its own, growing and expanding while you consistently feed it with monthly dollars. Your regular investing will be as natural and unobtrusive as getting dressed in the morning (night-shift workers may have a different frame of reference, of course).

No-load funds may not charge you for buying and selling shares, but they do have some expenses. After all,

QUICK n PAINLESS

If you're not inclined to study the stock pages in your newspaper every night or follow all the economic indicators, mutual funds might be just the investment for you. A well-diversified fund selection can cover all your bases.

they're not doing this simply to stay in your good graces. Expenses include:

- Management fees
- 12b-1 fees

Management fees can run from less than 0.25 percent—some of the Vanguard Group funds (800-662-7447 or www.vanguard.com) have particularly competitive fees—to around two percent; 12b-1 fees range from .25 percent to 1 percent and are charged for advertising and marketing costs for no-load funds.

As an investor, fees and expenses can quickly cut into your returns. Sticking pins in a voodoo doll in the form of the fund's president may give you some surprisingly unexpected results, but it won't cut the fees. You want this to be easy, but not at any cost. What can you do? Let the Securities and Exchange Commission (SEC) and their rules give you a hand.

By law, a mutual fund must send you a prospectus before you invest in the fund. A prospectus is a barely comprehensible document printed on tissue thin paper that describes:

- The investment objectives of the fund.
- A history of the fund and its risks.
- The fund's financial statement.
- Expense ratio (the percentage of a shareholder's investment that pays for the fund's operating expenses and management fees).

YOU'LL THANK YOURSELF LATER

Fees can really eat up the gains on your investments. All things being equal, look for funds with the lowest costs.

You can also find a fund's annual expenses, and other information, in *The Wall Street Journal*'s mutual fund listings. These listings will also include:

- The NAV (net asset value)
- Investment objective (growth, income, capital appreciation)
- Total return (one-, three- and five-year periods)
- The maximum initial sales commission
- The fund's ranking among funds with similar investment objectives (A through E; A = top 20 percent, E = bottom 20 percent)

Given the fee structure, why would anyone buy a load fund over a no-load, other than the fact that your sister is the sales rep and she'll tell your mom if you don't buy into it? A load fund would have to give you a marvelous return over a no-load, and studies show that there is no difference in return between load and no-load funds. The load only makes sense if you need someone, namely a broker or financial adviser, to help you choose a fund, and if you read this book, you won't need that help.

Remember, the fund has already swallowed the commission you paid—and that can be in excess of 5 percent! Add on management and other fees and you've got a higher cost than the return on a current Treasury bill— just for the your first year's expenses! For no-hassle wealth accumulation, no-loads are a no brainer.

QUICK n PAINLESS

Pay attention to the prospectus section on fees and expenses first. Avoid loads and 12b-1 fees, and pay no more than 1.5 percent in expenses for a stock fund and no more than 1 percent in expenses for a bond fund.

An Open and Shut Case

From a trading standpoint, mutual funds are divided into two major groups:

- Closed-end funds
- Open-end funds

Forget about closed-end funds that issue a limited number of shares and then close the door to new investors. They sell like stocks and are just as hard to pick, hardly a lazy investment.

An open-ended fund just keeps growing, kind of like the hamburger industry with billions and billions sold. New investors can buy in at any time, purchasing the fund at its net asset value (NAV) on that day. The NAV equals the value of the fund's investments less any liabilities divided by the number of shares outstanding. If it's got $2 billion in holdings (less expenses), you're buying a percentage of those assets. If more money comes in, you've got a percentage of all the newly purchased assets, too. When you sell, you receive your share of the NAV at the time of sale. The NAV is calculated on a daily basis by taking into account:

- The value of the securities in the fund
- The fund's expenses
- Any cash on hand
- The total number of shares in the fund that day

Mutual funds are great for the lazy investor. Large index funds or a balanced funds (ones that include stocks

and bonds), coupled with an automatic investment plan will put you heads and shoulders ahead of too many of your fellow Americans who take a spend-and-burn attitude toward money and think retiring is what you do when you go to sleep in the evening.

(Conversely, if you're at the point where you're using your funds for operating income, you can arrange for automatic monthly redemption as well.)

Above Average

Automatic investing works especially well when combined with another investing trick: DCA, or dollar cost averaging. This is simple, automatic, and habit forming, but a little healthier, than, say, whacking yourself on the head every time you miss an answer on *Jeopardy*.

Here are the mechanics of DCA for stock or mutual fund purchases:

- You invest the same amount of money at the same interval, usually monthly, regardless of market conditions.
- Each payment buys a certain number of shares based on the price at the time of purchase.
- You'll buy a different number of shares every month (more when the price is low, fewer when it's high).
- Your average cost per share is lower than the average price per share.

Don't believe it? Here's an example:

DCA for the Typical Investor

Monthly Investment	Price per share	Shares Purchased
$300	$10	30
$300	$6	50
$300	$8	37.5
$300	$10	30
$300	$15	20
$300	$7.50	40
$300	$6	50
Total $2,100	Average price: $8.92	Total: 257.5

Your average cost per share: $8.15

Average share price: $8.92

As an investor, you benefitted from lower costs by purchasing more shares—using a consistent dollar amount—during dips in the share price. By ignoring price changes and investing consistently you keep your emotions at bay—a good idea, especially when those around you are turning into screaming meemies. This works with good, solid investments—the ones this book advocates you buy—not with companies that are tanking and about to enter history's rolls of bankrupt corporations.

Basically, DCA is a discipline to keep you investing and saving come good times and bad. No one can time

A COMPLETE WASTE OF TIME

The 3 Worst Ways to Invest in Mutual Funds:

1. Invest your money based on advertisements.

2. Buy funds without checking out their fees.

3. Excessively trade in and out of funds.

the market, that is, know when to be in and when to be out, and it's easy to get spooked when fund managers start packing their bags and buying tickets to South America. Decide on a minimum amount of money you can invest monthly and stick with it, increasing it when possible. No-load mutual funds are especially receptive to modest monthly investments.

Index Investors Rule

Index funds have been the rage for at least the last 10 years. Depending on whose figures you believe, they have gotten better returns than:

- 80 percent of all managed equity funds for the last 10 years.

- 110 percent of every fund that ever existed in the last 75 years and every fund that will exist in the next 100 years.

- Every investment ever conceived since Hannibal took his elephants for a walk through the Alps in 218 B.C.

Okay, the first one is closest. An index fund buys a representative sampling of all the equities in its particular index and then does . . . very little. Index funds assume it's tough to regularly beat the average return of the index and for the most part they have been proven correct during these past years of a rising market.

The most publicized index funds have been based on the Standard & Poor's 500 Composite Price Index, which is composed of mostly large cap—capitalization, BIG capitalization—blue chip companies that account for about ²/₃ of the U.S. stock market value. These are the General Motors and Colgates and Exxons of the world. Other indexes include:

- Russell 2000 Index (small cap stocks)
- Wilshire 5000 Equity Index (all regularly traded U.S. common stocks)
- Lehman Brothers Aggregate Bond Index (U.S. taxable bond market)

Index funds will keep you in line with the returns of the index they represent. You won't do dramatically better or worse than the index, and that's okay! Fund managers and private investors scramble every day to beat the market and the vast majority fail. Remember, lazy investing is about decreasing your risk without having to spend your nights and free time poring over annual reports and the spouting of stock analysts. An index fund will keep you out of trouble and give you a healthy return.

Index funds are passive investors. Their portfolio managers don't have a lot to do except keep the fund balanced according to what's hot and what's not in their respective index. Consequently, their fee schedule normally is quite low. The Vanguard S&P 500 Index Fund has an expense ratio of just .20 percent, far below the average growth fund's expense ratio of 1.5 percent. That's a 1.3 percent disadvantage for the average actively managed fund. Managed funds are always on the hunt, ready to show the world their great trapping ability. This brings us to another aspect of mutual funds: tax-related costs.

IF YOU'RE SO
INCLINED

An index fund is a recommended core holding for your portfolio. Look for funds based on the S&P 500 or the Wilshire 5000 for starters.

QUICK ■ PAINLESS

A mutual fund is required by law to pass on dividends and realized capital gains to shareholders each year. As a proud investor, you're pleased when your investments increase in value. Uncle Sam shares your pleasure and then taxes it. The more trading, the more potential for capital gains—a taxable activity. Actively managed funds, because of their more frequent buying and selling (called turnover, and measured by the turnover ratio), typically have a greater potential for realized capital gains. This is especially true when end-of-the-year distributions are made, necessitating some sale of a fund's holdings. A well-managed fund will try and offset any capital gains with losses to mitigate taxes.

Since an index fund has relatively little turnover, you will eventually incur a tax when you sell off your shares. As time passes, you will have the advantage of compounded growth, which will dwarf any taxes due.

How do you avoid this nasty tax surprise? Easy. Several publications list and dissect mutual funds according to their performance, fees, and tax friendliness. Among these publications are:

- *Morningstar Mutual Funds* (www.morningstar.net)
- *Forbes* (September "Honor Roll" edition)
- *Barron's* (mutual fund edition)
- *The Wall Street Journal* (mutual fund edition)
- *The Value Line Mutual Fund Survey*

These publications are all available at many public libraries. Morningstar exists to evaluate mutual funds, so grab it and look for star performers. One caveat that can't be mentioned enough: Past performance doesn't predict future performance! It's true with basketball players, authors, and all investments. Last year's ace mutual fund may not even have the same management this year, so look for long term, steady performance. You want a fund that runs like a '66 Dodge Dart on fuel additives, not an exotic sports car that spends half its time in the shop. *Forbes'* Honor Roll, according to Peter Lynch, is an excellent source for well-performing funds and fund comparisons.

They're not perfect

Index funds have had a great trot during the bull market of the 1980s and 1990s. Like every other investment, there's a huge cartoon balloon over every index fund with the word "BUT" in capital letters. By their nature, index funds keep almost no cash on hand as they are essentially 100 percent invested. Thus, they are more exposed to the whims of the market and can have large declines just as they have had steady gains. A couple of other concerns:

- The popularity of index funds have loaded them up with new investors—and new money. This money has to be put to work and can artificially force up the prices of the stocks it purchases rather than have them increase in value on their own intrinsic merits.

- A really big fund like Vanguard cannot easily unload big stock positions without affecting the market and possibly driving prices down, again affecting the returns on your index fund.

YOU'LL THANK YOURSELF LATER

Keep all of your mutual fund records in a separate file for tax accounting. You can be taxed twice on reinvested dividends—once as income and a second time as capital gains— for instance, if you can't account for taxes paid.

Various financial advisors opine against index funds, claiming a good active fund manager can offer superior performance and greater risk control. Fine, but for how long? And which funds? What happens when the fund manager moves on? Do you want to spend your time moving your hard-earned money in and out of the fund of the month looking for bigger returns? Nothing lazy about that.

Let's face it, index funds are boring and predictable and go against our image as independent, go-down-the-road-our-own-way-come-hell-or-high-water Americans who can always do better than average. Nice image, except that we demand four-lane highways, air-conditioned sport utility vehicles, and convenient motels (with swimming pools) while we go barreling down that road to independence. Most actively managed funds haven't managed to beat index funds and those that do have higher expenses. Why bother with them?

There's nothing wrong with a mostly predictable, average return if it gets you the freedom—especially in retirement—to do as you wish. Constantly challenging the odds isn't going to do it.

All in the Family

Many funds are members of extended families whose siblings and cousins come in the form of sector funds, bond funds, income funds, and more. Some families, like Fidelity, Oppenheimer, Vanguard, and Dreyfus, are bigger than others and offer a great variety of funds. Owning funds within large-fund families allows for easy

QUICK n' PAINLESS

Since most managed funds don't manage to beat index funds, are they really suitable for a lazy investor? Index funds are custom-made for lazy portfolios.

switching among different funds should you choose to do so.

Fund families offer you the necessary diversification beyond index funds that every investor should have. Stocks are great investments, and many investors are more than willing to ride along while their values go up. When market physics starts to assert its own law of gravity, are all of these same investors willing to stick around or will they sell at a loss? Some diversification cushions the ride. You can even take the really easy way out and buy a balanced fund of stocks and bonds.

Every fund family sells a balanced fund. A balanced fund (roughly 60 percent stocks and 40 percent bonds) reduces your risk even further than an index fund since its bonds can kick in when stocks are weak. The returns won't make for great cocktail party chatter, but you won't be crying in your beer over big losses, either.

Remember, in the long run, stocks have historically yielded superior returns to bonds or cash. If you're in your twenties or thirties, there's little reason not to be heavily invested in stocks, whether it's through mutual funds or individual stocks. That said, for the sake of diversification, you can create your own balanced fund. Since mutual funds can be sliced and diced to produce any portfolio mix you want, you can buy an index fund and a short- or mid-term bond fund. The Vanguard 500 Portfolio, mixed with the Vanguard Intermediate-Term Bond Fund, for example, will keep you within one family and spread your portfolio risk.

IF YOU'RE SO
INCLINED

You don't have to stick with one fund family, although you may find it convenient to do so. Mix and match as you would any diversified portfolio.

BON BONDS

Bonds have a place in your portfolio. They're great for short-term investments when your money must be secure, that is, if you invest directly in U.S. Treasuries held to maturity. They can also be a safe haven when you want out of the stock market—maybe you're close to retirement—and you're satisfied to live on a fixed return. Bonds can be bought individually or through bond mutual funds. Bond mutual funds include those investing in:

- Corporate bonds
- Municipal bonds
- Government bonds

These funds cover a lot of territory, including international income bonds, high-yield (junk) bonds, emerging market bonds, you name it. Within that territory, comes some roadblocks:

- A bond fund does not behave like a bond. As interest rates change, portfolio managers trade bonds rather than hold to maturity. Bond funds never mature.
- If rates rise, the market price of the bonds can drop. You can lose both yield and principal since you have no control of the fund's trading.
- Even a fund that invests in U.S. Treasuries isn't safe from loss of principal.
- The degree of risk varies with each fund; a high-yield fund, for example, will be less stable because it invests in lower-rated bonds.

A COMPLETE WASTE OF TIME

The 3 Worst Ways to Diversify Your Retirement Funds:

1. Place more than 10 percent, if that, in a money market account while you're still young.

2. Invest too heavily in narrow sector funds, like high-tech or emerging markets.

3. Buy only bond funds.

- They facilitate the purchase and sale of corporate bonds, tough transactions for small investors.

- If the fees are low enough, a mutual fund can help you sort through the tangle of highways, hospitals, and civic improvement projects across the country who are vying for your money with their municipal fund offerings.

- Some bond funds allow for automatic investment deposits of modest amounts of money, far less than an individual bond purchase would demand.

Repeat this mantra: "I will never buy a government bond from a fund!" What's the point? Treasuries are already available from the Federal Reserve Bank (Treasury Direct) without any transaction fees, and recent changes in Treasury policies make any Treasuries available in amounts as little as $1,000 (see Chapter 13). Why pay a fund a fee when you can buy direct for free? If you decide to sell before maturity, a broker can handle the transaction or you can sell through Treasury Direct. The best approach with Treasuries, unless interest rates rise like the Goodyear blimp, is to buy them short term, buy them direct, and hold them until maturity. *The Lazy Way* mutual funds offer tremendous diversity, ease of investment, diminished risk, and solid returns to an investor. They are an ideal vehicle for monthly investing via dollar cost averaging—the perfect automatic account builder, especially for beginning investors. A low-fee, no-load index fund can spread your dollars over a broad range of the market easily and more cheaply than you can on your own.

YOU'LL THANK YOURSELF LATER

Compare a bond fund's fees with purchasing a bond directly, particularly Treasuries. If the interest rate is attractive and you intend on holding to maturity, why incur a fund's charges?

Professional management is another plus. Let's face it, portfolio managers have two goals they never state in a prospectus:

1. At the very least, they want to keep their jobs and will only do so if the fund maintains decent returns.

2. They really want the bragging rights—and salary—that comes with being one of the year's top performers (if not the number one performer).

There is no guarantee that the funds you choose will do well or even equal the index returns. There aren't any guarantees when you invest in stocks, or bonds not held to maturity, but a mutual fund will lessen your burden of choice and selection. They're an easy way out for the lazy investor.

The lazy investor can treat mutual fund investing like a birthday: Once a year, you'll have to deal with the numbers. These numbers include:

- Total return vs. other similar funds
- Expenses
- Allocation percentages

One year's return may not be a fair test of a fund's performance, especially if other funds are lagging. Two years is a different story and you should strongly consider selling, particularly if other funds are showing gains.

Has your fund gotten more expensive due to increased management fees or trading? Some funds gradually drift away from their initial cost structure—sometimes a new portfolio manager comes on board and

QUICK ⬭ PAINLESS

Mutual funds offer an ideal way of investing in such areas as foreign stocks, corporate bonds, and municipal bonds.

changes the stock mix—and may be too pricey for your tastes and investment goals.

Did you put together your own balanced fund with an index fund and a bond fund? Are the percentages of each still appropriate or has your outlook changed? A yearly adjustment will keep your funds on the right track.

Once-a-year number juggling isn't much, even for the lazy investor.

YOU'LL THANK YOURSELF LATER

Selling a fund at the first sign of a slow return can be a mistake. Watch it, along with the market in general, to see if the decline is specific to your fund or across the market itself before deciding to sell.

Getting Time and Money on Your Side

	The Old Way	The Lazy Way
Buying load funds because you liked their advertisements vs. saving money on no-load funds:	Well, the guys in the ads were very sharp dressers.	With the money I saved, I bought some new clothes.
Ignoring the fee structure of a fund vs. paying attention to fees and costs before buying a fund:	Hmm, I wondered why my fund's manager was listed in the *Forbes* 400 wealthiest Americans.	My fund gets terrific returns and the fees are rock-bottom.
Dealing with numerous monthly statements vs. buying no-load funds through one discount broker:	Hey, if I recycle these I might pick up five bucks.	I get everything in one statement. I like a simple life.
Buying a fund based strictly on recent past performance vs. understanding that this cannot always determine future performance:	How do I know if the management team all left and went over to a competing fund and the new guy is a known embezzler? The track record is great.	Well, these guys look okay, but their record only goes back four years. According to my research, the last fund they managed tanked during the fifth year.

Building a Fund Portfolio: Investing Like a Pro Without Working Like One

Imagine you were in charge of a wedding banquet, but you decided the only foods you would prepare would be made with kumquats and corn. You would serve kumquat preserves, kumquat cider, corn on the cob, creamed corn, roasted corn, and corn pudding with kumquat sauce. It's safe to say this would be an unforgettable wedding reception. A meal like this would even put you on a vegetarian's hit list. To decrease the possibility of bodily injury from the wedding party and guests, it would behoove you to spread your risk by availing yourself to a few other food groups, perhaps crispy roast duck in orange sauce, lobster salad, maybe some strawberries dipped in white chocolate, and to prepare a more diverse table.

Your portfolio is something like this wedding banquet: Invest all of your money in the Cleveland Indians (NASDAQ symbol: CLEV), for example, and you had better hope they sell a lot of tickets and T-shirts (hope a lot, the stock dropped around 60 percent as of autumn 1998 from its opening-year high of 15). Round out your portfolio, some large cap industrials here, some bonds there, a dash of foreign stocks, and you'll spread your risk and not be so dependent on a group of rich guys' prowess with a baseball.

Diversity in your investments will bring your mutual funds, stocks, bonds, and money market accounts in line with a lot of current state fireworks' regulations, that is, they'll be safe and sane. True, they won't be anywhere near as exciting as the cherry bombs, M-80s, and small hand grenades, which used to be available around the Fourth of July. Those were really the good old days from a pyrotechnic standpoint. But they will be safe and more predictable, unlike those barely smoldering fuses on unexploded fire crackers which dared you to pick them up and check for yourself.

The equity market offers the diversity and fee structure for the lazy investor to put together a well-rounded portfolio for a secure financial future. With as few as five funds, you can have a comfortable return with an acceptable level of risk.

A LITTLE OF THIS, A LITTLE OF THAT

Regardless of where you invest, there will always be a better investment two minutes later. It may be the Malaysian futures market or gold coins or an initial public offering of stock in a company that manufactures Portland, Maine, refrigerator magnets. Trying to chase down the hot buy of the day is usually futile and expensive. Day traders—individuals who buy and sell stocks the same trading day—are perhaps the ultimate example of this optimistic pursuit, but few can make a living at it yet alone build up any wealth.

Instead of fretting about your investments and keeping your eyes glued to a stock monitor all day, which makes eating and working a little problematic, work on building a diversified portfolio to carry you through all kinds of markets and let you sleep at night. A diversified portfolio can include:

- Large-company (large cap) stocks and mutual funds
- Small-company funds (small cap)
- Foreign stocks (an international fund)
- Bonds or bond fund
- Money market fund (cash)

Each of these choices has its strong points, which will carry the day in certain markets. With enough diversification in your investments, they can carry you as well.

The Big Guys

Large-cap companies are the stalwart listings on stock exchanges, typically with a capitalization of $5 billion or more. Cap, or capitalization, refers to the market value of the company, the product of the share price multiplied by the number of shares outstanding. For example, General Motors had a market cap of about $40 billion in mid-1998 based on 650 million shares and a per-share

QUICK **n** PAINLESS

A growth fund invests in growth stocks that aim for capital appreciation (an increase in the price of the stock vs. slow growth with dividend payments). Growth stocks can be volatile, with quicker gains in earnings than the average stock.

price of just over $61. Typically, these companies are steady, been-around-forever corporations like Procter and Gamble, Union Carbide, Bristol-Meyer-Squibb, and Ford. Many of them will continue to do well in a world that needs soap, plastics, cold medicine, and cars. Their returns and growth may not be eye-popping, but they will, for the most part, be stable, the perfect addition for a lazy portfolio.

Some mutual funds that invest in large cap stocks include:

- Index funds that buy into the S&P 500.
- Funds that hold the 30 stocks of the Dow Jones Industrial Average (DJIA), 30 large, regularly traded blue chip companies, whose list is created by Dow Jones & Company.
- Various subsets of the DJIA (i.e., the Dogs of the Dow, see Chapter 12).
- Index funds that track the market at large (Wilshire 5000).

A broad-based index fund should be a core holding in your lazy portfolio.

Small, but Feisty

Small-cap companies fall in the $150–$500 million range (The Vanguard Group defines "small cap" as under $1 billion). In mid-1998, Cirrus Semiconductor, for example, had a market cap of $463 million based on 63.3 million shares outstanding at $7.28 a share. Small caps are considered to have more opportunity to grow—and

grow quickly—since they are often in new, expanding markets.

It is presumed to be easier to double the size of Cirrus, for instance, than General Motors. The automobile market is more mature in many established markets while the software market is really growing. And long-term statistics do show that small-cap investors are rewarded for the greater risk. According to John Bogle, founder of the Vanguard Group, in a speech given at MIT's Distinguished Lecture Series (Jan. 29, 1998), the compound return for small-cap stocks between 1925 and 1997 was 12.7 percent vs. 11 percent for large-cap stocks. He cautioned, however, that the difference was largely accounted for by the returns between 1973 and 1983 and that the two groups had equal returns between 1925 and 1968. Templeton Funds steps into the debate claiming that the small-cap index grew at a rate 3 times that of the S&P 500 since 1927. Uh, oh, here we enter the trauma of my statistics, and their interpretation, vs. your statistics and interpretation.

What's the lazy investor to do? Stick with diversification and keep in mind the musings of Mark Twain ("There are three kinds of lies—lies, damned lies, and statistics."), George Gallup ("I could prove God statistically."), and the now politically incorrect observation of professor of business administration, Aaron Levenstein ("Statistics are like a bikini. What they reveal is suggestive, but what they conceal is vital."). Personally, I'll give some consideration to Hunter S. Thompson ("I have a theory that the truth is never told between the nine-to-five hours.").

QUICK ⬭ PAINLESS

A 70 percent stocks/30 percent bonds allocation works for most portfolios. If you're younger and just starting, increase your stock investments, even up to 85 percent, and decrease your bonds.

A COMPLETE WASTE OF TIME

The 3 Worst Ways to Invest in Small-Cap Stocks:

1. Buy them because they're cheap.

2. Try and pick individual winners instead of a fund.

3. Continue to buy a bad stock as the price drops, thinking you'll recoup your losses.

Remember, at one point a lot of companies were small-caps. Look at Microsoft. It took awhile for its capitalization to grow, in part because software was a new field and not well understood by traditional investors. Software companies don't have a lot of physical assets and must pump most of their earnings into research and development. How do you put a value on that vs., say, Eastman-Kodak, the easily understood film behemoth? Investors who did understand software and invested early in Microsoft can now buy all the Kodak film they want—and cart it home in their Jaguar convertibles.

Small-cap mutual funds aren't hard to find: The term "small-cap" in the name is a dead giveaway. As with any actively managed fund, you should check for:

- Its 10-year record.

- Any management changes (a longtime manager with a consistently good record is a plus).

- Its performance against other funds in its category and its particular index (if it can't beat the index, why buy it?).

- The fund's expense ratio.

Remember the rule: past performance cannot be an indicator of future performance, but it might be a safe hint. A fund's quarterly, semi-annual, or annual reports will note any changes in investment style or management. Morningstar will also list these changes, although they may be a month or two behind the information curve.

All things being equal, the expense ratio can be the real return killer here. A long-term return of 10 percent on a $10,000 investment, for instance, will provide, over 40 years, a lump-sum value over twice that of an 8 percent return (see below). If that two-percent difference is due to a fund's expenses, you gave away a big chunk of your retirement to keep a fund manager's kids in private schools.

The 2% Advantage

$10,000 invested for 40 years at 10 percent = $450,000

$10,000 invested for 40 years at eight percent = $220,000

(Source: Vanguard Group)

You Get My Drift?

Small-cap funds have a habit of drifting into mid-cap stocks if the fund manager runs out of bargains in the smaller capitalization stocks. Sometimes small-cap companies simply grow larger and are retained in the fund. As an investor, you should check the fund's median cap size—no, I am not referring to a head covering with a visor—to be sure it's in the small-cap range. You can avoid this by buying into a small-cap index fund which, by definition, should stay within the small-cap range.

Another drift to be aware of for the diversified investor is fund drift. If you want to stick to a 75 percent stock fund/25 percent bond fund portfolio, for instance, and your stock funds go up in value to the point that

QUICK *in* PAINLESS

The advantage of an actively managed mutual fund is that its portfolio manager looks at a company's fundamentals and decides whether or not to include it in the fund's holdings. Unless you're prepared to take on this time-consuming exercise, stick with mutual funds, especially for more volatile small-cap stocks (but always watch and weigh the funds' expenses).

they equal 85 percent of your portfolio, you need to rebalance your investments. You can either:

- Put additional money into bonds.
- Sell some of your stocks (and buy more bonds).

Whatever you do, remember one cardinal rule of investing: Reinvest your dividends and keep your cash to a minimum, especially in a retirement account. If you need to rebalance your account, do so, but stay invested.

Something with a Foreign Flare

Foreign stocks, especially emerging markets, have interesting potential for investors. America understands that consumers drive markets. As the rest of the world's economies grow, millions—billions!—will enter this consumption wonderland, paying for these new found goods with their exports. The local businesses producing those exports have strong growth potential. Some of these companies—Sony, British Steel, Cemex, and Elf Aquitaine—are already world players in their respective industries.

The easiest way to buy many foreign stocks is through a mutual fund. Some stocks are only available on foreign stock exchanges, which means you'd be messing with exchange rates in Swedish krona, Mexican pesos, and Swiss francs to buy them. A professional manager also has access to a great deal of information about companies and countries that is hard for individuals to get or understand. Let a fund manager handle the money and the stock selections for you.

Foreign funds are often marketed as:

- Broad international funds (Scudder International Growth and Income, for example)
- Sector funds by area (e.g., Strong Asia Pacific)
- Sector funds by country (e.g. JP Morgan Japan Equity)

Going with a single country, or area, fund is dicey. Currently, the across-the-board turmoil in Asia right now has sunk its funds and currencies into the basement. A broad-based international fund, when you're ready to add it to your portfolio, is a better way to go.

A Little Bonding

As discussed in the previous chapter, bonds are a safe haven if you can live with the interest rate and hold them to maturity. If you want corporate bonds in your portfolio, buy a bond mutual fund. Government bonds can provide some steady income, with a locked-in interest rate, and act as a kind of shock absorber when the stock market is dropping. The younger you are, as a general rule, the fewer bonds you need since you're more interested in growth that will meet or stay ahead of inflation than you are in a fixed return.

Cold, Hard Cash

In a retirement account, there's little reason to keep much cash around unless you're timing the purchase of some equities—a haphazard process at best. There are a lot of theories on market timing, i.e., when to be in one sector of the market, when to be out, and most of them

YOU'LL THANK YOURSELF LATER

Remember this difference: An international fund invests in foreign securities only; a world fund invests in both foreign and U.S. securities. For a pure investment in foreign equities, stick with international funds.

work about as well as fortune telling. In other words, some of them will be right some times by pure luck.

Cash normally gives the worst return of the three main investment vehicles (stocks, bonds, cash). Sometimes this isn't true, however. In 1998, circumstances made cash the place to be for a number of reasons:

- Crashing markets in Asia with lackluster government response.

- Devaluation of the ruble and general instability in Russia, despite the relative insignificance of the Russian economic output (it's only about one percent of the worldwide economy, hardly a powerhouse at this point; Russian mobsters and miscellaneous nuclear weapons floating around are considered significant).

- A flood of cheap commodities worldwide, thus skewing the balance of payments in many countries dependent on exporting these commodities.

- Rising labor costs in the U.S., as well as some disappointment with corporate earnings.

- A U.S. president whose adolescent behavior has thrown into question his leadership of the country; investors like boring, go-along presidents when things are going, as well as they have through most of the 1990s.

This neatly segues into some caveats about our diversified portfolio selections:

QUICK ⟨ ⟩ PAINLESS

A bond fund is a good way to invest in municipal bonds and give you some tax advantages at the same time.

- Large-cap stocks don't do well when the entire market is heading south. As an investor, you'll need the willingness to weather these downturns while re-examining your portfolio allocations. Erratic trading among funds and investments during down markets is a guaranteed way to lose money.

- Small caps are typically among the most volatile stocks. This volatility—the risk factor—is the Jeckyl/Hyde personality of these stocks. You can do very well or watch your money vanish without even getting the entertainment value of a nightclub magician. According to *The Wall Street Journal* (August 28, 1998, p. C-11), the Russell 2000 small-stock index was down 16.23 percent for the first eight months of 1998. For that matter, the Wilshire 5000 Index, which covers almost every U.S.-based publicly traded company, saw its market value drop $1.71 trillion from July 17 to August 28—$435 billion on August 27 alone!

- Foreign stocks haven't been faring all that well lately either. According to the same issue of *WSJ* (how timely for yours truly), demand for commodities, such as oil, copper, and grain, has dropped due to weakening economies, especially in Asia. At the same time, production capacity is up. Commodities are a major stock and trade with many developing countries. You don't buy my oil, I don't get any money to pay my bills, and my country's economy falters. Who's going to invest here? So much for the potentially booming markets overseas. And at any

IF YOU'RE SO
INCLINED

Watch the broad market for noticeable changes in one segment of it. These can affect your holdings as well if reactions spread across the market at large in a domino effect. When investors and fund managers rejoice over lower interest rates, for instance, just about everything goes up in value.

time, foreign stocks are subject to currency risks since they are valued in their national currency which can drop against the dollar.

■ Yields on 10-year Treasury bonds have fallen to their lowest level since 1967, while their prices are the highest since the end of 1968. Why? Because traders and investors are buying them at any price in a so-called flight to quality because Treasuries are a sure thing in an uncertain market. The higher their price—as driven up by demand—the lower their yield since their interest rate is fixed when they're issued.

■ Meanwhile, back at the bank, some money market rates are paying more than Treasuries, all the while giving you immediate access to your cash with less restrictive terms.

In terms of risk, from least to worst, your investment choices would look like this:

1. U.S. Treasuries

2. Federally insured bank accounts

3. Money market accounts

4. Corporate bonds

5. Blue chip stocks

6. Small-cap stocks

7. Junk bonds (high yield)

8. Options

YOU'LL THANK YOURSELF LATER

Despite setbacks, history is on your side. Healthy, solid companies will survive and prosper in good times and bad. A jump in interest rates or a country defaulting on its bonds isn't the end of the world, although it may slow down your returns for awhile.

9. Commodities

10. Lottery ticket purchases

Look at it this way: the market is like junior high school social life. Sometimes it's your friend, sometimes it ignores you, and other times it pulls the rug out from under you by stealing your boy/girlfriend and going on its merry way to the spring dance. In the long run, the market will be like those same school friends/nemeses at your 20-year reunion: friendlier, more mature, and willing to put the bad times—like our current dropping markets—behind them. (Well, maybe everybody except the jerk who stole all your clothes after gym class while you were in the shower.) How does this adolescent sociology apply to your investing? Simple: sometimes the market favors one investment over another. When things look bad, remember to:

QUICK **n** *PAINLESS*

If you're at a standstill, a blended fund—one that has both stocks and bonds— gives you the easiest way out of making investment decisions. Start with that and diversify later when you're more comfortable with investing.

- Stay diversified and keep yourself covered.

- Avoid emotional responses (scream all you want, just don't hit the "sell" button).

- Remember you're in this for the long run; time heals most wounds, as well as dropping stock prices.

- Look over your portfolio and ask yourself: Do I still have a good reason to own each of these investments? If not, which ones should I change?

- Maintain your asset allocation if it still suits your original plan.

- Remember the tax implication if you do sell.

PUTTING IT TOGETHER

You should be fairly convinced by now that index funds, at least for large-cap stocks, should be part of your portfolio. Skip the ongoing is/is-not/is-too debate dialog between indexers and managed fund advocates and look for index funds:

- With low expense ratios (.25 percent or less for most domestic funds).
- That represent the broad market (Wilshire 5000).
- For corporate and municipal bonds.
- For large capitalization stocks such as the S&P 500.

Foreign funds can benefit from active management and small-cap funds can go either way.

According to *Kipplinger's* (March, 1998), the Vanguard Group offers index funds with some of the lowest expense ratios around including:

- Vanguard Index 500 (0.2 percent expense ratio, call 800-635-1511 for a prospectus or www.vanguard.com)
- Vanguard Index Total Stock Market (0.25 percent; mimics Wilshire 5000 Index)
- Vanguard Index Total Bond Market (0.2 percent)

For more information than you ever wanted on index funds, go to:

- http://www.indexfundsonline.com
- http://indexinvesting.com
- http://www.vanguard.com

YOU'LL THANK YOURSELF LATER

Index funds are not created alike, even if they're both buying the same index. Examine the expense ratios carefully. Some index funds charge like managed funds!

You'll want to weigh your investing among large-cap, small-cap, foreign, bond, and money market funds. It may sound like a lot of work, but it doesn't have to be.

DECISIONS, DECISIONS

Ads for actively managed mutual funds take up a lot of room in financial publications. Often they show one or two guys—sorry, it's still mostly guys running these things—sometimes with their sleeves rolled up, letting you know they'll work hard for you and your dollars. Managed mutual funds are fine if:

- They have a low expense ratio.
- Their performance has been superior compared to their peers over a long time frame (5 to 10 years is good).
- The management team and management philosophy stays consistent (check Morningstar or the funds' own reports).

Remember, it's easy to pick a poor-performing fund so do your homework. You may decide to diversify your entire portfolio with index funds—even your foreign holdings—keeping your expenses down and not worrying about missing out on returns.

A core holding in your portfolio should be a large-cap fund. Unless the entire economy goes into an intermediate to long-term funk, which is always possible, established, well-managed blue chip companies will usually roll out steady, but not always outstanding, earnings. Choose the S&P 500 index as a starter (if you want a

YOU'LL THANK YOURSELF LATER

Fees and expenses eat away at your returns. Choose funds that outperform their peers and have a low expense ratio.

While you invest in your mutual funds through automatic deposits from your checking account, be sure to reinvest your dividends, as well.

broader index, choose the Wilshire 5000). Every major fund company has one of these and they're very competitive. You'll want to look for:

- A low fee structure (as always)
- A low minimum initial investment
- The fund's return on investment (since they all mimic the S&P 500—fewer expenses—the returns should be similar)

Every fund will list its recent returns, as well as incremental ones, such as the five-year return, and return since inception, on their website or prospectus. Sometimes the minimums can be high for non-retirement accounts. Vanguard has a $3,000 minimum for their Vanguard Index 500 fund, plus a $10 yearly fee for accounts under $10,000. The Schwab S&P 500 Index has a $1,000 minimum. However, there are some exceptions to these requirements and they fall into two categories:

- IRA accounts
- Automatic investment plans

IRA accounts, including the new Roth IRAs, get a break, sometimes a big one! Schwab drops its minimum to $500. Vanguard also drops to a $1,000 minimum, but Strong (www.strongfunds.com or 800-359-3379) goes as low as a $250 initial investment! If an IRA account is right for you, there's no excuse for not opening one at these prices. You can easily build up a healthy IRA balance with monthly contributions in these funds, which brings us to our second exception: automatic investment plans, an easy, tried-and-true wealth builder.

A number of funds will allow you to invest in their index funds, as a non-retirement account, for $500 or less if you set up an automatic investment plan, which entails monthly minimum investments from your checking account, starting as low as $50 with some funds.

Some of these funds include:

- T. Rowe Price Equity Index (based on the S&P 500; www.troweprice.com or 800-638-5660)

- Strong Index 500

- Waterhouse DJIA (Dow Jones Industrial Average; www.waterhouse.com or 800-934-4410)

- T. Rowe Price Total Market (Wilshire 5000 Index)

Be sure to check the expense ratio of these funds and any fees for account balances under certain minimums— I know, I'm sounding like a broken record, or CD as the case may be, but fees make a huge difference in your long-term returns. These can be great ways to get started on your portfolio building, whether it's for an IRA or a taxable account.

HOW TO SLICE THE PIE

Before you cut into the investment pie, you'll have to consider some questions:

- How big should your core holding of large-cap stocks be?

- What about your other holdings?

YOU'LL THANK YOURSELF LATER

Remember, your first investments should be for retirement. These tax-deferred accounts are really in for the long term and are an easy place to invest in mutual funds.

How do you balance performance with volatility?

Should I maintain the same diversification as I age?

It depends on your age and with whom you speak. It also depends on the type of account, retirement or taxable. One old rule even calls for subtracting 10 from your age and using the resulting figure as your bond allotment! That's about as good as saying your blood pressure should be equal to your age plus 100—an old belief, actually.

The younger you are, the better chance you'll have of recovering from periods of market decline. A 100 percent stock portfolio will win out in the end over other investments, but what if you're 70 years old and the market goes into a five-year decline, right when you want to retire and start drawing income from your investments? Diversifying your portfolio, regardless of your age, is like buying insurance—it's hedging your bets to cover inevitable events whose timing you cannot control.

Investment advisors have all kinds of variations on diversification, but even with index funds, you can start with:

- 40 percent large cap
- 20 percent small cap
- 20 percent foreign funds
- 10 percent bonds
- 10 percent cash (a retirement account should be fully invested with little if any cash balance until withdrawals start)

A COMPLETE WASTE OF TIME

The 3 Worst Ways to Diversify Your Portfolio:

1. Using formulas without scrutinizing your specific situation.

2. Holding onto too much cash.

3. Failing to rebalance your portfolio annually.

This is a starting point. Once you've set your allocation, stick with it despite temptations to follow the hottest investment sectors. If interest rates start going through the roof and stocks stagnate, then bonds could be very attractive. The Swiss might decide to declare war on Liechtenstein just to show the world they're not a bunch of neutral, pacifist, sissy watchmakers, and drive down international stocks in the process. And small-cap stocks could be on the ropes as they were in 1998, wearing a big hat—or, ahem, a large cap—that says, "VOLATILITY HAPPENS . . . GET USED TO IT." In the long run, which should be your time frame, a healthy mix of stock and bond mutual funds will serve you well into retirement.

Building your financial future isn't going to happen overnight, but that doesn't mean it has to be a laborious process. Mutual funds in general, and index funds in particular, can get you there without a lot of hand-wringing and stress. There will always be investments that get better returns, but how consistently? And with how much work on your part? Investing can be as hard—or as easy—as you want it to be. Getting an early start and investing consistently and regularly are more important than trying to pinpoint the perfect, good-at-all-times allocation. Investing the hard way won't guarantee you returns superior to doing it the easy way—and you may incur serious losses. Index funds, as well as managed funds, will have their losing periods, too, but without as much drama as, say, betting the house on a new chain of Ten-Minute Therapy Centers for the Truly Insane when they do their initial public offering.

YOU'LL THANK YOURSELF LATER

Trying to guess the direction of the market and jumping from one investment to the other is a sure way to rack up losses. Even seasoned investors take huge losses trying to latch onto bigger and bigger returns. Stick with a basic—and usually conservative—plan.

All in the Family

As mentioned in the Chapter 10, mutual fund families offer numerous choices to satisfy the most finicky investor. What if you think some families are more dysfunctional than others and you want to pick and choose among them? What if you want one from T. Rowe Price, one from Oppenheimer, and one from Vanguard? That's a lot of monthly statements to deal with. You need the one-stop shopping of a discount broker where you only need to fill out one application for all of your funds—and receive only one monthly statement. A single phone call—instead of a lot of calls to a lot of mutual funds—gets the ball rolling. Brokers to contact include:

- Charles Schwab & Co. (www.schwab.com or 800-435-4000; One Source, over 850 no-load, no-fee mutual funds)

- Jack White Discount Brokers (www.jackwhite.com or 800-216-2333, NoFeeNetwork, 1,300 no-fee funds)

- Quick & Reilly (www.quick-reilly.com or 800-222-0481; No Transaction Fee Network)

- Waterhouse Securities (www.waterhouse.com; Investors Fund Family Network, over 1,000 no-fee funds)

- Muriel Siebert (www.msiebert.com; 794 no-fee funds)

- Wells Trade (www.wellsfargo.com or 800-TRADERS; a new entry in the discount brokerage area and possibly a hint of banks offering this service in the future)

Active traders will find fault with just about every brokerage firm, especially those online. Newsgroups on the Internet always feature harangues—and kudos—for all of them. For your long-term investment purposes, you have little to be concerned about. Buy-and-hold investors (those who do little trading and hold on to their investments for years) will be content with most brokers, but check out all their costs. Long-established players offer a comfort factor that new Internet firms may not have established yet.

That said, there is no reason to use a full-service broker. Their guidance and research isn't necessarily going to be any better than yours—and it can be worse. Good or bad, they still get their money while you pay high commissions. Stick with a discount broker (many of whom are offering some services similar to a full-service broker) or even one of the steep discounters or web brokers (see Chapter 12).

Fund families can provide you with an easy way to buy international and small-cap index funds, too, but remember the rules:

- Look at each fund's 10-year record.
- Check how the fund has done against its peers and its equity grouping.
- Look for expense ratios under 1.5 percent for stock funds and under one percent for bond funds.
- Look for stable management; a change in management may mean a change in the fund's return.

IF YOU'RE SO
INCLINED

Check all the fees and services—not just the trading costs—at a discount broker. One firm may be better than another for your purposes, even if it doesn't have the lowest transaction costs.

THE LAZY WAY

Professional investors and active fund managers spend long days—and nights—reading annual reports, examining cash-flow figures, and sometimes visiting the companies they're considering investing in before making their final decisions. Despite their best efforts, many of them fail to match the returns of various indexes, whose portfolio managers do very little besides keeping the funds balanced according to their respective indexes.

Notwithstanding the vociferous arguments against index funds, they appear to meet their mark the better part of the time. They are an appropriate vehicle for a passive investor who neither has the time nor the expertise to decipher cash-flow figures and profit-and-loss statements. This isn't ceding control of your financial future to someone else; it's just recognizing a solid return when you see it, a good deal for your money, and a better use of your time. If you choose actively managed funds, pick ones with long-term winning track records and portfolio managers.

Even if you're a passive/lazy investor, you still need to:

■ Rebalance your portfolio once a year in order to maintain your chosen allocation.

■ Look at your time frame and any new circumstances (like marriage, children, or an inheritance), which may cause a change in your allocation.

■ Continue your monthly contributions to your portfolio, as well as dividend reinvestment.

QUICK ⬤ PAINLESS

Opening an account at a discount brokerage firm will greatly simplify your investing. One application and you can buy just about anything. Congratulate yourself for making this first step.

- Check the expense ratios of your mutual funds. If they've increased beyond what is acceptable to you, start looking for new funds.

- Remind yourself this is for the long term.

YOU'LL THANK YOURSELF LATER

Being a lazy investor isn't a license to be negligent. No one's going to tap you on the shoulder and tell you it's time to buy or sell an investment. With some basic monitoring—and yearly portfolio adjustment—you'll do fine.

Getting Time and Money On Your Side

	The Old Way	The Lazy Way
Sticking all of your money into a bond fund vs. diversifying:	Hey, this is great, I can retire when I'm 105.	Bonds have their place, but they don't always keep pace. I must be a poet and not even know it.
Buying into a fund when I scrape some money together vs. using automatic investment each month:	Looks like we overspent on the entertainment budget this month, but I did drop $8.70 into our index fund.	$200 a month off the top right into our retirement account and we don't even miss it.
Maintaining a large cash balance instead of buying equities:	Wow, I'm getting four percent interest!	I keep just enough cash in my brokerage account to pay for transactions fees and yearly account fees.
Buying a mutual fund based on its name recognition vs. doing some basic research:	I figured with a name like The Issac Newton Technical Fund it couldn't miss.	The fund name guides, research decides.

Chapter twelve

A Stock Fund With Your Name on It

In his book *Beating the Street,* Peter Lynch discusses a class of seventh-graders whose stock picks produced a 70-percent gain over two years, and outperformed just about every equity mutual fund in the universe. How? They researched products and services they understood and had interacted with everyday. They didn't work at this full-time the way fund managers do—the same well-paid managers who couldn't beat a group of 13 year olds.

Some investors—even lazy ones—find mutual funds boring and unchallenging. These same investors, by doing some research and taking a more active hand in their investments, can successfully pick individual stocks and unit investment trusts (SPDRs, DIAMONDs, and WEBs) for their portfolio. You can mimic the passive investment tactics of fund managers—on a more limited basis—through tentative approaches such as the Dogs of the Dow. The Dogs requires investing in the 10 highest-yielding stocks of the Dow Jones Industrial Average

QUICK ⬛ PAINLESS

and updating your portfolio on a once-a-year basis. Author and fund manager James O'Shaughnessy swears by the Dogs—and other advisors swear atO'Shaughnessy.

With careful planning and some monitoring, you can build your own fund and call the shots. You can determine when to take capital gains (increases in the value of the stock or bond that are taxable) and profits or sell for offsetting losses, whether it's in a taxable account or an IRA. You can have business cards printed naming yourself as king/queen of your newly founded fund, and then mention to card gawkers that the fund is currently closed to outside investors. Or, you can make it simpler yet by hiring your seventh-grade niece to take care of your investments for you while paying her a modest fee. If she starts demanding more, threaten to turn her into the SEC as an unlicensed stockbroker.

You already know about mutual funds. Now we'll snoop around some mutual fund clones as well as the equities that go into funds.

PARKING FOR STOCKHOLDERS ONLY

Remember what happens when you buy a share of stock: You become a part owner of the company issuing the stock. You can call Dell Computer and tell the help line, "Yeah, put Mike Dell on the line. Tell him it's one of his partners and I think my hard drive's a little slow." Single stocks sound a little too risky for your tastes? Try a SPDR, WEBS, or DIAMONDs.

Technically, these are unit investment trusts (UITs) that hold a portfolio of stocks and bonds and then sell shares of themselves in the secondary market. They're easy to buy and understand and offer the lazy investor professional management and diversification—without buying into a mutual fund.

Standard & Poor's Depository Receipt (SPDRs), World Equity Benchmark Shares (WEBS), and DIAMONDs are traded on the American Stock Exchange, or AMEX. An SPDR is similar to a S&P 500 index fund because it's based on the same basket of stocks. Buy a share of an SPDR (stock symbol: SPY) and you own a fraction of the S&P 500 stocks. A MidCap SPDR (symbol: MDY) tracks the S&P Midcap Index, those companies that haven't made it to large-cap fame yet. DIAMONDs (symbol: DIA) take in less territory, namely the 30 stocks in the Dow Jones Industrial Average. What you're really buying in each case is part of the trust that holds the stocks.

Price-wise, SPDRs and DIAMONDs are a good budget fit for the small investor. DIAMOND shares trade at approximately 1/100 the value of the Dow Jones Industrial Average. A SPDR share goes for approximately 1/10 the price of the S&P 500 index.

So far these sound like index mutual funds. But there are some differences for the independent investor:

- Mutual fund share prices are mostly end-of-the-day prices. If the market is quickly sinking, you can get out faster with unit investment trusts, which trade like stocks, thus, the prices vary throughout the day.

- SPDRs and DIAMONDs have low management fees (well under one percent) and no transaction fees

IF YOU'RE SO
INCLINED

Compare the transaction fees—basically the brokerage fee—of a UIT against the management fees for a no-load mutual fund. Additional purchases of investment trust shares, aside from dividend reinvestment, may cost more than the same purchase of mutual fund shares.

other than broker commissions (these can be quite low with web trading).

▨ There are no 12b-1 fees.

Unlike mutual funds, SPDRs and DIAMONDs cannot reinvest your dividends in partial shares, so any left-over cash—after full shares are purchased—will sit around until you reinvest it. These are both excellent vehicles for a passive/mildly aggressive investor who wants diversification and safety, but doesn't quite like the feeling of being in the public swimming pool of a mutual fund.

Before you go running off to buy SPY or DIA, become an informed investor first. A prospectus is available by contacting:

▨ www.amex.com (download)

▨ 800-THE-AMEX

▨ PDR Services Corp.
c/o The American Stock Exchange
86 Trinity Place
New York, New York 10006-1861

From Spiders to WEBS

Looking for a foreign flare? WEBS are the international set of the unit trusts. Each WEBS represents an index series (based on the Morgan Stanley Capital International Index, or MSCI) for each of 17 different countries. What does this mean for you? It means you can buy WEBS for as many of these 17 countries—no, I'm not going to list them all—as you want. It's not one-stop international investing, and it's riskier than a more

YOU'LL THANK YOURSELF LATER

Reinvest your SPDR and DIAMOND dividends for maximum return. You don't want unneeded cash sitting around idle, especially in a retirement account.

BUILD YOUR FINANCIAL FUTURE The Lazy Way

broadly based fund, but if you think a specific country is going to take off, WEBS are a great way to put your money down.

As always, be informed first by calling 800-810-WEBS for a prospectus.

REALLY BIG LANDLORDS

There is one other unit investment trust—a Real Estate Investment Trust (REIT)—that you've probably read about. A REIT is another hybrid investment. It sells like a stock, but looks like a mutual fund made up of commercial and residential properties and mortgages. REITs have been one of the Wall Street darlings in the 1990s, but their more recent performance has been quite mixed. Some REITs are very limited in their scope of property holdings and others are all over the board, including some Las Vegas casino properties, which would at least make the stockholder meetings fun. These are not necessarily for the lazy investor. Like most real estate related investments, they can be time-consuming to pick through—and then there are all those tenants to deal with.

For a list of REITs, go to http://realtymall.com/reits for links and names.

TAKING STOCK

Remember Peter Lynch's seventh graders? They didn't buy any mutual funds or unit trusts, only stocks. Of course, they weren't dealing with real money—too bad, they could have paid for an end-of-the-school-year party they would have remembered for the rest of their lives.

QUICK **n** *PAINLESS*

If you're uncomfortable with narrow-focused foreign stocks, then skip WEBS altogether. Single-country stocks are bigger bets than broad-based international mutual funds.

Buy what you under-
stand and can measure.
If profits from selling
toothpaste make more
sense to you than
depending on regional
rental property, then let
this guide you as you
choose investments.

You don't need to spend every one of your non-
working, waking moments chasing down every stock
chart and financial newsletter in sight. You can, for
instance, piggyback onto other people's research. There
are investors who simply follow the lead of Warren
Buffett, the billionaire guy behind Berkshire-Hathaway,
the most expensive stock on the New York Stock
Exchange (it hit a high of $84,000 a share in 1998;
Warren just doesn't believe in stock splits). They buy
what he buys and do just fine. This brings us to a short
lecture on investing and motivations.

THE LECTURE

In the cold, cruel world of business and the stock market,
all that's suppose to count are numbers: is the company
making money, how much cash does it have, what do the
sales look like, stuff like that. This is what all of these business guys—and it is mostly guys—would have you believe.
They see themselves as tight-fisted, steely individuals,
exuding rationality and precision thinking. Uh, huh.
These are the same smart guys like the head of Quaker
Oats who paid $1 billion for Snapple Beverages only to
eventually sell it at a loss. Apparently the idea of coming
up with their own ice tea product was simply too daunt-
ing of a task. If they had bought a billion dollars' worth
of stock in Coca-Cola instead of Snapple they would have
made a profit of millions—and millions—of dollars.

You can add Boeing to this list, too. They've had
losses and write-offs to the tune of billions of dollars this
past year because, among other things, they sold planes

for less than they cost to manufacture. That's under-standable—they admitted they actually don't know what it costs to manufacture a plane. Maybe the now ex-head of the commercial airplane group, who, according to the *Seattle Times,* referred to himself as "Top Gun"—needed a little more ammunition. A lot of angry stockholders probably wish they had some ammunition. As a potential shareholder, you want to buy into solid, well-run compa-nies based on long records of solid returns.

Too often we bring a lot of irrational behaviors to the marketplace, vestiges of our cave days when we had to hunt and skin wild beasts for their meat and fur and other fun survival activities. The only hunting we do now is stalking a sirloin steak at the grocery store. If we want a warm coat we open an Eddie Bauer catalog and order a down parka. But our emotional evolution hasn't quite caught up with our technological evolution. We have to take it out somewhere and one handy place is the stock market.

How so? By hunting stocks, taking risks that don't make any sense on paper, trying to get a jump on every-one else to show how smart we are, even continuing to buy into a rapidly deteriorating company because we feel like it's on the edge of a turnaround even though we know from the numbers that it's on the edge of a cliff. This might be a little more like cognitive dissonance at work, but that's another story.

Understand how your feelings affect your investing, keep them at bay, and limit your hunting and gathering to the grocery store. Investing is a humbling experience.

QUICK ⬛ PAINLESS

An easy way to find bar-gains? Start by reading the news! At this writing, the government is trying to snuff out the tobacco companies and their stocks are looking very cheap. Same with some tech companies whose sales are lagging due to the downturn in Asia.

It shows that it's tough to outsmart the market and you'll get a lot further as a thoughtful observer than recklessly punching away.

The stock and bond markets are not unlike large farmers' markets, except that you don't see as many overalls or get to sniff truckloads of Walla Walla onions. The market is simply buyers and sellers coming together and agreeing upon terms of purchase. Heads of lettuce, automobiles, those funny eyeglasses with googly eye-balls hanging out on springs, or shares of Xerox—they all have one thing in common: Someone is usually selling and someone is buying. The prices are determined simply by the willingness of both parties to come up with a figure they can both live with. This is why some people will pay thousands of dollars for one of Elvis Presley's old socks and someone in Newfoundland may pay the same amount for a house.

From a practical viewpoint, some prices don't make any sense at all. Emotions have a huge influence on the final price tag—witness Elvis's socks. Well, actually, you'd probably rather not think of his footwear, but aside from being associated with a long dead singer (sorry to break the news, he really isn't living incognito in Montana) socks are socks.

Once a stock is out in stockholder land, anything can happen. It can shoot up way beyond any tangible worth of the company. Just look at Amazon.com, the on-line bookstore. It has lost money since the day it opened its doors, yet the stock has gone crazy. Analysts and buyers have shoved any and all discretion and fiscal caution into a closet and locked the door. Why? Oh, because they feel

A COMPLETE WASTE OF TIME

The 3 Worst Ways to Invest in Brand-Name Stocks:

1. Invest without investigating the company.

2. Invest without checking out competitors.

3. Hold onto a stock out of misguided expectations.

like it will do well since it has such a prominent Internet presence. If there's one easy rule to remember in the stock market, it's this: Feelings can make you go broke.

Investing is a show of faith in the future. It shows you believe that the world will keep on turning, despite some setbacks, and grow more and more prosperous. As it does, it will demand more computers, soap, diet sodas, and boxed sets of kitchen knives guaranteed to cut through tuna fish cans with just a couple of swipes—as seen on TV! It's your belief that the companies you invest in today will be part of that prosperity and growth tomorrow.

The easy way to be a successful investor is to:

- Buy large-cap stocks (you can expand your scope of buying later)

- Invest for the long haul

- Avoid panic selling

- Not buy into fads

You've heard the phrase, "I'm playing the market now." Playing is something you do with basketballs and Scrabble boards (although probably not at the same time). This is your money we're talking about—the green stuff that doesn't come to you all that easily! Until you have so much that you can treat large amounts of it like so much play money, you have to take your investing seriously. No playing!

Stocks will give you a long-term, financially secure future. No two ways about it. People who bury all of their money in bonds and CDs may feel safe, but, with

IF YOU'RE SO
INCLINED

Some solid companies go into decline. Chrysler almost went broke in the early 1980s. Penn Central Railroad did go broke. IBM hit the skids a few years back and has since recovered. Read up on the histories of these companies to get some idea of the problems any large company can face—including the ones you invest in!

Long-term fixed rate instruments like bonds can lock you into a low rate of return that may not even keep up with inflation. Avoid long-term investments like these unless rates start dropping and you have locked in a fabulous rate.

these investments, they can't protect themselves from inflation and taxes and interest rate changes. With stocks you can:

- Spread your risk.
- Build a broad-based portfolio.
- Gain both income and equity appreciation.
- Retire gracefully.

Think of the stock market as your savings account, except with much bigger numbers, and an invisible warning label that reads:

- Despite history, you can't predict future returns.
- There will be down periods, maybe with losses.
- The market is a long-term investment.

Hmm, sounds like raising a child. In a sense, that's a compelling analogy. You start cautiously, have your ups and downs, and ultimately watch your baby grow up—as a brilliant, wealthy scientist-business-owner-award winning athlete, of course!

End of lecture.

SO WHAT ARE YOU GOING TO BUY?

You have thousands of individual stocks to choose from among the stock exchanges. For starters, stick with the blue chip, large company stocks that pay dividends. These are not the fastest growers, but they're a good for beginners and are generally reliable in the long term. Geraldine Weiss, who publishes *Investment Quality Trends,* is a big believer in dividends as an indicator of a solid company. The ability to pay dividends, especially with regular increases, suggests a well-managed company with confidence in its future. After all, you don't go around sending your shareholders checks if you think you'll need the money to pay the light bills. Weiss's newsletter, which has been published for over 30 years, has received a high rating by the *Hulbert Financial Digest,* which rates the performance of investment newsletters.

A word about newsletters: Many of them offer dubious advice as evidenced by their inability to match the market, let alone beat it. By all means send for and read complimentary copies, as well as those at your local library. Be sure to check out the *Hulbert Financial Digest* before subscribing to any newsletter. Some are fairly expensive and your money can be better spend doing some actual investing.

Woof!

A popular—some would say fanatical—investment strategy for the past several years, based in part on dividends, is the Dogs of the Dow, or Dow Dividend Approach. In a nutshell, the Dogs approach entails:

- Picking the 10 highest-yielding stocks of the Dow Jones Industrial Average (highest dividends per price of the stock).
- Buying roughly equal dollar amounts of each stock.
- Holding the stocks for one year.
- At the end of a one year period, rebalancing the mix to include any new highest-yielding stocks.

This is a ridiculously simple, mechanical approach to investing. It proposes that a high yield on a big blue chip

QUICK 🔳 PAINLESS

The future will bring a large number of aging boomers (think pharmaceutical stocks), computers in every room (tech stocks), and more consumers all over the world clamoring for soft drinks (beverage companies). With this in mind, you can narrow your choices, fill up a portfolio, and sleep easily.

company suggests that its price is depressed and probably a temporary situation. Various practitioners of this theory quote studies going back for years (showing how the return of the Dogs beat the S&P 500 index) to support their claims that it's the best thing since the invention of cordless phones.

With the Dogs, you don't have to research anything and at best spend less than an hour a year on balancing your portfolio. Investment advisor Frank A. Jones, former director of the Eighth District Federal Reserve Bank, describes the Dogs as "a simple, mechanical, disciplined approach for investing in large-capitalization, blue chip companies." He's right—and the billions of dollars invested in the Dogs and mutual funds based on the Dogs agree with him. The Dogs are fine for the lazy investor looking for large-cap exposure without having to work through the stock listings from Abbot Laboratories to Xerox.

You can find the Dogs listed monthly in *The Wall Street Journal*, with all 30 stocks in the DJIA ranked by dividend yield. Faster yet (and available daily) is the website www.dogsofthedow.com, or go to the Motley Fool's website (motleyfool.com). The Motley Fool—a we're-smarter-than-those-dumb-Wall-Street-guys investment site—is a big advocate of the Dogs theory and explains it and its variations at length.

As this is written, you can buy shares in all 10 companies, albeit only a few shares in each, for a little over $2,000 by going to a deep discount broker on the web. At $7.95 per trade, you can make 10 separate purchases as the chart below shows.

QUICK n' PAINLESS

The Dogs approach is not a substitute for more in-depth research before you invest. It's a simple way to get started in blue chip stocks without much of a downside.

Top Yielding DJIA Stocks (as of 8/28/98)

Company	Price	Shares	Total Price
Phillip Morris (MO)	$42^{13}/_{16}$	4	$171.25
JP Morgan (JP)	97	2	$195.50
General Motors (GM)	$61^{1}/_{16}$	3	$183.19
Chevron (CHV)	$75^{1}/_{4}$	3	$225.75
Minn. Mining & Man. (MMM)	$75^{5}/_{8}$	3	$227.88
Caterpillar (CAT)	44	5	$220
International Paper (IP)	39	5	$195
Exxon (XON)	$67^{9}/_{16}$	3	$202.68
Dupont (DD)	$58^{1}/_{16}$	3	$174.19
Goodyear (GT)	$49^{13}/_{16}$	4	$199.25

Total: $1,994.69
Commisions (10 @ $7.95): $79.50
Total Cost: $2,074.19

According to www.thedogsofthedow.com, this approach has returned an average of 17.7 percent since 1973. Detractors are less generous, claiming the interpretation of various studies is distorted, that the more people buy these stocks the higher their price due simply to the popularity of this investment approach, thus skewing the prices, and, hey, they have their own studies that prove the Dogs are appropriately named. Daniel Kadlec (*Time* magazine, 12/8/97), for instance, quotes a study by Morningstar, Inc., that suggests that the most pronounced gains occurred during the first 12 years of this time frame. James O'Shaugnnessy—a true believer—would say you have to look at the bigger picture and not pick specific periods of time for your measurement. Everybody jumps in with an opinion on this one. Nevertheless, a lazy investor can easily buy into these stocks (all substantial companies) for a relatively small amount of money. As our case above demonstrates, yields ranging from 2.41 percent to 4.11 percent are possible with only once-a-year maintenance. Overall return over a 12-month period cannot be determined, but if history is any guide you should be ahead.

Once you buy into the Dogs, leave them alone for the year and let the approach do its job. This is truly passive, long-term investing.

NO BROKERS AT ALL . . . ALMOST

Corporations get people to invest in them by offering them something in return—money, in one form or another, although it would be fun if Hershey would ship out a box of candy bars with each annual report. Dividends, as well as share price appreciation, are the two ways you make money with stocks. A healthy

QUICK 🖾 PAINLESS

The Dogs can be started anytime. You decide when to start the one year holding period. Your day going to the dogs? Invest in them!

dividend—and a history of increasing dividends—can make a stock very appealing, all other things being equal.

Dividends are usually paid quarterly. Complete stock listings will note a stock's dividend and its yield (the dividend divided into the stock price). A $90-stock paying a $2.80 dividend has a yield of 3.1 percent. As a lazy investor, you can put dividends to work for you and avoid brokerage commissions at the same time.

Dividend Re-Investment Plans (DRIPs) allow you to automatically reinvest your stock dividends toward the purchase of additional shares, even fractional shares, such as 1.3799 shares. There are entire books, websites, and newsletters devoted to dividend reinvesting which, when used properly, can advance you toward your financial goals almost without your thinking about it.

DRIPs offer a number of advantages:

- Low fees (depends on the company).

- Some have automatic investment.

- Some companies actually sell you the stock at a discount (around three to five percent) on the prevailing share price.

- Optional cash purchases (OCP) allow you to buy large amounts of stock with funds besides dividends and without broker commissions.

What's not to like? You buy direct from the issuing company without any middle men/women/people taking a cut of the action. DRIPs are a great idea, with some DRIP participating companies, but they're an investment approach to be avoided with others.

IF YOU'RE SO
INCLINED

There are hundreds of investment newsletters. Many will send a complimentary copy of their most recent edition. Check out the newsletters at your public library as well.

The 3 Worst Ways to Invest in DRIPs:

1. Ignoring the true cost and fees.

2. Investing in a company because it has a DRIP rather than because it's a good company.

3. Not taking advantage of optional cash purchases.

Bad DRIP, Good DRIP

The only way DRIPs make sense is when the costs are low enough to compete with deep discount brokerage fees. DRIP fees include:

- The purchase of at least one initial share registered in your name (usually through a broker)

- One-time enrollment fees

- Yearly administrative fees

- Transaction fees

Many DRIP plans require that you own at least one share of their stock and that it be registered in your own name. Almost all brokerage accounts hold the stock and other equities in the broker's "street name." Instead of issuing you a paper stock certificate, which is very artistic and cool to look at, your equities are merely an electronic entry in the broker's bookkeeping system. This system allows for easier trading and safe keeping. Otherwise, you would have to physically possess, securely store, and transfer the actual certificates, a nuisance in the electronic age. There is usually a fee for holding them in your name and requesting the certificates. A DRIP company requires you to register at least one share in your own name so you can be identified as the owner; they don't know it's you when the stock is in the street name. Some DRIPs will sell you the initial share, but most don't.

Set-up and yearly fees vary with each DRIP. The transaction fees also vary. They're almost always cheaper than a broker for small purchases, but not always with larger optional cash purchases. But if you're selective, DRIPs can work very much in your favor. Remember, if the fees are too high, your shares have that much further to grow for you to get a positive return.

Two companies that have wonderful DRIPs are Coca-Cola and Exxon—just try to overlook that little tanker problem they had in Alaska a few years back. Coca-Cola (800-446-2617 or FCTC@DELPHI.COM for the plan administrator) pays all purchase and maintenance costs after you buy the first share. They'd have to pay you to buy their shares to make it any cheaper. And it's a great stock. Coke is driven. Their last couple of annual reports have made it clear that they are currently supplying only about two ounces of the daily fluid requirement for human beings—based on the then world population—of 64 ounces a day, and they clearly have a long way to go. Granted, that 64 ounces usually refers to plain water, but Coke doesn't let details get in the way. As far as Coke is concerned, water is their main competitor. They'll probably have the first bottling plant on Venus (Motto: "The drink that refreshes when you're a colonist living in an atmosphere of almost pure carbon dioxide that is absolutely hostile to human life.").

Exxon (800-252-1800), a premiere DRIP company, lets you in for a $250 minimum initial purchase, no purchasing fees, and automatic investment is available. If you're feeling really flush, Exxon allows you an optional cash purchase of up to $100,000 worth of stock each year, or a low of $50. If you're a long-term holder, DRIPs like this offer great value and ease of investing. Send off a

YOU'LL THANK YOURSELF LATER

Even if you're reinvesting your dividends, they are still taxable. You will receive a "1099 Misc. Income" form with the amount of paid dividends. Include this form with your tax return.

monthly check when you do the rest of your bills while the dividends are automatically reinvested. For more information on DRIPs, contact:

- http://stocks.miningco.com (hit their DRIP link, which will lead to more links)

- www.netstockdirect.com (dedicated to direct investing)

- www.dripinvestor.com (Charles Carlson's site, a big advocate, newsletter publisher, and writer about DRIPs)

- The Money Paper, (800-388-9993, ext. 301; ask for a list of no-fee-to-buy DRIPs)

You'll have to keep stringent records for your DRIP investments (hold onto your monthly statements). Since you're buying shares at different prices and reinvesting your dividends, you'll have to know your cost basis for both tax on the dividends and capital gains tax if you're holding these stocks in a taxable account. Some plans, like Exxon and Morton International, allow for IRA participation so the record keeping is less of an issue.

Selling your DRIP stock isn't as quick or as automatic as selling stocks in a brokerage account. Many companies require written notice from you (so much for capturing today's price) and in some cases telephone or FAX requests are accepted. This may change in the years to come given the popularity of these plans. Increasing demands from DRIP shareholders, and an increase in the number of plans themselves, will no doubt bring about more competitive terms and conditions.

Really Lazy DRIPs

You like the idea of a DRIP, but want the convenience of a broker? No problem. Charles Schwab & Co., for example, offers free dividend reinvestment—that's right, no transaction charge. And you can buy fractional shares, too, Schwab doesn't care. Instead of automatically investing additional money every month (this would get too expensive with their commission rate) wait until the fee structure makes sense. Currently, their cheapest eSchwab (Internet) commission is $29.95. If you're buying a large number of shares, making a purchase two or three times a year might pay off for the convenience factor. Compare Schwab's fees with those of direct investment and other brokers offering free dividend reinvestment.

Treat a DRIP like any other investment. Research the companies available and scrutinize the fees. You don't need to waste your money on any of the newsletters with all the free downloads available on the Internet. Read each prospectus just like you would those from mutual funds. If the fees are too high, toss it out—and drink a Coke. If you participate in their DRIP, you'll be adding to your own bottom line.

NOT-FOR-PROFITS TO THE RESCUE

At this point, you might be thinking this doesn't sound all that lazy. How can I fit in recreational time on my rollerblades if I'm tracking down stocks, DRIPs, SPDRs, and WEBS? In America, there's an organization for everyone and in the case of the independent investor, there are two major ones:

QUICK 🔳 PAINLESS

DRIPs are really a long-term investment strategy. Use them this way, take advantage of the optional cash purchasing, and watch your stock value grow. This is very lazy investing.

- The NAIC (National Association of Investors Corporation, http://investmentclub.mining.com; 248-583-4880 or write NAIC, P.O. Box 220, Royal Oak, MI 48068)

- The AAII (American Association of Individual Investors, www.aaii.org; 800-428-2244)

Both of these are not-for-profits (which is a bit ironic considering they are mostly about you making profits). The NAIC was founded in 1951 with the intent of educating investors and investment clubs. The benefits of a NAIC's $39 individual yearly membership include:

- *Better Investing* magazine (monthly)

- NAIC's Official Guide (for starting and running an investment club)

- Low-Cost Investment Plan (a DRIP, with a low-cost first share purchase in selected companies)

- Investor's Information Sheets (information on individual companies)

- Other educational services and advice

Not to be outdone, the 20-year-old AAII, at $49 per yearly membership, provides:

- *AAII Journal* (published 10 times per year)

- The Individual Investor's Guide to Low-Load Mutual Funds (published in March, valued separately at $24.95)

- Additional educational materials

QUICK **n'** PAINLESS

Memberships in either the AAII or the NAIC, along with their investor educational materials and publications, can save you hit and miss research on your own. And that means more time for more important pursuits—like napping.

Both of these organizations are well worth looking into for the independent investor, especially one who's just getting started.

If you're not quite the joining type, look into the Value Line Investment Survey (www.valueline.com for subscriber information or available at many libraries). Value Line is an investment advisory service that ranks stocks according to such criteria as safety and volatility. Many investors use Value Line, which usually has an introductory rate available (currently $55 for 10 weeks). This is definitely for the hands-on investor.

One of the most popular websites is the Motley Fool (www.motleyfool.com), which was started by two brothers with the premise that Wall Street types tend to be self-aggrandizing, but not very helpful. Independent investors, the Gardner boys concluded, could do without the dubious advice of well-compensated analysts and advisors while at the same time doing with the advice of the Gardners. They have a point—they just say it about four hundred different ways. Still, it's worth visiting the site to get a you-can-beat-the-street-guys viewpoint.

Why They're Called Brokers

DRIPs won't offer you access to all stocks, so at some point you'll have to go through a stockbroker who acts as an intermediary in the secondary market, matching up buyers and sellers. We deal with intermediaries all the time, from car sales to buying groceries. They make modern life convenient and workable. So far, so good, until we get to the topic of commissions, the fees charged to handle the transactions.

YOU'LL THANK YOURSELF LATER

Read a broad range of investment information while avoiding trendy market predictions. Headlines like "The Best Hot Stocks" don't exactly imply objective data.

Before the SEC did away with fixed commission rates in 1975 and Charles Schwab & Co. shook up the investment world as the first major discount broker, you had little choice but to go to a full commission broker for your trades. In theory, you're buying advice and wisdom, a guiding hand to your financial future. In reality, you're paying a lot more money than you need to for . . . opinions. Right or wrong, good trade or bad, buying or selling, a broker gets paid with your money. Do yourself a favor, skip the high commissions, open an account with a discount or steep discount broker, and invest the difference.

I'll put it another way: don't ever bother to go to a full commission broker. In my own experience, brokers are called brokers because, if you deal with them long enough, you become just that—a little bit broker. Even a lazy investor can make informed decisions with a little investigation and reading. In these days of information overflow and competitive commission rates, full-service brokers may well become an institution of the past—or at least a very different one than it is now.

Case-in-point: For all the research, studies, charts, and advertising materials put out by brokerage houses (and mutual funds and newsletters, for that matter) how many of them managed to beat the returns of Coca-Cola, which has handsomely beaten the S&P 500 since the mid-1980s? Who doesn't know about Coca-Cola? Apparently not too many analysts, who keep calling it overvalued. And they want to charge you for this kind of advice?

A COMPLETE WASTE OF TIME

The 3 Worst Ways to Open a Brokerage Account:

1. Going to a large, full-commission broker because you think your account will be safer.

2. Shopping strictly by price rather than service and reputation.

3. Not understanding the complete fee structure of each firm.

You Get What You Pay For

Since Schwab first put its toe in the brokerage waters, a number of discount brokers have hung out their shingles and grabbed accounts from full-commission brokerage firms. All the national firms have websites where they compete with the new steep discounters—firms which charge as little at $7.95 for a trade. Many of them allow for telephone trades, as well. As mentioned in the previous chapter, every broker has its detractors and supporters, especially in the discount/steep discount arena.

Discount brokers are broken into approximately three categories:

- Discount (Schwab, Kennedy–Cabot, Accutrade)
- Moderate discount (Aufhauser, Jack White, Muriel Siebert, DLJ Direct)
- Steep discount (Ameritrade, Brown, Datek, E-Trade, SURETRADE)

The fastest way to access these and dozens of other discount brokers is to go to www.thewebinvestor.com and view their list and links. Commissions vary depending on the size of your transaction and the services performed by the broker. Most lazy investors aren't going to do much trading. Remember, you're saving for medium- and long-term goals like college education and retirement. You're not trying to be a wiseguy commodity trader, which is almost a guaranteed way to go broke, by the way. This is a building process, one in which you want to keep your costs down and your returns high. Buying

QUICK n' PAINLESS

Are you looking for discounted fees, but not bargain-basement service? Regular discount firms such as Charles Schwab now offer more services than ever before for low fees. You can feel smart and economical at the same time.

and holding quality equities always works in the long run.

THE LAZY WAY

The lazy investor can put together a winning, long-term stock portfolio using the easily available tools including:

- Newsletters and Internet sites
- Discount brokers
- DRIPs
- SPDRs, DIAMONDs, and WEBs

Internet sites (see Appendix B) are full of information and daily columns by financial reporters. I stress that much of this will be opinion, but it's a starting point for narrowing down your investment choices. Newsletters are also informative, but check their performance history in *Hulbert's Financial Digest* and read what they say with a skeptical eye.

Discount and deep-discount brokers have leveled the playing field for the individual investor. They offer trades for a fraction of the cost of a full-service broker who, in my opinion, has no place in your investment strategy.

DRIPs offer even lower costs on select stocks and, with automatic investing, offer the lazy investor an inexpensive way to build up a portfolio. SPIDRs, WEBs, and DIAMONDs provide a back-door way into a basket of stocks without having to buy into a mutual fund.

Build your stock portfolio using the same guidelines as a mutual fund portfolio:

QUICK ⬤ PAINLESS

Worried about losing your money once it's in a brokerage account? Relax. Your account at any SEC-registered firm is insured by the SIPC, the Securities Investor Protection Corporation, for up to $500,000.

- Buy a diversified group of stocks.

- Keep your transaction fees low.

- Examine your stock mix once a year and readjust if necessary.

Stock picking isn't an occult science and really is like learning to ride a bicycle—or skateboard. The more you do it, the better you'll get at it. Just be sure to keep your helmet on.

QUICK n PAINLESS

If an investment doesn't make any sense, then it's probably a bad idea. It's easy to get taken in by convincing sales tactics or media hype. It's also easy to sell an investment because of exaggerated negative news. Keep a clear focus and tune out the noise.

Getting Time and Money On Your Side

	The Old Way	The Lazy Way
Buying stocks based on the hottest new picks in Gimme Money Magazine vs. research-ing stocks that fit your investment goals:	It had a 5$$$$$ rating. That's good enough for me. No, I don't know what the company does, but it sounds techy.	I wanted a blue chip drug company and picked Merck based on my research.
Buying growth stocks when you really wanted income stocks vs. understanding the difference and buying what you really wanted:	Oh, so that's what "div" means in the stock listings.	Man, this is great, Phillip Morris is paying almost four percent.
Going to a full service broker vs. a discount broker:	Fortunately, I wore my new suit when I went to my broker's office. They have a very strict dress code, you know.	These guys are terrific: efficient, fast, and inexpensive.
Buying into a DRIP program without examining the cost vs. carefully comparing one DRIP with another:	What's it costing me? I'm not sure, but at least I'm skipping those brokers. No one can call me a chump.	This DRIP was fine, but the other two I looked into cost more than a steep discount broker.

Chapter

thirteen

The Laziest Investing: Bonds

The current accounting system of the Federal government produces the Public Debt Outstanding—our huge national IOU—each morning around 11:30 a.m., EST, after chewing over approximately 50 reports from such entities as the Federal Reserve Bank. This means that for all of you just getting settled in at work on the west coast, the U.S. Treasury (www.ustreas.gov) can provide an updated figure for our approximately five-and-one-half-trillion dollar national debt. With a population of over 270 million citizens, your share of that debt is over $20,000—think about that over your cappuccino and biscotti. The interest cost alone for fiscal year 1998 has totaled over $300 billion.

Depressing? It doesn't have to be. Much of that interest is payable to holders of Treasury bills, notes, and bonds, more familiarly known as Treasuries. Buy a T-bill, note, or bond and you can join the legions of international creditors to whom the U.S. government owes big bucks. These debt instruments are all guaranteed and backed by the government, the cash

register of last resort. Of course, when you run the printing presses, you can stamp out $100 bills as long as the paper and ink hold out. It doesn't quite work that way, but suffice to say these investments are the most guaranteed in the world.

If you're looking for absolute safety (i.e., your principal returned when held to maturity and the interest rate assured) consider Treasuries as part of your portfolio.

THE T-GUYS

The Bureau of Public Debt issues and redeems U.S. Treasuries, which mature between 13 weeks and 30 years. Treasuries are:

- Conservative
- Boring
- Easy to purchase
- Available in a variety of flavors
- Simple to understand

Remember, boring can be a good thing! In times of low inflation, dubious investment choices, and international turmoil, Treasuries are a safe port in which to park your money. Foreign investors certainly think so—they own over one-third of all privately held Treasury bonds.

Like other bonds, Treasuries are IOUs, in this case issued by the government. You can legitimately say that the Feds owe you money and you're helping them out of a rough spot by loaning them a thousand bucks or more.

Treasuries usually work best when:

- You buy them short term (unless inflation has peaked—impossible to predict—and you can lock in a high interest rate)
- They're purchased direct and held to maturity
- You need a guaranteed return

Why does the government sell so many Treasury securities? And why do their interest rates vary? And what about all this talk about a balanced budget?

We're a Little Over Budget . . .

The U.S. government has a lot of mouths to feed. Those mouths demand everything from honeybee studies to bronze highway placards reminding drivers that, yes, you're still in South Dakota. When the government's revenue is less than its outlays or spending, it runs up a deficit. Add enough deficits together and you get the national debt.

When the government sells a bond, bill, or note, they are sold at an interest rate established during an auction process. No take backs, no "I didn't mean it my fingers were crossed," and no returns, receipt or not. They take the money and run, content to spend it until the maturity date. They don't have to worry because they can always issue new debt.

When you buy a Treasury, you're locked into a set interest rate. If market interest rates drop during the maturity of your specific issue, well, gee, it's still paying

YOU'LL THANK YOURSELF LATER

Treasuries are time-sensitive investments. You don't want to get penalized for cashing in too early or in a down market, so consider your financial goals before purchasing, especially intermediate and long-term Treasuries. If your cash needs are uncertain, you may want to put off buying these investments.

an old, higher rate and now it doesn't look like such a fuddy-duddy, unexciting investment anymore.

Say you have a $1,000 bond that pays out seven percent interest. A month later, the Mr. and Mrs. President of the United States decide it's about time to do a real spring cleaning in the White House and darn if they don't find a few billion dollars kicking around in the attic in boxes marked "Xmas Ornaments, Mamie Eisenhower." After taking a 50 out to buy a pesto/garlic pizza, a six pack, and a couple of cannollis, they turn the rest of the money over to the Treasury. The Treasury now:

- May cut back their next round of borrowing.
- May call in some of their debts and pay off some bond holders.

If the Treasury makes one or both of the above choices, the markets will react. With less demand for money, the government can pay lower rates for the Treasuries it sells. It's okay with you if the interest rate drops because your rate and return are locked in. Now you can demand more money for your bond should you decide to sell it before its maturity. How come? Easy math!

Your $1,000 bond is paying seven percent, or $70.

If rates drop to six percent, you can up the price of your bond until its $70 yield equals six percent of the larger dollar amount, which in this case is $1,166.50.

Okay, it doesn't work quite that cleanly. You won't get such an exact dollar amount in the secondary market, but you get the idea. You just made some quick money! But, what the market gives, the market takes away.

Now, what if Mr. and Mrs. President were poking around and discovered tons of dry rot in the basement of the White House, maybe a few billion dollars worth and the whole place had to be put on house jacks and the foundation rebuilt. Meanwhile, the First Couple need some digs for a few months and check into the Watergate. Uh, oh, time to go looking for money. Now the government needs more funds than usual.

The market reacts again. It might say, "Well, well, looks like Uncle Sam needs another loan, but a lot of other people want one, too, like the Fund for Friends of Wood Boring Insects and Cellulose Loving Fungus. With all this demand, we want a higher return if we're going to loosen up with the bucks." Now, interest rates are higher than what you're getting for your bond.

If you want to sell it, you'll have to adjust the price and you'll have to drop it.

Your $1,000 bond is paying seven percent, or $70.

The new rates are eight percent.

All you can get now is $875 for your $1,000 bond. At $875, the $70 your bond is paying will be an equivalent of an eight-percent return.

Some investors are big holders of Treasuries. Just how do you go about buying them?

Treasuries-to-Go

Treasuries are broken down into different maturities:

- T-bills come in 13-week, 26-week, and 1-year maturities.

- T-notes have maturities of more than 1 year, but no more than 10.

QUICK ᴺ PAINLESS

Bond prices react the opposite of interest rates. If rates go up, an existing bond, with its lower rate, will drop in price. If rates drop, the bond, with its higher rate, will go up in price. None of this matters if you keep it to maturity.

- T-bonds have maturities greater than 10 years (up to 30 years).

- As of 9/16/98, all Treasuries are available in $1,000 increments, making them very affordable, while avoiding bond funds or brokers.

Treasury bills are sold at a discount on their face value—or par—and do not pay interest before maturity. At maturity, the investor receives full face value. Treasury notes and bonds pay simple interest, that is, interest on the principal only, and only semi-annually.

Treasuries are issued in a book-entry system, similar to stocks held in the street name by a broker. Both are simply electronic entries in a computerized ledger. You won't receive any paper certificate and will have nothing to physically deal with when you want to redeem or sell the issue. This makes for easy—and secure—bookkeeping.

The over $3.4 trillion dollars in treasuries are held in one of two book-entry systems:

1. TRADES

2. Treasury Direct

TRADES is the commercial book-entry system used when Treasuries are held by brokerage firms or other intermediaries who sell them for a commission. The Treasury cannot identify the owners of the 99.7 percent of its outstanding debt held in TRADES. If you buy your Treasuries through a broker, they will be registered via TRADES.

IF YOU'RE SO
INCLINED

Compare costs, returns, and tax consequences of Treasuries vs. CDs before deciding on your purchase. Both are safe and guaranteed against loss of principal, but the tax consequences are different and may effect your decision.

Treasury Direct investors only hold a fraction of that amount of securities. The Bureau of Public Debt, however, has made Treasury Direct easier and more affordable than ever for the individual investor. Why pay brokerage fees when you can save money this way?

Treasury Direct offers the lazy portfolio:

- Direct purchasing via the Internet at www. publicdebt.treas.gov

- Opening a Treasury Direct account at this same Internet address (request or download P D 5182 New Account Request); you can also open an account at any of the 37 Federal Reserve Banks around the country (list on the website)

Treasury Direct Electronic Services offer:

- Pay Direct: keeps your money in your bank account until the security you're buying is being issued; you don't even have to mail a check (fill out P D F 5381, Treasury Bill, Note, and Bond Tender and mark for automatic withdrawal; purchase price will be transferred from the same bank where Treasury Direct interest and redemption payments are currently sent).

- Reinvest Direct: allows you to reinvest in more Treasuries upon redemption of current holdings.

- To sell your Treasuries for you without your having to transfer them to a broker or other dealer; for a current fee of $34 a trade, Treasury Direct will get quotes from different brokers, give you the best price, and then deposit the proceeds in your bank

QUICK **n** PAINLESS

Treasury Direct is a great way to buy Treasuries and avoid brokerage fees. It's simple to open an account. You can even do so over the Internet.

account (you must complete P D F 5179-1, Security Transfer and Sale Request)

- A Statement of Account whenever you establish a new account or have a transaction that changes your par value amount in your account from buying, redeeming, or selling Treasuries.

Treasury Direct is the government's equivalent of buying stocks directly from the issuing company. Fill out an account form and cut the brokers out altogether. You can also start with a minimum purchase of $1,000 for all Treasuries—try that with most brokers!

What other advantages to Treasuries offer the lazy portfolio? Well, they're exempt from state and local taxes—a big plus in hyper-tax states like New York and California. This feature alone may make a Treasury more advantageous than some taxable interest-paying investments. Federal tax on T-bills isn't due until redemption; T-bond and note interest is taxable in the year it's paid.

STRIPS—Nothing to Do with Exotic Dancing

Started in 1985, the Department of the Treasury STRIPS, which stands for Separate Trading of Registered Interest and Principal of Securities, is better known in the market place as Treasury zeros or Treasury zero coupon bonds. STRIPS separate and package the interest payments from the principal payment and allow them to be traded individually. This separation is done by financial institutions and government securities brokers after they buy Treasuries.

QUICK 🔲 PAINLESS

Treasury Direct even allows for direct payment from your bank account. That means no additional paperwork on your part.

What's the point? STRIPS are just another means of trading—and a volatile one at that—but they have some advantages:

- For those who need a specific amount of money at a specific future date.
- Their guaranteed payoff makes them useful for college funding or retirement accounts.
- They are very conservative when held to maturity (conversely, they're very speculative if sold before maturity).

STRIPS do not pay periodic interest—they have only one future payment date—and they are deeply discounted. According to the Bureau of Public Debt, a $1,000 STRIPS component with 30 years to maturity would normally sell for less than $100 (mid-1998), paying $1,000 at maturity. Tax-wise, STRIPS aren't so great. In taxable accounts, you are obliged to pay a portion of your original discount—your future payoff less the discounted purchase price—each year of your ownership, even though you won't get any return for years! For this reason, STRIPS are a good investment for tax-deferred retirement accounts (see IRS Publication 550, Investment Income and Expenses).

STRIPS are guaranteed the same as Treasuries, but are only available through brokers. Are they a good idea for the lazy retirement portfolio? Certainly, if for no other reason than you don't have to reinvest periodic interest payments, such as are paid by bonds and notes, in what may be a lower-yielding environment.

A COMPLETE WASTE OF TIME

The 3 Least Profitable Ways to Invest in STRIPS:

1. Buy long-term in a taxable account.
2. Buy at a premium price.
3. Sell in a volatile market.

YOU'LL THANK YOURSELF LATER

STRIPS are quite volatile. Be sure they fit into your investment plans before taking the plunge.

Zero-coupon Treasuries' returns are set in stone if kept to maturity. For taxable accounts, look for something else with less volatility and tax friendliness (such as it is).

Since STRIPS are only available through brokers, shop around for the best commission rate.

OLD STANDBYS—SAVINGS BONDS

U.S. Savings Bonds are kind of a patriotic blast-from-the-past. The first Series E bonds were issued in 1941 and were followed by series EE and HH in 1980. There are currently more than $6 billion in U.S. Savings Bonds in homes all across the country—and some overseas, too.

Series EE Bonds are one of the easiest investments to make because:

- The minimum purchase price is $25.

- They are sold through many banks and payroll savings plans.

- The principal and interest payments are guaranteed by the U.S. government (however, there is no guaranteed minimum interest rate).

- They can be cashed in after six months without penalty.

- No commissions or fees are due at purchase.

- They are exempt from state and local taxes.

- Federal taxes on the interest aren't due until the bond is cashed or it stops earning interest in 30 years.

- They are guaranteed to reach their face value in 17 years (you're buying at 50 percent of face value).

Interest rates on the Series EE bonds is set at 90 percent of the average yield on five-year Treasury notes for the previous six months; new rates are announced in May and in November—you don't know what you'll be stuck with! Series EE bonds are worth looking at if you want a guaranteed investment that's easy to purchase with relative liquidity—but don't expect to retire on them. A big advantage is the $25 minimum purchase through payroll savings. But remember, some money market mutual funds can be started for $50 a month contributions.

There is a qualified tax exemption available for bonds used for higher education. For more details, go to http://www.publicdebt.gov or inquire at your local bank that sells U.S. Savings Bonds.

Series HH bonds are only available in higher denominations ($500 minimum) and are purchased by exchanging series EE bonds that are at least six months old.

A new addition to the savings bonds group is the Series I bonds— "I" for inflation. The first of these bonds, issued in September 1998, offer a whopping fixed rate of 3.4 percent plus a 1.24 percent added on for inflation as measured by the Consumer Price Index for Urban Consumers, or CPI-U (apparently purchases in rural Kansas don't count) for a total return of 4.66 percent. The inflation rate will be adjusted every six months. Series EE bonds currently pay 5.06 percent.

Are these a good idea? Only if inflation heats up, in which case new EE bonds would probably pay a higher rate, as well. What investor would welcome a bout of inflation? And if deflation sets in, your series I bonds

IF YOU'RE SO
INCLINED

For serious savings bonds investors, there are on-line calculators available to determine the current redemption value of your bonds. Try http://www.mmrsoft.com or http://www.bondsonline.com

won't be paying any inflation rate, but their return will slowly sink back toward their guaranteed 3.4 percent fixed rate.

Think twice before betting on an inflated future. Judiciously buying short-term bonds will keep you from getting locked into low returns if inflation returns from its current extended vacation.

And just how do you go about doing this?

Get Me a Ladder

Laddering your bond purchases is an easy way to spread your risk against changing interest rates while enjoying the security of bonds. By purchasing Treasuries of varying maturities, you can maintain a portfolio partially invested at current rates while other bonds are approaching their redemption dates. You simply buy six-month Treasuries along with longer term securities (one year, two year, three year, five year) and reinvest as each bond matures. If rates drop, your five-year bonds will maintain a higher return. Rising rates can be captured as your shorter term bonds get redeemed.

The following would be one example of laddering:

- 26-week or one year T-bills to hold tax money due later.

- Three- and four-year T-notes to go toward first two years of college tuition for a child currently in high school.

- 20-year T-bond for retirement (assumes good interest rate).

THE LAZY WAY

For guaranteed returns, you can't beat Treasuries. They won't yield the highest interest in town, but there's something to be said for stability and dependability. Stocks may produce an overall historically higher return, but they won't do this at all times. They've even been known to retreat on occasion (note the crash of 1987)! Bonds are ideal for meeting short-term financial goals, where security of principal is critical, like the imminent beginning of college tuition bills three or four years down the road. Treasury Direct gives the individual investor cheap, easy access to purchasing Treasuries without brokerage fees, as well as direct deposit of interest and redeemed principal into your bank account. This investing pretty much takes care of itself!

YOU'LL THANK YOURSELF LATER

No one can predict interest rates. Five years is plenty of time to commit to holding a bond. Any longer and you may be compelled to sell it before redemption and incur a transaction fee—and maybe a loss of principal.

Getting Time and Money on Your Side

	The Old Way	**The Lazy Way**
Buying Treasuries, but not holding them to maturity vs. sitting tight with them after having planned on doing so:	I thought these things were guaranteed! I didn't even get my purchase price back.	Yep, Uncle Sam paid me off in full, all my principal and interest to boot.
Having a huge attack of buyer's remorse when your STRIPS start losing value vs. understanding that they are volatile if not held to maturity:	Nooooooo!!!!!	What do I care about the price? They've got two years left before I redeem them. Duh!
Buying Treasuries from a broker vs. Treasury Direct:	Man, these commissions really bite into the return.	No commissions, I like it, I like it.
Regularly buying Savings Bonds as your main investment vs. stocks, mutual funds, and other bonds:	Nothing beats good old Savings Bonds.	Just about everything beats Savings Bonds.
Selling your Treasuries through a broker vs. Treasury Direct:	They get you coming and going with these commissions.	I still like no commissions.

Taxes: Keeping Uncle Sam at Bay

Ben Franklin was right.

For a guy silly enough to take a chance frying himself big time by flying a kite during a lightning storm, Ben Franklin came up with some fine bits of wisdom. He had it right the day he was hanging around the French Academy of Sciences and told a M. LeRoy that " . . . nothing in this world is certain but death and taxes." He could have added the annoyance of small, yappy dogs if he'd thought about it, but that may not have endeared him to the poodle-loving French.

Taxes are a constant expense for most people. You may not earn enough to pay federal income tax, but in many states you're hit with either a local income tax or a sales tax. Add in property tax, rental car taxes, hotel tax, and taxes on personal property, and the price of everything we do or purchase goes up.

The United States Tax Code is a forbidding collection of laws, subparagraphs, and exemptions. It would be easier to follow a lecture on post-ganglionic cell functions delivered in

Norwegian than to try to fully comprehend our tax regulations. (Of course, if you're a Norwegian post-ganglionic cell biologist who also happens to be an accountant, this doesn't apply.)

Over the last few presidential administrations, various tax exemptions have been eliminated, but that doesn't mean you can't be tax-smart. Legally keeping more money in your pocket is a smart investment of your time.

THE PAPER TRAIL CAPER

What's the number one stumbling block to accurate, clear tax reporting? In a couple of words, record keeping! Trade in that shoe box full of receipts and forms for a simple system that will keep your taxpaying a little less painful (it will never be completely painless). Good record keeping means you should have a file for:

- State, local, and federal taxes
- 1098 Statements (interest you paid out)
- 1099-Dividend Statements (dividends you received)
- 1099-Interest Statements (interest you received)
- W-2 (Wage and tax statements)
- 1099-MISC Statements (Miscellaneous income statement)
- 1099-B Statements (Proceeds from brokerage activity)
- Out-of-pocket medical costs
- Day care expenses
- Elderly and dependent care expenses

- Moving expenses

- Foreign taxes

- Other deductions

When it comes time to do your taxes, it is hands down easier to open a file drawer and efficiently pull out your paper work than it to hunt around your office, or closet floor, for it. You must maintain a paper trail to back up your claims to the IRS—a note from your parents won't do the trick. If you want to make it simpler yet, record all of your deductions and income statements in a separate accounting ledger or tax organizer as you incur them. When your 1040 arrives in the mail, you'll be ready for it.

I Deduce This Is a Deduction

There aren't a lot of fun deductions left these days, so citizen taxpayer high jinks are a little more subdued. Nevertheless, there are major opportunities—if you itemize and don't take the standard deduction on your form 1040—-available to everyone to cut or postpone taxes. These opportunities include:

- Contributions to retirement programs

- Purchasing a home

- Tax-deferred annuities

- Charitable contributions

- Municipal bonds

- Self-employment expenses

YOU'LL THANK YOURSELF LATER

If you're going to apply for a loan in the coming year, especially a home loan, make at least three copies of your tax returns. Do this when you file your taxes and they'll be ready for your potential lenders.

Did you receive a raise this past year or a bonus? More money means more taxes. Consider putting this "found money" into a qualified retirement account. You'll defer taxes and save for retirement at the same time.

I cannot stress enough the importance of contributing to a retirement program, especially one sponsored by your employer. What could be easier? You never see the money—it's taken out of your salary automatically—and it's tax deferred. As an added bonus, many employers kick in a matching contribution. You save money and earn money at the same time!

For taxpayers in low tax brackets, the greater advantage of retirement programs is the return on their money rather than the deduction itself. If your current bracket is lower than the bracket you anticipate when you retire and start drawing taxable money out of a 401(k) or other plan, you may be better off contributing to a Roth IRA (see Chapter 9). Compare the advantages of a Roth against the additional earnings from employer contributions to a 401(k) before choosing one over the other.

The home mortgage interest deduction is a very visible and blatant piece of social engineering, but it's great if you own a home. A nation of homeowners is somehow thought to reflect a more stable society than a nation of potentially anarchic renters. Funny, I thought George Washington and his contemporaries were all homeowners before they did their Declaration of Independence thing.

A home purchase brings a bundle of deductions such as:

- Points paid to the lender
- Mortgage interest
- Property taxes
- Home improvements to offset capital gains

Recent changes in the tax laws allow a married couple to take a profit of up to $500,000, or $250,000 if you're single, on their home without paying any capital-gains tax. Think of your home as a tax deduction machine. Every mortgage payment keeps a roof over your head and a little less cash in Uncle Sam's piggy bank. For many people, a home provides the quickest and most uncomplicated path to reducing their taxes. In addition to your primary mortgage, a home equity loan—based on the amount of equity you eventually build up—also has tax deductible interest. These loans are useful, if used with discretion, for home improvements or other large-ticket items like automobiles or college education.

Charity Begins on Schedule A/Form 1040

We can all consider charitable contributions as another possible deduction. Contributions can be in the form of:

- Cash
- Household goods
- Stocks and bonds
- Real estate
- Valuables such as art and jewelry

Cash, stocks, and bonds are the most straightforward to deduct because their value is set—a dollar is a dollar, after all. The best part about giving stocks away is that you can deduct their current value, on a stepped up basis, a real tax treat if they've appreciated since you bought them. The same is true for real estate and other valuables. Just be sure your appraised value is a fair one.

YOU'LL THANK YOURSELF LATER

The mortgage deduction, although important, shouldn't be the prime consideration when choosing purchasing a home over renting. Look at the whole picture, including the likely period of time you'll be living in the area, before making a final decision.

The same principle holds true for donated furniture and clothing. Household goods are regularly given away. Where do you think the Salvation Army stores get all their ultra cool 1950s dinette sets? You can deduct them—and the charity to which you donate will give you a small form for your records—but you must be realistic in setting a value. You might really like your driftwood table lamps, but the IRS isn't going to buy your $200 a piece deductions.

Buy a Bridge and Write It Off

Municipal bonds, issued by states and local governments to pay for roads and schools and such, pay interest that is exempt from federal taxes. This interest is also often exempt from state and local taxes in the state of issue. Municipal bonds can be a good tax strategy for higher income brackets. If you live in super-high-tax states like New York or California, locally issued municipal bonds, if exempt from all taxes, can be a great defensive strategy. Note: should you sell them before they mature, you will pay tax on any increased value in their principal.

Use It or Lose It

The government is like an annoying cousin who's always trying to borrow $20 and doesn't pay it back until a year later. If you are due a big tax refund every year, you have effectively given Uncle Sam free use of your money. Why would you do that? Ideally, when April 15th rolls around, you will neither owe money nor be due a refund. This is probably impossible to achieve, but adjusting your withholding with your employer is not.

IF YOU'RE SO INCLINED

Municipal bonds are often easier to buy through municipal bond funds, unless you're familiar with individual issues. As always, watch out for a fund's expense ratio.

If your circumstances change during the year—you may receive a raise, for example—then file a new W-4.

Our Little Tax Deduction

Don't look to your kids for any great tax breaks. Tax regulations allow:

- A deduction per child
- A qualified child care tax credit

You can write off, tax-wise, that is, each child with a $2,650 deduction for 1997. You can also get up to a $720 tax credit for child care for one child (up to $1,440 for two or more children) depending on your income. Be sure to check IRS Publication 503 for some of the small print requirements. Remember, a credit comes right off your tax bill! If only the government would give you as big a deduction for your kids as they do for your property tax bills!

There are also tax provisions for child adoption, up to a $5,000 credit for each child (see Form 8839).

Everybody's My Boss—I'm Self-Employed

Self-employment has one simple, easy rule: Just about everything you do that's related to your business is tax deductible: printing, legal fees, transportation, uniforms, the works. But you must keep scrupulous records and be prepared to back up your claims. The IRS figures they lose billions of dollars a year to self-employed individuals who don't report all of their income or fudge their returns too much in their own favor.

YOU'LL THANK YOURSELF LATER

Talk with your payroll department at work and fill out a new W-4 (for tax withholding) if your refund, or amount due, is too large. It's easy to adjust your withholding once a year and quit giving the government a free loan!

Sole proprietors who work alone have it the easiest. The biggest tax advantages for sole proprietors include:

- SEP-IRA and Keogh retirement plans
- Writing off automobile expenses
- Writing off tools and office equipment
- The home office deduction

SEP-IRAs and Keoghs (see Chapter 9) allow you to sock away more money than individual IRAs allow. In contrast to employer sponsored plans, you control your own SEP-IRA or Keogh. The bookkeeping for a SEP-IRA is uncomplicated and easy to maintain.

If you need a car in your life anyway, it's great if you can write it off whenever you use it for work. Some people will buy or lease the sleekest imported sedan on four wheels and have a wonderful time tooling around in it on Uncle Sam's dime. Spend $5 to park it for an hour—or maybe three days if you're in the middle of Oklahoma (land of the first parking meters)—mark it in your book, and write it off.

There are some restrictions, of course, especially if you use the car partially for personal use.

At the end of the year, you can either deduct the portion of your costs actually incurred for business use or take a deduction per business mile.

The home office deduction is a double-edged sword. If it's in your house, it has to be used exclusively for your business and be critical for its functioning—no letting it double as a playroom for the kids! A separate structure, like a cottage or converted garage on your property would be easier to justify. You can depreciate the square footage of your office as a percentage of your home. Although this depreciation can affect how you figure your taxes when you sell the house (you have to recapture the depreciation, which affects your basis for capital gains) it's not much of an issue anymore since the increase in capital gains limits.

The easiest approach? Unless you really need the write-off, consider skipping the office deduction. Why? The IRS, which will not officially confirm this, has an automatic sensor that lights up their entire audit department when a return comes through showing an office deduction is being claimed. At that point, a SWAT team runs in, pocket protectors askew, and grabs those returns. You don't want to know what happens next.

Not So Capital Gains

All of those wonderful stocks and bonds this book advises you to buy can also add to your tax bill. So much for rewarding frugal, conscientious living! Nevertheless, with some planning, these taxes can be a little less taxing if you time your selling and buying right.

As a rule, you shouldn't base investments strictly on tax avoidance. This can blind you to other, more advantageous investments which may be taxed, but yield a better return.

Taxable interest and dividends from stocks, bonds, bank accounts, and installment loans payable to you are taxed as regular income on your federal tax return. Interest is earned throughout the year, and even if it isn't

YOU'LL THANK YOURSELF LATER

An IRS audit—or scrutiny—simply isn't worth the trouble. If you have a dubious deduction, skip it. Don't try and write off a hobby as a business venture. Play it straight, pay up on time, and get it over with.

paid out (such as with zero coupon bonds) you will still owe tax on it for the year it was incurred. No escapes here, unfortunately, unless the investments are in a tax-deferred account. Even if your stock dividends are automatically reinvested, you will still owe tax on them.

Capital gains—the difference between what you pay for an asset and what you sell it for if the price goes up—have their own special rate structure, which was adjusted in the last IRS Reform Act effective January 1, 1998. The new, improved capital gains are established at four rates:

- 20 percent rates for assets held over 12 months (or 10 percent for those in the 15 percent tax bracket)
- Rates of 28 percent for assets held for less than 12 months
- Assets held 12 or fewer months are taxed as ordinary income
- Assets acquired after the year 2000 and held for five years are taxed at 18 percent

How can you turn this to your advantage? Keep it manageable! You may not want to pay the tax during a given tax year, so wait until the following year to sell the asset. The same applies to purchasing. A stock or mutual fund that's just about to declare a dividend will stick you with a tax liability right away! If it's close to the end of the year, consider putting off your purchase until January and take the gain the following year.

Another technique is to use any capital losses you may have in underperforming, losing assets to balance against your capital gains. Say your investment in Yakima Yo-Yos appreciated $2,000 because yo-yos are really hot right now. You're ready to sell and grab your profits, but your investment in Dial-a-Scent Home Deodorizers loses $2,000 and you want to dump it and forget you ever set eyes—or nose—on it. Sell them both and the gain in one offsets the loss with the other. Ideally, you wouldn't take any losses, but they come with the territory, so use them to your advantage.

Proper record keeping is critical when you determine capital gains, especially if you hold an investment for years and years. Keep all of your transaction slips showing your stock and bond purchases and sales, as well as your monthly statements! You'll never remember your actual costs otherwise. Simple solution? Keep them in a separate folder in your file cabinet.

THIS ISN'T THE BOSTON TEA PARTY

Some people take a dangerously easy way out of their taxes—they don't file and they don't pay! Some of them even voice their intentions to the IRS in protest letters or on mutilated tax returns. It sounds very revolutionary, but I wouldn't recommend it.

Arguments that challenge the legality of the federal tax system have all been heard before in various courts, and all have been dismissed. Tax protesters, on top of owing taxes with penalties, also pay legal costs, and may end up in jail. No one is eager to pay taxes, but they go with the territory called civilization, such as it is. Pay them and forget about them, but keep them as low as legally possible.

YOU'LL THANK YOURSELF LATER

Save any canceled check or receipt that is reflected on your tax returns. Keep your old returns for at least seven years.

TAX SOS

Every change in the tax code is greeted with muted cheers by tax attorneys and accountants. More changes, more frustration, more clients! No one on the face of the earth, including IRS employees, understands the code from beginning to end. If your return is fairly basic, doing your own taxes is pretty painless. Once you start adding depreciation schedules, self-employment, passive activity loss limitations, and rental property, you should also think about adding an accountant to your list of telephone numbers on the refrigerator.

In addition to preparing your returns, a good CPA can also educate and guide you toward an advantageous tax strategy. If you use a CPA:

1. Set an appointment as early in the year as possible.

2. Completely fill out any tax organizer your accountant gives you prior to your appointment.

3. Bring clear, orderly records; this makes the work easier and keeps the billable hours down.

Not quite the same as a CPA, but definitely a help, are software programs like Intuit's TurboTax or Microsoft Money 99. A tax program will speed up your calculations and produce a neat, professional looking return. Both Turbo Tax and Money 99 offer on-line downloads, too. For $9.95, if you don't want to buy the entire program, TurboTax offers web-based interactive tax preparation for doing your Federal taxes. You can do it all online, including filing your taxes, or download and print the forms.

IF YOU'RE SO
INCLINED

Accountants come in all shapes and sizes, but I would go for someone on the conservative side. Some accountants are a little more daring than others, pushing the deduction envelope until the seams bulge. If they're wrong, it's your signature on the return.

THE LAZY WAY

Taxes are always with us, lurking in the background, rearing their ugly heads every time we read a paycheck stub. Everyone, in most income brackets, has to pay federal income tax, but state taxes vary across the country. Washington state has no state income tax, but it does have a hefty sales tax. Oregon is just the opposite. As a result, some wise guy Washingtonians buy big ticket items across the border and then drive them home, a very much frowned upon behavior. Pay your taxes, but keep them simple:

YOU'LL THANK YOURSELF LATER

Even if you use an accountant or a software program to prepare your taxes, always recheck the information before signing off.

- Keep all of your documentation and receipts neatly filed away.

- Take advantage of all tax-deferred retirement programs.

- Adjust your withholding as often as necessary to avoid having too much, or too little, tax withheld.

- Plan the purchase and sale of equities to minimize tax consequences.

- Take all possible deductions and retain all related documentation.

- Know when to call an accountant.

Getting Time and Money on Your Side

	The Old Way	The Lazy Way
Scrambling around on April 14th looking for receipts, cancelled checks, and W-2 forms vs. calmly opening your files in February and doing your taxes:	What's this? $40 to the Hamster Humane Society? Is that deductible?	This was tough! Open file draw, remove file, open file. I'm exhausted.
Ignoring your tax withholding vs. adjusting it as your circumstances change:	Hey, look at this fat tax refund. I'm rich!	Wonder if we can cut that refund in half next year? I hate the idea of the government getting free use of all this money.
Selling your investments without regard to timing and capital gains taxes vs. selling when it's tax-advantaged for you:	Capital gains? What are those?	I held off selling until January. I've got some losses coming and they'll balance each other out.
Not keeping track of your charitable deductions vs. accurate record keeping:	So, what did we give away last year, $4,000–$5,000 worth of clothing and kitchen utensils to GoodWill?	Let's see here, okay, here's the charity file with all the receipts from GoodWill.

Chapter fifteen

Get-Rich-Quick Schemes Aren't for the Lazy

Ever since the Cro-Magnon folks migrated into Europe at the end of the Ice Age some 40,000 years ago, people have been making get-rich-quick investments. Back then, it was buying waterfront property, sight unseen, on the Arctic Ocean. More recent times have seen more elaborate real estate scams, sales of non-existent gold mines, and Ponzi schemes.

The latter were named for that fine American Charles Ponzi, who set up an investment swindle in which he paid early investors with the money from later investors. This worked out just fine until he ran out of new investors.

Con artists and scammers come in every size, shape, and dress code. They're present in every culture. A thousand years from now, they'll be selling ground floor opportunities to buy oxygen rights on the planet Zymar, two solar systems and

three suns past Mars. Even sophisticated investors get taken in when their greed gene is buzzed. You don't need to join their ranks.

There are plenty of easy, solid ways to invest your money and get good earnings. They may not appeal to your sense of armchair adventure, but they won't drain your piggy bank, either. Avoid the risky, speculative, high-flying venues and you'll do just fine.

I'm Selling Shares in This Big Bridge in New York

Commerce is a necessary part of the culture. We work, produce stuff, sell it, pocket the money, and go out and buy someone else's stuff. Some people like to skip the production part and go right to taking the money. Spending even one minute listening to their proposals— usually during a dinner-suspending telephone call—is a waste of your time.

If anyone ever interrupts your evening with a phone call guaranteeing a big return with no risk if you sign up now, you should do any of the following:

1. Hang up the phone.

2. Tell them you work for the Securities and Exchange Commission and you'd love to hear all about it.

3. Act interested and then ask for their address and Social Security number (usually works quickest).

These solicitors offer nothing but a cue to the rumblings of avarice (a trait we all have) to go up a few decibels. Once again, we return to our ancestors' cave dwelling days when no one knew where the next meal was coming from, so people just grabbed food when they got the chance. You may remember this propensity was mentioned in Chapter 12 to explain irrational investment behavior, i.e., grabbing at risky investments because they hinted at higher returns (more food). These days, we're not living in cold caves anymore.

With 24-hour grocery stores and door-to-door teriyaki delivery, we're not as likely to be left behind to starve, but we still get these prehistoric rumblings. Someone comes along and offers a deal too good to be true—a dead giveaway that it's a bad idea—and we're tempted to take it and run back to our cave.

Take the easy way out and ignore all of these scams. Think of it this way: If these ideas are so terrific, how come guys like Warren Buffett and George Soros—a couple of current mega-investor billionaires—don't seem to know anything about them? Don't you think they'd like to double their money with little risk and do it in a short time instead of waiting for all of their dumb stocks to go up?

Good Advertising, Bad Investments

Fantasy beats out reality every time, at least for an hour or so. Then you get a tap on the shoulder. It's reality asking, um, now that you've spent $300 for these video tapes and cassettes on how to buy and sell apartment buildings and double your money in seven days, and have found out the claims were just a teeny bit exaggerated . . . what next?

The solicitations are very appealing. The wording is seductive and the pitch enthusiastic. That's why they

YOU'LL THANK YOURSELF LATER

The simplest way to check out any unsolicited offer to invest is to demand references from the solicitor. It may be a new stockbroker trying to drum up some business—or a highly dubious operation selling risky securities. Never reveal your bank account or credit card number to an unsolicited caller.

work so well for the solicitors, but they won't work for you!

Certain investments (and I use the word very loosely here) make the rounds from time to time, including:

- No-money-down real estate
- Mysterious sales techniques
- Highly speculative securities

Avoid them all. The only profits in these deals will be the ones made from selling you the videos and books—and even some of these guys go bankrupt! The only money you'll recover is what you can get for selling the stuff at a garage sale.

Engaging Ideas, Disengaged Dollars

There are legitimate, albeit risky, investments that you may want to consider—and then reconsider! There are reliable books and seminars available that offer advice on how to maneuver in the edgy world of:

- Short selling
- Options
- Futures

Short selling goes like this. Picture yourself borrowing your neighbors' big screen TV while they're on vacation (you're watching their house) and taking it to a pawn shop. You receive 250 big ones for it. The pawnbroker tells you that your redemption price will be $250 plus or minus what you roll with a pair of dice. Then, you'll multiply the dice total by five. And you'll

QUICK **n** PAINLESS

determine whether it's plus or minus by flipping a coin, heads for plus and tails for minus.

It's your belief that you'll buy back the TV for less than the $250, keep the extra money, and get it back to your neighbors' living room before they return from Ft. Lauderdale. You'd better hope you roll a 12 and get tails. Either way, you still have to replace the TV.

As a short seller, you're thinking that the price of a stock is going to drop. You borrow some of that stock from your accommodating broker, who charges a fee, and then you immediately sell it, pocketing the money. You're betting that the price is due to drop because of some upcoming financial news or a market "correction," because, in your opinion, the price is too high. If the price does drop, you cheerfully buy enough stock at the lower price to pay back what you owe and keep the difference.

What if the stock price goes higher? Uh, oh, you still have to replace the stock, but now it's going to cost you more than you got when you sold the stock you borrowed.

To add insult to injury, if it happens to be a stock that is being heavily played by short sellers, they will start buying a lot of it to cover their positions since they're on the losing end, too. All this buying will shoot the price up even further!

That's why I call it betting. If you really want to wager, go to a casino. At least you get cheap drinks. Lose enough, and you might end up with a free room and a coupon for the nightly buffet.

YOU'LL THANK YOURSELF LATER

If you want to avoid coming up short then skip short selling—even if you're longing to try.

Still interested in short selling? Set up a practice portfolio first and follow it for a few months. I guarantee you that if you keep accurate records, you'll be glad it was just practice!

PUT IN A CALL

Life is full of options. Cars come with options, so do houses and TV sets. Options in the financial world are a little different. Here, you pay your money, but you don't have to take anything if you don't want it.

An option gives the option holder the choice to buy or sell a piece of property or security at an agreed upon price by a specified date in the future. The holder can exercise the option or let it expire. Either way, it's been paid for and the seller gets to keep the money the buyer paid for the option, which is called the option premium. In the stock market, the traded options are puts and calls, which are very appropriately named.

A call simply means that the buyer can contact (well, a broker handles the transaction) the seller of the call—yoo-hoo, remember me?—and demand that the stock in question be sold to the buyer at a price the buyer and seller already agreed to (the strike price). The buyer believes that the stock would go higher than the agreed upon price and wanted to lock it in that price by buying a call.

A put allows the buyer to "put" the stock back to the seller of the put. Why would anyone sell or buy puts? Gambling fever aside, the seller thinks that the price will rise and the buyer thinks it will drop. If it drops, the buyer says, "Hey, remember me, you sold me the right to put the stock back to you at $50 a share. Too bad it's now dropped to $12 a share, but pay up." If the price goes up, the buyer would be nuts to offer to give it back to the seller because the strike price they agreed to would be less than its new, higher market price. It would be something like the old Abbott and Costello routine, "Here's a 5, give me two 10s."

Puts and calls give you the right to buy or sell shares of stock. Let's say you sell a call for 100 shares of Billy Bob's Bodacious Best Beer Company to your cousin for $1 a share. He's buying it because he really likes the beer. You agree to sell him the stock at $15 a share a couple of months down the road. You think Billy Bob's will never make it that high, but even if it does, that's okay since you only paid $8 a share for it. You get the $15 plus the dollar a share your cousin paid for the privilege of buying it from you.

Why would your cousin do this? He thinks Billy Bob's Beer is going to go up. He should know, he's one of their biggest consumers. Two months later, your old cuz gives you a call and says, my, my, isn't it wonderful that Budweiser is buying out old Billy Bob's for $100 a share. It's so nice of you to let me have it for the $15 we agreed to, and maybe now we're even for the time you tattled on me about my dad's missing cigars.

It could be worse. After all, you did make $8 a share (a $7 increase in price plus $1 for the call). You could have sold the calls and not owned the stock at all! This is called a naked option. It means that if the option holder calls

Trying to keep the rules straight for puts and calls can be like an Abbott and Costello routine. Do some practice trades first before you even consider any actual trading. Most options are never exercised so think twice before trying them.

you—hey, hey, guess who?—you have to come up with the goods. It can be very expensive, even if you know what you're doing. It's like playing bluff poker, having nothing in your hand, and hoping everyone else folds!

The conclusion? Puts and calls can be both volatile and risky. They have little place in a hassle-free, long-term portfolio. Ignore certain current advocates of option trading, and stick with long-term investments. This is supposed to be easy, not stressful!

If you're in for the long haul, you should be able to ignore options.

IS THERE A FUTURE IN FUTURES?

Futures, like options, involve the passage of time, but that's where the comparison ends. As a futures holder, you don't have any choice like you do with options (puts and calls). You've got to make good on the contract. A futures agreement says that you'll come up with the bucks to buy the underlying commodity or financial instrument on an agreed upon date at an agreed upon price. Commodities include wheat, oil, cotton, and pork bellies. Play your cards wrong and you'll end up with a truck load of bacon in your driveway. If you live in an apartment, you'll really have a problem.

Futures trading is a strange, even arcane business carried out primarily at various trading centers in the Midwest and New York City. Traders work their trades via strange hand signals and shouting, something like Shriners practicing primal therapy. At the end of the day, these trading centers are piled high with small mountains of paper scraps and comatose traders.

IF YOU'RE SO
INCLINED

Options can offer some protection in a volatile market, but they are nothing to jump into without study and calculating the costs. Treat them like short selling: Set up a practice portfolio and see how you would do. Go to http://www.moneynet.com and click on option chains after you've done some research.

Futures are even more speculative and volatile than most options. Keep it simple and stay away from them. If you're interested in pork bellies, order yourself a BLT for lunch and enjoy yourself.

GOLD-PLATED TROUBLE

Aside from opposable thumbs and a willingness to consume non-fat salad dressing, it is our ability to trade and establish commerce that separates us from other animals. Before coined gold was introduced as a medium of exchange, most people traded with a garage sale mentality: Uh, how much you want for those oxen? Gold, as it became universally accepted, simplified trade and allowed it to expand. Ultimately, gold is just a pretty metal that we all agree represents a certain value.

Gold, and to a lesser extent, silver, are viewed by true believers as a hedge against inflation. When the economy is tanking, these investors may buy up gold, which then helps drive up its price. When the economy, at least on the surface, appears to be strong, and inflation is nowhere in sight, gold is a mediocre place to put your money. First, there are practical considerations. Do you buy:

- Gold coins?
- Bullion?
- Gold mutual funds?

In times of high or severely increasing inflation, gold can be seen as a good hedge. That is, it tends to keep up with inflation over the long run. An advantageous

An easier approach to putting your money in an inflation-sensitive investment is to buy a house in a strong market. There are no guarantees, of course, but at least you'll have a roof over your head and a refrigerator for Bodacious Bob's Beer.

purchase of gold, along with other heavy metals, requires good timing, and that requires a lot of monitoring and fretting about many economic factors.

BUILDING AN ESTATE WITH REAL ESTATE

Real estate promoters really like to own buildings and land. They were the kids that never lost at Monopoly and usually ended owning everything on the board. A personal residence, over time, often works out from an investment standpoint, although that's not a good reason to purchase. Remember, it's a home first; invest your money somewhere else.

Other real estate purchases can be a little more problematic, especially:

- Raw land
- Vacation rentals
- Time-shares

Vacation rentals, typically condominiums, depend on a lot of factors that are beyond your control including:

- The quality of the on-site management and their upkeep of the property
- Local tourism
- Vandalism
- Competition from newer developments

It's a big price to pay just to have a place to crash when you go off to the islands. An easier idea: Invest your money in a nice income stock, and use the dividends to pay for a hassle-free rental.

(In the long run, you're better off reinvesting the dividends, but if spending them keeps you from buying a dumb vacation rental, I'm all for it.)

Read this twice: Time-shares are not real estate investments! If you really need some convincing as to their investment merits, check out their resale prices. Then, the next time you're walking down Front St. in Lahaina, Maui, ignore all those guys offering you free luaus if you'll listen to their time-share spiels.

I KNOW ART WHEN I SEE IT

Art falls into the category of collectibles such as:

- Rare coins
- Stamps
- Antiques
- Memorabilia
- Oriental rugs
- Baseball cards
- Beanie Babies

Raw land can be highly speculative. If you can't get any income from it, say, by leasing it to a farmer for crops, it can be a constant money drain. Consider buying land with some partners to decrease your costs.

Repeat this statement aloud several times: these are not investments! Sure, they can go up in price. Maybe. A baseball card doesn't produce a tube of toothpaste or a software program the way a corporation does. Its entire value is dependent on a very fickle market that's tough to measure.

Millions of people are ready and willing to invest in stocks and bonds. How many people want to chase down a Babe Ruth baseball card? Or a 1909 S-VDB Lincoln head penny? The pool of individuals making up these markets is comparatively limited so selling your little treasure can be difficult.

Are there other problems? Sure, like security measures. One burglary, and you can lose all those first issue stamp sets in a heartbeat. If you get illiterate burglars (not unlikely!) your stamps could end up as postage on a utility bill!

The easy rule to remember is this: If you like the painting or antique dresser or 1955 proof set, and they give you some degree of enjoyment, commensurate with the price, then buy them and be happy. Buying them strictly as an investment will probably be disappointing.

Keep your investments manageable and uncomplicated. Put your money where it belongs: stocks, bonds, and money markets—all starting with your retirement accounts. Then, when all your other bills are paid, you can think about buying antique teddy bears and Belleek china.

THE LAZY WAY

The old adage about something sounding too good to be true is a sound one when it involves your investments—or a notice in the mail announcing that you've just won a national sweepstakes contest. Our day-to-day existence isn't as precarious—or as exciting—as our distant ancestors. We may try and duplicate the missing melodrama of chasing (and being chased by) any variety of wild beasts by chasing risky investments, enticed by

YOU'LL THANK YOURSELF LATER

Some people buy new issue proof sets from the U.S. Mint every year as an investment. They're not. If you want a government-sponsored investment, buy Treasuries.

slick sales brochures or TV infomercials. Tips from in-laws who have already bought in can add credibility to dubious ventures, depending on how much you believe your in-laws.

How can you protect yourself?

- Never buy anything you don't understand or can be easily explained in five minutes or less (some would say less than a minute).

- Ignore any solicitations via telephone, mail, television infomercials, or Internet.

- Always check the credentials and track record of those doing the selling; if necessary, contact the local Better Business Bureau or state attorney general and inquire about any registered complaints, law suits, or official investigations of the promoters.

- Skip short selling, options, and futures.

- Time-share properties are not investments—and not necessarily a good deal for vacation rentals, either.

- Collectibles are for your enjoyment and pleasure, not investing.

You already know where to invest your money: stocks, bonds, money markets, and mutual funds. They may not give you the same short-lived bragging rights you'll get from telling your friends about your killing in the futures market, but you'll sleep at night. And as everyone's favorite 19th century German philosopher/poet Nietzsche said, sleeping is no mean art.

QUICK 🄽 PAINLESS

Equities like stock and mutual funds don't require storage, in-home security measures, or any storage space larger than a monthly statement. What could be simpler?

Getting Time and Money on Your Side

	The Old Way	The Lazy Way
Investing big time in baseball paraphernalia vs. equities:	I know this Mariners T-shirt will be worth a fortune someday So what if they never made it, moved out of town, and changed their name?	Hey, I got a dividend check today. Let's go to a ball game.
Short selling stocks vs. buying and holding:	Uh, oh, the price of my shares is going up.	Great, the price of my shares is going up.
Buying a time share as an investment vs. listening to the sales representative's pitch and taking advantage of their free tickets on the sunset island cruise:	We should have just taken the cruise.	He was annoying, but the cruise was free.
Pursuing a "safe" investment, you buy gold vs. buying Treasuries:	Hmm, I see our gold has dropped once again.	Tried and true Treasuries. Boring, but guaranteed.

Monitoring Your Plan and Investments: The Least You Need to Know to Keep Your Plan on Track

It would be great if our money and investments could be like trees in the forest: growing of their own accord without any attention from us. Better yet, they might even yield some maple syrup. Somehow, those trees seem to make it without anyone watering, fertilizing, or trimming them. No one ever calls either a tree surgeon nor a tree psychologist ("Your leaf shedding is an obvious sign of body image problems and your failure to bond with your parents. You're simply trying to disguise it as seasonal stress disorder because it's autumn."). An investment portfolio, unfortunately, isn't so autonomous.

Unlike the philosophical inquiry as to whether a tree falling in the forest makes any noise if there's no one there to hear it, a fast-falling portfolio would be accompanied by plenty of noise—from its owner. Losses are part of investing. Your job is to minimize them. Regular monitoring, coupled with solid stock, bond, and mutual fund selections, will keep your investments upright and growing, although you may lose a few branches now and again. As much as I really hate sports analogies—just what relation do millionaire ball players engaged in children's play have to do with real life?—remember that even the seemingly indomitable Chicago Bulls lost a basketball game once in awhile.

Would You Rent This if It Were a Video?

Monitoring your investments can range from being about as interesting as watching paint dry (in the case of Treasury bonds) to going into a free fall waiting for your chute to open (if you're a day trader, moving in an out of the market every hour). Your financial monitoring will include:

- Rebalancing your account from time to time.
- Deciding to sell an equity.
- Assuming more debt.
- Establishing new goals and examining existing ones.
- Budgeting more money for investing.

A portfolio that does well in heady times when the economy is charging ahead may be out of balance when things slow down. It may be way out of balance when portfolio managers are wandering the streets with signs reading, "Will Trade Stocks for Food, Preferably Northern Italian." Even a lazy investor in for the long haul has to consider portfolio allocations from time to time.

Many investment advisors will tell you one of the biggest problems many people have, once they've finally made the leap to saving and investing in equities, is knowing when to sell. Do you:

- Take your profits after reaching a certain pre-determined price or hold out for more?

- Hold onto a falling stock in hope that it will recover?

- Consult your local tarot reader when you can't decide?

A mainstay of this book has been to get you out of debt and keep you out. As that household name 17th century English cleric Thomas Fuller once said, "Debt is the worst poverty." As we've seen, though, judicious debt can be a good thing, including:

- Mortgage debt

- Money to start a small business

- Funds for schooling (both your own and your children's)

There are times when you will have to reconsider your debt load and this can affect your investment strategy.

As you get older, your goals may change. You may seek earlier retirement or you may want to change jobs—the call and camaraderie of the espresso-slinging

A COMPLETE WASTE OF TIME

The 3 Worst Ways to Monitor Your Investments:

1. Strategize on a day-to-day basis.

2. Hire an advisor and unquestioningly follow the advice you're given.

3. Leave your portfolio alone without ever scrutinizing it.

barristas may just be too strong to resist and the heck with this corporate law job at $150,000 a year plus a free parking space in midtown Manhattan. Or, you may have accomplished earlier goals, look around, and say, "Now what?"

Conversely, you may run the numbers and decide you have to pump more money into your retirement account pronto. The way you figure it, at the rate you're saving, your last day of work will be one month short of your 97th birthday, and that's only if your salary triples between now and then. The money has to come from somewhere which suggests some combination of the following:

- You'll have to earn more.
- You'll have to save more.
- Your investments will have to earn more.
- You'll have to get really lucky at the racetrack.

Not Quite a Tightrope Act

High-wire performers seem to have a colossal, almost pathological need for attention; it's not exactly normal behavior to ride a motorcycle across a cable 75 feet in the air with a dozen people dressed in glittering, silver costumes hanging off it like so many Christmas tree ornaments. Their occupation demands a strict understanding and development of balance, as well as a cousin in the life insurance business. As the members of the performing troupe change—as in gain or lose weight, or new members come in (suggesting that some have "dropped"

YOU'LL THANK YOURSELF LATER

Some debt—such as a home mortgage—is prudent as long as it fits into your budget. If it doesn't, and will jeopardize your financial stability, it should be avoided. Buy it when you can afford it.

out?)—a new balance has to be obtained in order to reach the troupe's goals of not falling off the wire.

The same principle applies to your money and portfolio management. Over time, you may need to adjust:

- Your mutual fund allocations
- Your stock and bond allocations
- Your cash position

Look over your funds and ask:

- How are these funds doing compared to past performance?
- Has one been stagnant for a year or two?
- Is this fund behind its peers (not an index) in performance?
- Has the fund's manager or investment strategy changed? (Is a small-cap fund, for instance, buying more mid-cap stocks?)

These are reasons to consider a new allocation. Maybe one fund group has grown beyond the original percentage you had allowed for it in your portfolio and it's time to either reduce it or invest more money in other areas.

The same principles hold true for your stocks and bonds. If you're dead set on keeping 30 percent of your money in bonds, for instance, but your stocks have gotten ahead of their 70 percent allocation, it's time to adjust.

Some changes will come with age as you approach retirement. You may want the perceived security of

QUICK **n** PAINLESS

Keeping all your investments—or as many as reasonably possible—with one broker greatly simplifies your monitoring. Year-end statement comparisons tell it all.

bonds and, in the case of Treasuries, their guaranteed returns instead of the inherent risks with stocks.

You should reconsider your investment balance:

- At least once a year
- As you've reached certain financial goals and milestones
- If the economic climate radically changes
- As you get closer to retirement

Sell, Sell, No, I Mean, Buy, Uh, Sell . . .

No one really knows when to sell, at least, no one knows the optimum time to sell, although everyone knows when to sell in hindsight. Time travelers might know, but then they end up breaking all the movie fiction rules about changing the past and they might end up really messing things up. Are there any guidelines for selling? Some, including:

- Sell when a stock has appreciated to your own pre-determined "sell" levels (for instance, a 50 percent appreciation, at which point you would take your profits).

- Sell if a stock drops to a pre-determined level (you agreed to sell if it drops 15 percent, for instance, believing it would be too difficult to recover your original cost vs. investing elsewhere).

- Sell a sagging stock for tax purposes (to offset capital gains).

- Jettison a mediocre or poorly performing mutual fund after one to two years, not because the overall market has gone down but because the fund's returns lag behind other funds of its type.

- Sell to change your allocation or get out of a risky segment of the market.

There is one automatic way to sell a stock and that's through a stop-loss order. This is a directive to your broker (the deep discounters may charge for this) to sell your stock at a price below the current market price. Say you bought Mad Dog Sam's Canine Guard Service at $10 a share and it's now at $18. You're a little nervous about Mad Dog Sam—they've had a few lawsuits lately due to some overeager German shepherds—and want to protect your profit. You put in a stop-loss order with your broker to sell the stock if it drops to $16. There are no guarantees your broker will get this price; Mad Dog Sam could be trading very heavily and you may end up with less. But the sell order will kick in automatically so you won't have to worry about calling your broker. This is a very lazy way to protect yourself in a descending market in general or a specific stock that's having hard times.

The drawback to stop-loss orders is they kick in regardless of the reason the stock price has dropped. If a spurious rumor hits the street—Mad Dog Sam is really a closet cat lover, for instance, and his dogs are all snarl and no bite—a stock can quickly plunge, only to recover a short time later. No one can time the market, but a stop-loss order can protect you from potentially large losses.

QUICK **n'** *PAINLESS*

A stop-loss order protects you on the downside with no work on your part. You can put the order in with a "Good Until Cancelled" restriction and forget about it.

QUICK n' PAINLESS

If a stock has dropped irretrievably, the pain has already been felt. If the circumstances call for it, sell the stock and move on.

Selling is never easy for two reasons:

1. It suggests we made a poor choice in equities and it's never easy to admit our errors.

2. There's always that disembodied voice telling us that it may go up again, like an hour after we sell it.

You can second-guess forever. There is no point in compounding a mistake by embracing the principle that hope springs eternal. Sell, walk away knowing you're in good company (every famous investor had made mistakes, sometimes huge ones), and find a better place for your hard-earned money.

"I don't owe a penny to a single soul—not counting tradesmen, of course."—P.G. Wodehouse, humorist (except to tradesmen).

I'd be lost without a good book of quotations. When others can get a point across more pithily, I'm all for it. Chapter 3 rallied on against unnecessary debt, but some debt can improve your life:

- A home mortgage keeps a roof over your head instead of your landlord's and builds equity at the same time.

- A small business loan can get you started on a new career—or advance an existing one.

- A college education, either for yourself or your children, is an almost guaranteed road to more wealth accumulation and security.

You may have started investing and putting money into a retirement account, carefully budgeting your money—then your life changes. Mr./Ms. Right comes along, you decide to start the killer software application company in your garage, or your new bundle of joy comes screaming into the world and your crystal ball tells you Columbia Law School tuition is looming in your future.

In a sense, this is rebalancing your life portfolio, which will certainly affect your investment portfolio. You don't want to stop contributing to your retirement account, for instance, but you may have to decrease your contributions. Acceptable new debt allows you to do this without losing sight of your other goals. Relax, change is usually a positive force in our lives even if we get rattled by it. A little less money into your retirement account is better than none at all.

Shiny and New

Changes in your life give you an opportunity to re-examine your existing goals and set some new ones. When you're 27, the idea of retiring at 55 may be so appealing that you aggressively fund your 401(k) or IRA. At 40, you may decide early retirement isn't at all important, that waiting until 67 is just fine by you, and paying down the mortgage or a few more vacations are in order.

New goals, such as starting a business, may necessitate your selling some taxable investments. If so, keep your tax costs in mind when calculating the amount of cash yielded by the sale. Should you decide on late retirement, you can keep your bond allotment down to lower levels than you might otherwise have done. Your original allotments and regular cash contributions—based on

YOU'LL THANK YOURSELF LATER

Long-term goals are great guideposts, but they don't have to be set in stone. Allow yourself some leeway to adapt to new situations.

earlier plans and goals—will most likely change with the introduction of new goals. Lazy investors will examine their expenses and cash flow and then rebalance their portfolio.

I Want More . . .

What if your time frame changes? You want to retire at 40, for example. Or you've gotten more comfortable with the idea of risk and are willing to increase your allotment of stocks over bonds and cash. Maybe your boss has decided you really are the valuable employee you've been hinting at in anonymous e-mails the past two years and has given you a nice raise. You want to invest the money following the lazy investor's tenet of living below your means today so you can really have a blast later.

These are all valid reasons for changing and rebalancing your stocks, bonds, and mutual funds. Stick to the principles of your original goals—establishing investment allocations that will reach those goals—and you won't have any problems. Consistency in investing and saving is the guiding canon here, regardless of changes in goals or changes in your life.

THE LAZY WAY

Actively managed mutual funds rebalance their holdings constantly. In a looming era of 24-hour-a-day trading, portfolio managers will be more sleep-deprived than ever before, walking around with tanks of espresso strapped to their backs and cellular phones hanging around their necks. The lazy investor doesn't have to go quite that far to maintain a balanced portfolio and make intelligent decisions when it comes to selling stocks, bonds, or poorly performing funds.

Watch out for telltale signs including:

- Underperformance (based on its history) of a stock or mutual fund or in comparison to its asset group.

- A drop in stock or fund price to your pre-determined sell price.

- The equity has appreciated to your sell price.

Like fund managers, you will need to rebalance your portfolio from time to time due to:

- Change in the nature of your goals or lifestyle.

- Change in your equity holdings.

- Economic problems that may greatly disfavor part of your portfolio allocation.

A COMPLETE WASTE OF TIME

The 3 Worst Ways to Balance Your Portfolio:

1. Frequently trade without any sense of allocation.

2. Never establish any reason for a particular allocation.

3. Never give an allocation time enough to do its job.

Getting Time and Money on Your Side

	The Old Way	The Lazy Way
Trading in and out of equities, convinced that you can beat the market vs. buying and holding and only trading when necessary:	Hey, where did all these brokerage fees come from? I may have to sell something just to pay these guys.	Three trades a year is getting pretty racy.
Holding on to a real loser software stock vs. selling it off and moving on:	It's down to 75¢ and I just know this is rock bottom. It's blue skies from here, I can feel it.	All right, it was a bad buy, but it's gone. Live and learn.
Sticking to your existing goals and portfolio allocations even if your situation has changed vs. reevaluating and changing as needed:	You mean, just because I got married and we have triplets I can't keep putting all my extra money into my IRA?	Okay, looks like less money into retirement for awhile while we pump money into the college funds.
Selling at the first onset of a sudden drop in stock price vs. finding out why the drop happened and then deciding:	Sell, sell, sell!!!!!	What a bogus drop. The Federal Reserve said they'd appraise current rates, not raise them.

Single, Married, Divorced: How Family Life Affects Your Finances

Did anyone ever tell you that two can live as cheaply as one? Single individuals have repeated that joke since the first post-honeymoon Neanderthals discovered that the old studio bachelor cave just wouldn't do anymore. Marriage or partnering can quickly outlive small living spaces and casual lifestyles can suddenly seem too casual.

Kids usually come along with marriage, although not quite as many per family as a couple of generations ago. And the kids are still there if a marriage ends—a trauma for everyone involved—and often they pop up when there is no marriage or long-term relationship. Second and third marriages—and maybe more kids—aren't uncommon.

A prenuptial agreement can seem pretty rude—and not at all romantic! Consider it if you have considerable assets, and especially if you have assets from a previous marriage. Love may conquer all, but if a prenuptial chills it, wouldn't you rather find out before the wedding?

What does this mean for you? Your legal status—married, single, divorced, living together, parent, legal guardian for aging parents—will greatly affect your finances. It will certainly effect your head and your heart! Not all decisions come down to money, fortunately, but your life can be more stress free if you give some major changes some deep thought before jumping in.

BIRDS AND THE BEES

Marriage or partnering, aside from answering the pull of the heart strings, raises some interesting financial issues. Some things are cheaper; you don't need two sets of major appliances, for instance. You may decide to keep one car instead of two. And until a one-bedroom apartment starts feeling cramped, your housing costs may stay pretty much the same as when you were single. Okay, this assumes you weren't previously living in your parents' basement or in a house with 15 roommates. If you decide to greatly expand your household now that there are two of you, all the savings equations go out the window.

However, with two incomes, and a little bit of frugal living, you can really start stuffing some money into your savings. To do this, you should:

- Clearly establish your financial goals before marriage.
- Agree about bill paying.
- Decide major purchasing decisions together.

If you want to live like a monk (well, money-wise anyway) and save up for a house, but your spouse wants to rent or buy a waterfront condo, you have a definite conflict. Money issues are one of the main causes of marital stress and divorce. It's a hundred times easier to get finances out in the open first instead of coming home and not-so-calmly asking your sweetie what that new $3,000, no-money-down-90-days-same-as-cash stereo system is doing in the living room.

Couples may end up keeping both separate and joint checking accounts. Some split all the bills right down the middle; others are more relaxed, especially if they have different incomes. Still others throw everything into one pot and pay from there. This is something else you should discuss early on. It's understandable to want to hold on to your independence with separate accounts—and maybe even advisable for some people—but one account keeps the bank fees down and the bill paying simpler. Your biggest problem might be in picking the kind of checks to use—"Save the Black Bear," for instance, vs. checks that say, "American Rifle Association Member and Proud of It."

One not so amusing, government-sanctioned fun-killer is the so-called marriage tax penalty. Uncle "We-Promote-Families . . . kind of" Sam has managed to develop a tax code that can cost a married couple more in combined taxes, depending on their individual incomes, than if they were single and paid separately. You're stuck with this one if you both have similar earnings. A fun evening activity is to write your legislator stating that this penalty is so onerous that you'll probably have to divorce and live in sin.

Congratulations! You've settled some big money issues before making the big commitment. Many people never figure this out and end up with money problems later. Go out and inaugurate your checking account somewhere fun.

The Lazy Way

SPEAKING OF SIN

There is a noticeable legal distinction between living together and being married. Marriage allows an estate to be passed on to a surviving spouse without any tax penalty, regardless of the estate's value. Unmarried surviving partners for instance, face estate taxes if the estate's value is over $625,000.

Unmarried couples must be much more exacting in how they register property—in one name or both—and how they deal with joint purchases. Who gets the car if you split up? Will my partner get the house if I die? What if my partner challenges me for the house if we go our separate ways?

The simplest and most stress-free approach? Find a lawyer who specializes in estate planning. This is a good idea for married couples as well and is covered in more detail in Chapter 8. Document major purchases and write up contracts spelling out the ownership. All right, it's not very romantic, but neither is screaming at each other over the Saab or the Louis XIV sideboard if you become relationship-impaired.

THOSE DARN KIDS

You've read the figures. Each child will cost you approximately $6 billion dollars to raise from the moment Mom becomes pregnant to the sunny June afternoon years later when you see a black-gowned figure waving a college diploma from the stage of a graduation ceremony. Any way you look at it, deciding to carry on the family names is an expensive proposition. You should certainly

A COMPLETE WASTE OF TIME

The 3 Worst Reasons Not to Put It in Writing:

1. It's so unromantic.

2. It's too much trouble.

3. We don't have to, we trust each other.

carry on, but considering the timing and planning for the blessed event(s) can make family life a little calmer—except for the 2 a.m. feedings.

Financially, when you start a family, you will probably:

- Start thinking about a larger home.
- Require a second car.
- Watch your clothing allowances go through the roof.
- Arrange for child care or stop working.
- Foresee years of music lessons, soccer games, toys, and shoes that fit for about a month.
- Consider private school and camps.
- See college looming in the distance.
- Increase your health care coverage.

It's a lot easier to enjoy your kids if your finances aren't strained. Many people are waiting until they're in their thirties before starting a family, but waiting too long can bring its own problems. Strike a balance. Know what you're getting into so your voyage into parenthood is manageable and, when the kids are asleep, even relaxing!

College . . . Yikes!

You may have seen these figures, too. A post-secondary education is expected to be very expensive 15 years from now—it's already expensive! Currently, $25,000 a year is not an unusual price tag for a private college—and that's just for tuition and fees! You can easily figure another 20

QUICK n' PAINLESS

Think of your future family as an investment, even though you'll never be able to measure the returns in dollars! Start a separate account so some money is ready and waiting. This can make a big difference in easing some of your initial child-related expenses.

A college fund shouldn't take absolute precedence over your retirement account. The two can coexist. It's just as important that you look forward to a comfortable retirement as your children look forward to college.

percent for room and board and the ever present "miscellaneous." Many public universities can run as much as half that amount. It would almost be cheaper to offer to cash out your kids before they start and get a discount from them—offer them $10,000 and get off the hook! Who knows, maybe they'll start a really hot new Internet company with their little nest egg and never miss college at all!

Barring that, which isn't as likely as the business magazines would have you believe, you'll need a plan. The key is starting early and being consistent.

Few people have a big enough piggy bank to break open and cover all of a child's college expenses. Most families will depend on an aid package, loans, savings, and the earnings of both the parents and children. What you shouldn't depend on includes:

- The expectation of a sports scholarship.
- Money from grandparents.
- A full aid package.

Never depend on a scholarship! This is a lousy—and presumptuous—strategy. Same with depending on grandparents, although it would be a great way for them to start dispersing an estate—and do it at a time when you could really use it. No one can predict the limits or availability of financial aid years from now, so figure you may be paying or financing a good part of the costs.

The most manageable approach? Set up a separate account for college only. Add to it regularly and leave it!

Your best investments—at least in the early years—will be in stocks or stock funds. And keep the funds in your name, not your child's. If it's in Junior's name, the money goes to him at 18 or 21, depending on the terms of the account. He can do whatever he wants with it at that point, which might mean taking off to Europe for a few years instead of school. So much for years of planning and sacrifice! Maintain your sanity and stay stress-free at the same time by keeping these funds under your control.

SINGLE . . . SUDDENLY AND OTHERWISE

Some people prefer being single while others find themselves unexpectedly single. Legally, if you're living unmarried with a partner you are also considered single. Exceptions are made in 12 states and the District of Columbia that recognize common-law marriage. This is a leftover from the pioneer days. Check out your state laws—you just might meet their criteria and be married without knowing it!

It's easy to figure out who you have to depend on for all of your legal and financial needs if you're single—you! Mom may be a close second, but you're still number one on the list. It means you don't have to share your freezer full of Dove Bars with anyone, but you do have to figure out how to take care of your affairs:

- If you're ever ill and incapacitated.
- If you cannot work.
- In the event of your death.

IF YOU'RE SO
INCLINED

Follow the increasing costs of a college education as your child gets older. Note the conscientious schools that try to hold the line on fees and expenses. Get to know more about these schools—you may be pleasantly surprised!

This is where your single world will have some visitors in the guise of estate lawyers, trustees, and insurance agents. Insurance is covered in greater detail in Chapters 5 and 6, and wills in Chapter 8. As a single person, you should:

- Obtain adequate health and disability insurance.
- Write and maintain a current will.
- Name a trustee with power of attorney.

Facing your mortality doesn't have to sound so ominous—it's just good planning! This will keep your life uncomplicated during the times when you don't want any complications. A trustee, for instance, a family member, will see that you're taken care of should you ever be critically ill or hospitalized. A trustee will oversee your financial affairs during these times, as well—you don't want to end up with any surprises. It's critical that you be very clear with your trustee about your wishes. You might wake up from a coma and discover that your Buddy Holly records were sold to pay for some of your hospital care instead of tapping into some of your other investments.

Disability insurance and good health care coverage are especially critical for single people. If you're laid up from work due to injuries, you'll want a disability policy to kick in and lessen your sudden financial burden. These days, health care coverage is almost mandatory!

You may not have given any serious consideration to your estate. If you don't, the state will! Probate—a

YOU'LL THANK YOURSELF LATER

If you're single, but living with a partner, keep your financial affairs separate and distinct. This is much simpler than untangling bank accounts and portfolios later in the event of a death or parting of the ways.

process by which the courts validate and carry out wills—can be very complicated and expensive—depending on your state of residence and size of your estate—if you leave a vague will or no will at all. Give some thought to how you want your goods and money dispersed—and then get it down in a will.

GOING IT ALONE

Single parents can have a tough time, especially if the other parent isn't helping out or is deceased. There can be money problems, of course, and huge emotional issues. Becoming a single parent by choice isn't the picnic many people seem to think it will be—even for millionaire Hollywood actresses who seem to see it as one more movie script.

A single parent whose finances are tight may have a harder time putting money aside for investments and retirement. Take it one step at a time—don't panic!—and you can pull this off. For a single parent, the main ways to save are through:

- Automatic payroll deductions
- Strict budgeting
- Enforcing child support collection

Out of sight, out of mind, and into the bank! That's the advantage of automatic deductions from your paycheck. Even $20 or $30 at a time will add up. As far as you're concerned, this money doesn't exist. Let it accumulate and build up interest and earnings—you'll be pleasantly surprised at the end of the year.

A COMPLETE WASTE OF TIME

The 3 Worst Assumptions Made by Singles:

1. I'll never get sick.
2. I can live off of my savings.
3. I don't need a will.

Honestly discuss your situation with your kids. Make them part of your budget process. You'd be surprised how enthusiastic and supportive they can be. Make it clear that smart spending is a sign of a smart person, just like them.

Budgeting isn't much fun, especially with kids who may not understand why life has changed. Wanting to give our kids everything (at least not depriving them of much) can blow a budget out the window. Provide the essentials and a few treats and get over your guilt. You'll feel worse from the strain of having no savings.

As a single parent, a will is a very big deal, especially if the other parent is deceased or unreliable and your children are still minors. This is one time it's worth busting the budget and paying for legal advice. Do your own research first by checking out your local library for books on estate planning and wills. Don't use these as the final word regardless of how reliable or up-to-date they may seem! Instead, use them for basic information so you can talk intelligently with an attorney and not run the clock any longer than you have to. You'll probably be paying by the hour after all.

Single parents have to pay attention to:

- Naming a guardian for their children
- Considering establishing trusts
- Reviewing child custody and money arrangements regularly

You'll sleep easier knowing that your children will be taken care of according to your wishes should anything unexpected happen to you. And, if you've established trusts, knowing that they won't get all the money until the trust decides to give it to them. You set the terms! Otherwise, as much as she may miss you, your 16-year-old daughter might buy a new Miata in your memory.

ONE MORE TIME AROUND . . .
OR TWO OR . . .

Second marriages—and second sets of kids, dogs, and houses—are not uncommon. If either or each spouse has kids from previous marriages, the equation can go something like this where (H = husband; HK = his kids; EW = ex-wife; NW = new wife; NK = new kids; EWNK = ex-wife's new kids; NWK = new wife's kids):

$$(H + HK) - EW\ NW\ (NK) + EW - EWNK + (NW)(NWK)$$
$$= \$1,000,000)$$

In other words, you will be completely consumed by emotional and financial demands. Communicating your mutual expectations prior to a new marriage is even more critical now than with the first marriage. Everyone's bringing baggage into this one and it's not all shiny new Gucci luggage. Child support may be due on top of the expense of raising a new family. Take a long, hard look at your situation and be prepared for some big changes.

The more you talk and plan, the fewer hassles you'll have later with issues such as:

- How far does each partner go in supporting their new partner's children?

- Dealing with conflicting demands of children from the first marriage and children from the new marriage. For instance, who goes to private schools?

- Estate planning.

Take your time, plan it out as best you can, and enjoy your new life!

IF YOU'RE SO
INCLINED

Be sure any child custody issues, such as child support, are also clarified and dealt with appropriately in your will if your ex-spouse is not to get custody of the children.

Be sure you and your spouse-to-be have cleared away any joint accounts you may have held with your former spouse, especially credit card accounts. Order a credit check from Experian or another credit agency to be sure you're clear.

BREAKING UP IS HARD TO DO

With or without children, divorce is often tough—on the heart and on the wallet! As *The Wall Street Journal Lifetime Guide to Money* (Dow Jones & Company, 1997) points out, it's a good idea to hire a tax professional and a financial planner in addition to a divorce lawyer. These professionals can help you determine:

- The best settlement from a tax standpoint.
- Which assets are worth keeping.
- How to invest any settlement.
- Clearing your name from any joint obligations from the marriage.

Your goals during a divorce should be to make it as amicable as possible, take care of your children, and split up the assets fairly. Setting up battle lines will cost everyone involved.

Getting Time and Money on Your Side

	The Old Way	**The Lazy Way**
Entering into a marriage with little discussion of present finances vs. reviewing each others finances:	Uh, honey, what's this letter from MasterCard about you maxing out a $20,000 limit?	I think we should get these bills paid off first before we start planning a wedding, okay?
Entering into a marriage with little discussion of your new joint finances vs. talking first:	Well, excuse me if I have a problem with your going off to Atlantic City every weekend with the grocery money.	Okay, penny ante poker with the guys it is.
Jointly buying major assets—without a written contract—with an unmarried partner and eventually splitting up vs. getting it in writing:	That grand piano is mine, understand? I'll gut it out before I let you have it.	Remember what we agreed to? It's right here in our contract, you get the freezer and its contents and I get the condo in Aspen.

More Lazy Stuff

How to Get Someone Else to Do It

We hire professional help for all kinds of tasks in our lives from cleaning our homes to cleaning our teeth. Not that I'd rate the two equally! It's one thing to tidy up the house, but quite another to look in someone's mouth and say, "Open" about 50 times while scraping away with dental tools. Sometimes it's just easier to hire the work out and pay the tab.

Money management and planning can also be hired out. Advisors, accountants, brokers, and lawyers are there for the asking—for a price! You may find it's a better use of your time and money to seek advice while building your financial future. And there's plenty of advice to be had!

LET ME GIVE YOU A LITTLE PIECE OF ADVICE

Financial advisors and planners can be broken down into two categories:

- Fee-only advisors
- Commission-based advisors

Fee-only planners receive no commissions or compensation from selling investment products, such as mutual funds or annuities. They charge a flat rate, either:

- An annual fee
- An hourly rate
- A percentage of your portfolio value

Commission-based advisors are like car sales people—except for those anarchists at Saturn dealerships who don't negotiate prices and pay straight salaries to their sales crews. The argument against commission-based advice—and in favor of fee-only advice—is the assumption of a conflict of interest. How objective will an advisor be about the returns on Okefenokee Swamp Improvement Bonds if his or her salary is in part dependent on the sale?

America being the land of infinite choice, there are two additional variations on the financial planning scheme here. In addition to fee-only and commission-based planning, you also have:

- Fee-based planning
- Fee-offset

These advisors charge both a fee and receive a commission from selling products—talk about having it both ways! There are even CDPs—Certified Divorce Planners!

Just a Few Questions, Please

A good financial planner will poke and probe to find out more about you and your finances. They should ask about:

- How you track and follow your finances
- Your tax planning
- Your current life insurance coverage
- Any estate planning you've done
- Your long and short term financial goals

- Current investments and debts
- Your comfort with risk

  After this financial inquisition, you and your advisor will:
- More clearly define your goals
- Create a plan to reach those goals
- Review the plan from time to time as your finances change

  The plan should include:
- Developing an investment portfolio
- Managing your cash flow
- Income tax management
- Planning your estate
- Retirement planning
- College funding
- Consideration for taxes and inflation

In other words, everything we've already talked about in this book! At least you'll know what to expect from a paid professional.

Questions of Your Own

If you're going to hire a planner, do your homework. Get some referrals from your friends, your banker, even your church or synagogue—they have money to deal with, too! Talk with at least three advisors and inquire about:

- Their background and number of years working in this field
- Billings
- Current clients with whom you could speak

There are two main designations for financial planners:

1. Personal Financial Advisor (PFA)

2. Certified Financial Planner (CFP)

It's easy to get some more info on PFAs and CFPs: Go to their websites! Click on http://www.napa.org to find out about the fee-only National Association of Personal Financial Advisors. Next, go to http://www.icfp.org for the Institute of Certified Financial Planners, the larger—and older—of the two groups.

NOT CHEAP, JUST SPENDING AVERSE

Budget-minded? Take the really easy way out. Take advantage of advice on the web and incorporate it into your own planning. Let these sites do some of the work for you—for free! Some sites include:

- **www.fponline.com**   This is the "Home of Financial Planning on the Web." That may take in a little too much territory, but it is a site for financial planners. Check out their discussion group.

- **www.americanexpress.com/advisors**   An interactive advisory page.

- **www.slia.com/analysis.htm**   This is the site for the St. Louis Investment Advisors. They offer a free financial analysis; key in the information and send it off.

- **www.comfind.com**   Community Financial Planning Services. Offers both free and fee-based services plus an estate tax calculator, retirement information, and explanations of financial terms.

- **www.laicfp.org/consnews.html**   A free consumer newsletter; slanted toward a CFP, but still useful.

- **www.cybercu.org**   A site sponsored by credit unions with links for car purchases, college funding, retirement, and home purchases. Some wonderful loan and compound interest calculators, as well as tax forms and insurance information.

It's great to let these guys do some of the work for you, but in the end you'll have to decide if the advice suits you or not. Even professionals can be wrong: Just look at all the guys who advised Richard Nixon!

THE BEAN COUNTERS

A guy turns to the guy next to him in a bar. "You want to hear a joke about accountants?"

The second guy says, "I'm 6' tall, 200 lbs. and I'm an accountant. My friend next to me is 6'2" tall, weighs 220 lbs., and played fullback at Stanford. He's also an accountant. You still want to tell that joke?"

The first guy replies, "Nah, I don't want to have to say it twice."

Accountants, it seems, get no respect. Their work is tedious and will keep you in good stead with the IRS and following your financial goals. Unless you're self-employed and have business concerns, your main use for a CPA, or certified public accountant, will be for your tax work.

How complicated is your tax return? Do you take deductions or use the 1040A or 1040EZ forms? Any passive losses or rental property you're depreciating? For simple returns, a nationwide firm like H&R Block can do the trick. Their preparers can check your figures and guide you through your return if you have a certain aversion to filing your taxes. These guys have offices everywhere and provide an effortless solution to those vexing tax forms.

The next step up could be a CPA who specializes in tax preparation. Accountants may have knowledge in many areas of their profession, but not all individual CPA practices deal with taxation. Some specialize in audits, others in setting up business plans. If your CPA has a large sign on the door with the letters "IRS" inside a black circle with a slash across it, you're probably in the right office.

You may have a complicated return, one that includes your business taxes, perhaps an inheritance. In this case, consider a CPA firm with partners or associates with different specialties. They can all grab a page or two, run back to their offices and calculators, and put together a beautiful return.

Taking it Easy With an EA

You have another profession to add to your alphabet soup of financial advisors and helpers. An EA is an enrolled agent—a tax specialist, licensed by the Federal government, and authorized to appear in place of a taxpayer at the IRS. EAs must:

- Demonstrate technical competence in the area of taxation.
- Pass a rigorous two-day test given by the IRS.
- Have worked for the IRS for a minimum of five years in lieu of taking the test.
- Pass an equally rigorous background check.
- Take 72 hours of continuing education every 3 years.

You never heard of these guys? Most people haven't, but they've been around since 1884. The NAEA (National Association of Enrolled Agents) requires their members to take 30 hours of continuing education classes every year. You can contact them for an EA referral at their website, http://www.naea.org/find!us.htm or call 800-424-4339.

LEGAL EAGLES

It would be far too easy to start this section off with a lawyer joke—you could fill this book and more! Do a web search under lawyer jokes and stand back, you'll get plenty of responses. But, a good lawyer can keep you out of trouble before it happens and get you out of trouble when it shows its ugly face.

Normally (we'll leave criminal law out of this book, thank you very much) you might need an attorney in the following situations:

- Reviewing a will and doing your estate planning
- Real estate transactions and disputes
- Tax representation
- Divorce

Attorneys are specialists just like accountants, physicians, and chefs. You wouldn't expect a fry cook at Phil's Pancake Palace to whip up an order of lobster Newburg—go light on the paprika—with a side of risotto milanese, so don't expect a bankruptcy attorney to write up your will. There is little virtue in going into a business transaction, tax dispute, or divorce proceedings without hired help when you need it. Attorneys can keep your life hassle-free by tending to nagging details you would just assume ignore.

TAKE THE BROKE OUT OF BROKER

Stockbrokers make their money through commissions. You buy an investment—a stock, bond, or mutual fund, for instance—and the broker gets a share of the commission you pay to the brokerage firm. I'm not any fan of full-commission brokers, but if you're uncomfortable making your own investment decisions, a good broker should both make you money and help you keep an eye on your long-term goals. You want an experienced broker, one recommended by a friend or colleague, especially if they're suddenly driving around in a new Bentley six months after they started investing.

The problem? You want an experienced broker, but typically a broker at this level isn't interested in small accounts. A new broker, just getting started, would most likely work with you, but you may well lack confidence in his or her recommendations. In either case, if your account is only in the low thousands of dollars, it's questionable how much attention you'll get from an individual broker. Look at it this way: If the market is dropping rapidly, whose account will get tended to first, your $5,000 in holdings or a cardiac surgeon with $400,000?

If you're looking for a broker to hold your hand, figuratively, that is, throughout the investing process, you're probably out of luck unless you have sizable funds.

When engaging a broker, be sure to arrange a personal meeting before forking over those dollars. Ask about the broker's background and investment style. You want to avoid excessive trading and the commissions they generate. And you don't want any weird, risky investments that you don't understand—like Guinness stout options played out in the Dublin stock market.

SPEAKING OF BANKERS

Don't underestimate the advice and resourcefulness of your own bank. Your local bank branch manager can guide you through a loan process before you need it. This will give you some idea of what kind of customer profile is most likely to get a loan, i.e., how much savings you should have, how much debt, what kind of records you'll need. If your bank also sells investments through a brokerage partnership, they can be helpful here as well.

THE LAZY WAY

Advice is a wonderful thing—and everyone has some to offer, whether you ask or not! The final decisions are yours, so choose your advisors carefully—and get a second opinion. You're entrusting your savings (and at least part of your future) to someone else, but you still need to keep your eye on your account.

Financial planners, accountants, brokers, and lawyers can keep you on the straight and narrow path—when you're not ready to walk it on your own or need specialized help—to a secure future. Use them when you need them, weigh their fees against the results, and if you find good people, stick with them.

B

If You Really Want to Learn More, Read These

Financial planning lends itself to as much reading as you want to do. It's a lot faster to look up and read a stock or mutual fund share price than listen to someone go through the entire listings of equities. It would be like listening to an entire oral history of your family when all you want to know is if your uncle Ned really got those scars in a knife fight with five escaped convicts he claimed to have captured—or from an appendectomy as you suspect.

As an independent investor, your biggest tool will be information. Okay, it helps to have some money, too. In an age where anyone with a desktop publishing program or an Internet website can churn out their own forms of wisdom, accessible information has grown like a sumo wrestler on an all-day cheeseburger diet. Your job is to sort through it without getting overloaded.

GO TO THE SOURCE

It used to be that investors were at the mercy of stockbrokers for up-to-the-minute financial information. Not any longer. We're in the hyper-information age. Your two major sources of money info will be:

- The public library

- The Internet

Why the library? Because it's like a huge smorgasbord of free samples. You can browse through current financial publications, recent—and not so recent—books, various financial digests, and newsletters. *The Value Line Investment Survey*—an excellent stock rating tool—is used by tens of thousands of investors. A couple of Saturday mornings snooping around the stacks and you can quickly whittle down the publications worth the price of a subscription. The library will give you access to thousands of dollars worth of magazines and newsletters free—a price any lazy investor can relate to. Many libraries offer Internet access as well if you don't have your own.

Too lazy to go to your local library? Forgot where it's located? You can always go to your local bookstore/newsstand and pick up some recommended magazines at several dollars a pop and read them at your leisure. Or, take the easy way out and hit the Internet. Some of the sites listed below will link you to free e-zines (the electronic equivalent of magazines) put out by major financial publications.

Warning! Info-Load Ahead

With information come caveats, of course. Like wines, theatrical performances, and relationships, not all information is created equal. We're human, we look for answers and if someone offers them, we often accept them with little questioning about credibility if someone sounds convincingly authoritative. Pick your way through a variety of publications—the ones that make sense to you and appeal to the direction you want to go will make themselves known soon enough. Magazine subscriptions are inexpensive; you should consider subscribing to two or three of them to help keep you focused on financial issues. Internet browsing is cheaper yet—one monthly fee and you can read 24 hours a day. You probably could, too, if you consumed enough caffeine and Snickers bars.

Newsletters are another source of financial information, but be careful. Ever since Guttenberg put together movable type, the world has been flooded with opinions, including financial dogma. The first investment newsletter was probably pushing shares of The Ponce de Leon Fountain of Youth Water Company, as well as land sales in the new world. Unlike periodicals, investment newsletters are often expensive, sometimes more than $200 for a year's subscription. Consult *The Hulbert Financial Digest*, available in many libraries, which ranks dozens of investment newsletters according to the returns a subscriber would receive by following each newsletter's recommendations. It's hard to argue with the numbers, although some publishers offer what they view as valid criticisms of Hulbert's reports. You won't hear any of the winners complaining. Surprisingly, mediocre, even awful, newsletters manage to sustain subscribers—true believers waiting for their day to come.

IF I HAD A BUCK FOR EVERY FINANCE BOOK . . .

Finance and investment books are something like diet books: There are a million of them and they never go out of style. For every book advocating one investment style you'll find one that contradicts it or recommends another approach as superior. Studies are quoted, figures and charts fill the pages, and every author will lead you to financial enlightenment if you would only follow. In the end, they mostly agree on two things: investing—good, not investing—bad!

With that in mind, here are a few books, in no particular order, to consider in your quest to secure your financial future.

- *The Dow Jones-Irwin Guide to Using The Wall Street Journal* by Michael Lehman, McGraw-Hill, 1997. (Lehman explains *The Wall Street Journal* section-by-section, along with economic background; a wonderfully useful book.)

- *Die Broke: A Radical 4-Part Personal Finance Plan* by Stephen M. Pollan and Mark Levine, Harper Business, 1998. (Explores the notion of enjoying your money while you're in good health to do so, giving it away while you're still alive, and ensuring you'll have enough in your later years to live well.)

- *The Millionaire Next Door: The Surprising Secrets of America's Wealthy* by Thomas J. Stanley and William D. Danko, Longstreet Press, 1996.

- *The Wall Street Journal Guide to Money* by *The Wall Street Journal*'s Finance Staff, Dow Jones & Co., 1997. (Financial planning for every stage of your life.)

- *How to Be Rich* by J. Paul Getty, Mass Market Paperback, reissue 1996. (A blast from the past by the original billionaire.)

- *Two Incomes and Still Broke? It's Not How Much You Make, But How Much You Keep* by Linda Kelley, Time Books, 1998. (The title tells it all.)

- *Dictionary of Finance and Investment Terms* by John Downes & Jordan Elliot Goodman, Barron's Finance and Investment Book, 4th Edition, Barron's Educational Series, 1995. (From ABC agreements to zero-plus tick, a definition for everything financial.)

- *Buffettology: The Previously Unexplained Techniques That Have Made Warren Buffet the World's Most Famous Investor* by Mary Buffett and David Clark, Scribner, 1997.

- *Warren Buffett Speaks: Wit and Wisdom From the World's Greatest Investor* by Warren Buffett and Janet Lowe, John Wiley & Sons, 1997.

- *Beating the Street* by Peter Lynch and John Rothchild, Fireside, 1994.

- *Learn to Earn: A Beginner's Guide to the Basics of Investing and Business* by Peter Lynch and John Rothchild, Fireside, 1996.

- *A Random Walk Down Wall Street,* 6th Edition by Burton Gordon Malkiel
- *The Only Investment Guide You'll Ever Need* by Andrew Tobias, Harvest Books, Jan. 1999.
- *The Beneficiary Book* by Martin Kuritz, Active Insights, 1992.

There are hundreds of investment and personal finance books available. If you want to get readers' reactions, go to Amazon.com, call up the book title, and read reviews done by Amazon's customers.

Magazines

- *Worth*
- *Fortune*
- *Your Money*
- *Forbes*
- *Individual Investor*
- *The Economist*
- *Kiplinger's*
- *BusinessWeek*

Newspapers

- *The Wall Street Journal*
- *Barron's*

CASTING A NET

You cannot describe the Internet with enough hyperbole. It will keep programmers and web page designers and archivists busy for the next 20 years. From an investor's standpoint, it both levels the playing field and adds to the confusion.

The Internet provides a willing audience for brokerage firms, investment advisors, musers, and preachers of all stripes to advertise their wares and offer their opinions. Message boards allow stockholders and observers to comment without discrimination on specific stocks and financial instruments, as well as on other musers. A good percentage of the messages have little to do with the security under discussion and more to do with previous messages and the opinions of the sender. Some do offer in-depth commentary, though, and are worth looking at.

At this time, a lot of information, including stock and option quotes, is free, but don't expect this to last forever. Eventually, many requests will probably be billed to your account, even if for a nominal amount. A captive, hooked audience will pay before giving up the access.

The Internet goes on, essentially, forever. The quality of the information varies, of course, but for easy summaries of the day's stock and financial activity, you can't beat the Internet. How does it level the playing field? By providing much of the same information that a broker would have previously provided—for a fee.

Do you need a summary of a company's financials? You'll find it on the Internet. How about background information on Tanganyikan bonds? No problem. Current rate for Treasury bills? Click on their website and take a look.

You'll never lack for information—just cast a skeptical eye when you go fishing for it.

Websites

General Investing and Financial

- www.investorama.com (more information than you can ever use; sit down with your keyboard and a big snack and type away)
- www.yahoo.com/Business
- http://quicken.com
- www.armchairmillionaire.com

- www.motleyfool.com
- www.lombard.com
- www.investorlinks.com
- www.moneynet.com
- www.dailystocks.com
- www.kiplinger.com (try their calculator page at /calc/calchome.html)
- www.cyberinvestor.com (a site full of links on Internet-related sites, banking, company research, mutual funds, and links to free financial e-zines)
- www.webinvestor.com ("thousands of links," news, quotes)
- www.investorguide.com
- www.cob.ohio.state.edu (for an awesome Financial Data Finder)
- www.morningstar.net
- www.hovers.com (free research on publicly traded companies; may not always be up-to-date)

Credit Card Rates and CDs

- www.bankrate.com and www.ranresearch.com (both for credit card rates; bankrate.com also has certificate of deposit rates)
- www.banx.com

Debt

- www.dca.org (Debt Counselors of America 800-680-3328)

Credit Reports

- Experian
  www.experian.com or 888-397-3742
- Equifax
  www.equifax.com or 800-685-1111

Insurance Quotes and Information

Insurance

- www.quotesmith.com (800-556-9393)

- www.moneyclub.com

- www.insure.com

- www.aarp.org (American Association of Retired Persons, especially for long-term care insurance, other retirement issues)

Retirement Calculators

- www.troweprice.com/retirement/retire.html

- www.quicken.com/retirement/planner

DRIPs

- www.moneypaper.com

- www.dripcentral.com

- www.dripinvestor.com

- www.netstockdirect.com

Brokerage/Fund Sites (good general info)

- www.troweprice.com

- www.schwab.com

- www.vanguard.com

- www.fidelity.com

- www.strongfunds.com

- www.indexfundsonline.com

- http://indexinvesting.com

- www.fundsinteractive.com

SPDRs, DIAMONDs, and Dogs

- www.amex.com (800-THE-AMEX)
- 800-810-WEBS
- www.dogsofthedow.com

Discount Brokers

- www.thewebinvestor.com

Investor Organizations

- www.better-investing.org (National Association of Investors Corporation, 248-583-4880)
- www.aaii.org (American Association of Individual Investors, 800-428-2244)

The Federal Government

- www.ustreas.gov
- www.publicdebt.gov
- www.irs.gov
- www.ssa.gov (Social Security Administration)
- www.sec.gov
- FDIC Consumer News (a free quarterly publication from the FDIC; call 800-276-6003 or e-mail at publicinfo@fdic.gov)

The U.S. Securities and Exchange Commission (SEC) is a quasi-judicial regulatory agency that administers federal securities laws. They protect investors and ensure that they have access to any disclosed information by or about publicly traded securities. The centerpiece of their Internet site is EDGAR.

EDGAR, aside from being one of the names of at least two of America's stranger characters—Edgar Allan Poe and J. Edgar Hoover—

stands for Electronic Data Gathering Analysis and Retrieval system. This system contains most, but not all, of newly filed information on publicly traded securities.

College Financial Aid

- Request a copy of The Student Guide from the website of the U.S. Department of Education (www.ed.gov/offices/OPE) or call 800-433-3243; the most comprehensive resource on student financial aid; it lists aid, grants, work study, etc. available through the Federal Student Financial Assistance Programs.

- The Student Loan Marketing Association (SLMA or SallieMae) has a college planning calculator available at http://salliemae.com: 80/calculators/content/html.

- Go to www.finaid.org, a great site that offers a free, comprehensive, guide to student financial aid; the site was created by Mark Kantrowitz, the author of *The Prentice Hall Guide to Scholarships and Fellowships for Math and Science Students,* and lists all kinds of scholarships and links to research them.

- The U.S. Department of Education offers the Free Application for Federal Student Aid (FAFSA) either through their website (www.ed.gov) or by calling 800-433-3243.

- The U.S. Department of Education is also your source for federal Pell Grants for undergraduates (these are not loans and are not repaid), as well as subsidized and unsubsidized Stafford loans available from the Federal Family Educational Loan Program.

C

If You Don't Know What It Means, Look Here

AGI, or Adjusted Gross Income: What's left over after you subtract deductible Keogh and IRA contributions, alimony, deductible moving expenses, and other select expenses from your total income. Subtract itemized deductions and personal exemptions from your AGI to find your taxable income—the number that really counts!

After-tax dollars: Money left over after taxes have been paid. An after-tax return may figure in other costs, such as commissions, and inflation to yield a true return.

ADR, or American Depository Receipt: The means by which an American investor can buy shares of foreign companies without buying directly in overseas markets. An ADR sits secure in a U.S. bank vault and grants the U.S. shareholder all rights and privileges of ownership.

American Stock Exchange: A New York–based stock exchange of mostly small- to medium-sized companies.

Analyst: An individual, often at a large brokerage house or bank, who studies different companies, recommending some as worthy investments. Analysts get paid whether they're right or wrong and are often seen flipping coins.

APR, or Annual Percentage Rate: The interest rate you pay on a loan.

Annuity: An insurance company contract that pays the recipient—that's you if you purchased it—regular payments, usually as a retirement vehicle. Language, terms, and fees of an annuity contract can be only semi-comprehensible for the average person.

ARM, or Adjustable Rate Mortgage: A mortgage with a changing interest rate that is lower in its early years than prevailing long-term rates

Asset allocation: How you spread out your investments into different sectors or areas of the market such as stocks, bonds, cash, real estate, etc.

Bear market: Lots of sellers, fewer buyers, and dropping prices.

Blue chip: Big, fat and happy, well-capitalized corporations with solid histories and reliable returns (General Motors, etc.). Also, a weird looking tortilla chip made from blue corn flour.

Bond: An IOU from a corporation, government, or municipal bond issuer. The buyer earns interest in regular payments, both tax free and taxable depending on the type of bond.

Book value: Simply put, it's the stockholders equity, what a company's assets are worth after you subtract its liabilities.

Budget: Something human beings avoid, but a good way to list and deal with expenses and income.

Bull market: Lots of buyers, fewer sellers, and rising prices.

Call: A demand for repayment of a loan; an early redemption of a bond; the right to buy shares of stock at a set price by a certain future date.

Capital gain: The difference between your purchase price for an asset and its increased selling price; a capital gains tax is what you pay the government on your capital gain profit.

Capital loss: The difference between your purchase price for an asset and its decreased selling price.

Cash flow: Cash in and cash out (with the hope that more is coming in or at least staying in).

CD, or Certificate of Deposit: Interest-bearing, insured debt instrument sold by banks; terms may run from a few weeks to several years.

CFP, or Certified Financial Planner: Folks who will help straighten out your money affairs and recommend investments and strategies; certified by the CFP Board of Standards in Denver, CO.

CPA, or Certified Public Accountant: A smartypants person, often dour, who finds the U.S. Tax Code to be fun reading.

Closed-end funds: Mutual funds, listed on a stock exchange, with only a set number of shares issued; the value of the shares can be greater or lesser than the value of the funds' assets.

Common stock: Basic unit of ownership in a public company.

Compound interest: Interest on both the principal and the accumulating interest itself; also, a formula that Einstein thought was very cool.

Disability insurance: Covers you when you are unable to work due to injury or accident.

DIAMONDs: Units in the DIAMONDs Trust, which buys shares in the companies composing the Dow Jones Industrial Average.

Discretionary spending: The spending you can control.

Diversification: Spreading your investment risk among various equities and asset classes; similar to allocation, but includes diversifying within each asset class, i.e., a dozen different stocks rather than just one.

Dividend: Income payments made to stockholders by dividend paying companies.

DCA, or Dollar-Cost Averaging: Investing the same amount of money regularly into the market, regardless of conditions; over time, the average cost of your purchases should be lower than their eventual appreciated value; some investors set aside a sum, say $200, and invest it monthly.

DJIA, or Dow Jones Industrial Average: A religiously followed market indicator composed of 30 blue chip stocks.

DRIP: Dividend Reinvestment Plan.

Durable power of attorney: Allows someone to act as your agent or representative if you are incapacitated; no, this usually doesn't apply for the morning after an all-night poker game.

Equity: The amount or percentage of a property that you own; ownership in a corporation as represented by your amount of stock.

Executor: The individual who executes your will and sees to it that your wishes are carried out.

Fixed rate: A rate that doesn't change, regardless of the market.

FICA, or Federal Insurance Contributions Act: Your Social Security payment.

FDIC, or Federal Deposit Insurance Corporation: Covers bank, money market, and CD deposits at its insured banks and thrift institutions.

401(k): Employer-sponsored, voluntary retirement plan, which deposits pre-tax dollars into a tax-deferred account.

Full-service broker: The most expensive type of broker who provides more services than discount brokers.

Futures: Agreements to buy or sell a specified commodity—oil, wheat, metals—or financial instrument for a specified price by a specified future date; mess with these, and you won't have much of a future.

Growth stock: Stock of fast-growing, somewhat volatile companies that usually don't pay a dividend.

Health care directive: Expresses your personal wishes regarding medical care if you are incapacitated, a.k.a. a living will.

Home equity loan: Borrowing based on the percentage of equity you have in your home.

Index fund: Mutual fund that tries to match the return of a broad section of the market, such as the S&P 500.

IRA, or Individual Retirement Account: Tax-deferred account with various participation limitations; you put your own money into this one.

Inflation: Too much money flying around trying to buy too little stuff thus driving the prices up.

Keogh: Tax-deferred retirement plan geared toward small businesses and self-employed individuals; more paperwork demands than either a SEP-IRA or IRA.

Liquidity: A measure of how fast you can change an asset into cash; Treasuries convert really fast, your collection of antique plates will not.

Load fund: Mutual fund that charges you a sales commission; your return is lowered by this charge.

LTC, or Long-term care insurance: A policy that covers, for example, any nursing home care or in-home assistance you may need due to health problems.

Market timing: Mostly futile attempts to move money in and out of different areas of the market as conditions change; rarely works, but does build up broker commissions.

Medicare: Another deduction from your paycheck.

Money market deposit account: Federally insured, liquid account paying a higher interest rate than standard savings account; some check-writing limitations and account minimums.

Money market fund: Mutual fund that invests in safe securities, like a money market, but is not insured.

Municipal bonds: State and local government debts, used to pay for roads, hospitals, and anything else that tickles the fancy of local governments; interest is normally exempt from federal income tax and often from state income tax.

Mutual fund: An investment company; popular investment vehicles in which funds from many investors are used to buy usually diversified portfolios of mostly stocks and bonds.

NASDAQ: Computerized, mostly over-the-counter stock market for what are generally smaller, more volatile companies, although both Intel and Microsoft are listed on it.

Net worth: Assets minus liabilities; pay all of your bills and look at what's left—that's your net worth.

No-load funds: Mutual funds without a sales commission.

Option: The right, but not the obligation, to buy or sell something, within a specified amount of time, for a fee.

Penny stocks: Appropriately named, volatile, sometimes virtual stocks that should be avoided completely.

Points: Usually associated with mortgage costs, an up-front fee, a percentage of the loan, paid to the lender; currently deductible from federal taxes.

Preferred stock: Almost like a bond, a special class of stock that pays an established interest rate to its holders; preferred stockholders get paid off before common stockholders.

P/E (price-to-earnings ratio): Result of dividing stock price by its per-share earnings based on a one year period; the P/E can be found in your newspaper's stock listings.

Probate: A state procedure to validate a will.

Put: An option that gives the holder the right to sell shares of stock at an established price by a certain future date.

REIT, or Real Estate Investment Trust: Essentially a mutual fund of properties and mortgages, which distribute 95 percent of its income back to shareholders; often pays a good dividend; income based on rising property values and rents.

Roth IRA: An IRA which takes after-tax contributions, but does not tax the returns.

Sector: Specific grouping of stocks by type, such as tech stocks.

SEC, or Securities and Exchange Commission: The guys who keep the markets kosher (non-religiously speaking).

Short selling: A losing stock trading strategy just about guaranteed to bring you up short; the seller borrows stock from a broker and sells it, hoping to buy the shares back at a lower price in the open market at a later date to replace the borrowed shares.

SEP-IRA, Simplified Employee Pension IRA: Another retirement plan for self-employed individuals and their employees.

SPDR: Standard & Poor's Depository Receipt.

S&P 500 Index (Standard & Poor's 500): Group of 500 commonly held stocks in large, established corporations looked to as a measure of the general stock market; Standard & Poor's itself is a securities rating and advisory firm.

STRIPS, or Separate Trading of Registered Interest and Principal of Securities: Also known as zero-coupon Treasuries, sold at a steep discount by brokers and redeemed at full value.

Taxable income: The one you pay your income taxes on.

Tax deferred: An account in which no taxes are due until you begin to withdraw funds.

Tax-exempt: Interest earnings not subject to tax.

Term life insurance: Basic life insurance; insurance company promises to pay a set amount in the case of death.

Total return: The big number, what you get annually from an investment after figuring dividends, interest, and appreciation of the investment itself.

Treasuries: debt instruments issued and guaranteed by Uncle Sam; include T-bills, T-bonds, and T-notes.

Value stocks: Considered undervalued by investors willing to do some snooping into a company's numbers; often, stocks whose price has been beaten down, sometimes for no good reason.

WEBS: World Equity Benchmark Shares.

Whole life insurance: Broader policy than term insurance, builds up a cash value; not necessarily the best investment for tax-deferred earnings.

Yield: Generally, interest and/or dividends paid on your investment over a year's time; the percentage of your invested money that you receive back (not to be confused with return).

Zero-coupon bond: A bond sold at a big discount to its face value because it doesn't pay any interest; the investor, upon redemption, receives the full face value of the bond; volatile investment unless held to maturity; best used in a tax-deferred account because although the bondholder does not receive interest, taxes are due annually on imputed interest.

It's Time for Your Reward

Once You Do This	Reward Yourself
Made a list of your assets	A bottle of champagne if you feel rich, imported beer if a bit more modest.
Set up a budget	E-mail the White House to get on the ball with their budgeting.
Open a retirement account	Go to a Mercedez-Benz dealer and tell the sales rep you're checking out colors for an impending purchase.
Start saving a down payment for a home	Stop in at an open house for that $2 million high-rise condo and loudly announce, "Well, this might do for our guest house."
Implement some tax saving strategies	Let the IRS know they had better not depend on you for your normal contribution next year.
Open an account for your kids' college money	Tell your friends you'll just pay cash for college instead of filling out those boring financial aid forms.

Once You Do This	Reward Yourself
Invest in the stock market on a monthly basis	During Thanksgiving dinner at your insufferable in-laws' home, mutter, "I just hope our broker got our Microsoft order in yesterday."
Buy a three-month CD	Tell your brother you would really like to loan him some money, but you have a "major CD" deal going right now with a new recording label and you're doing the financing.
Write a will	"Accidentally" leave fake copies of it around when your friends are visiting, indicating you're leaving $1 million to each of them.
Take out a life insurance policy	Challenge your cousin to go bungee jumping.
Subscribe to *The Wall Street Journal*	Open it to the stock prices, circle different companies with a thick red marker, and write, "Buy 2,000 shares" and leave it open on your desk.
Buy an index fund that invests in the S&P 500	Casually mention to your date, "Oh, last time I looked I had holdings in 500 companies, give or take."

Where to Find What You're Looking For

Now you can do these tasks, too!

The Lazy Way

Starting to think there are a few more of life's little tasks that you've been putting off? Don't worry—we've got you covered. Take a look at all of *The Lazy Way* books available. Just imagine—you can do almost anything *The Lazy Way!*

Clean Your House The Lazy Way
By Barbara H. Durham
0-02-862649-4

Handle Your Money The Lazy Way
By Sarah Young Fisher and Carol Turkington
0-02-862632-X

Care for Your Home The Lazy Way
By Terry Meany
0-02-862646-X

Train Your Dog The Lazy Way
By Andrea Arden
0-87605180-8

Take Care of Your Car The Lazy Way
By Michael Kennedy and Carol Turkington
0-02-862647-8

Keep Your Kids Busy The Lazy Way
By Barbara Nielsen and Patrick Wallace
0-02-863013-0

*All Lazy Way books are just $12.95!

additional titles on the back!

Cook Your Meals The Lazy Way
By Sharon Bowers
0-02-862644-3

Shed Some Pounds The Lazy Way
By Annette Cain and Becky Cortopassi-Carlson
0-02-862999-X

Organize Your Stuff The Lazy Way
By Toni Ahlgren
0-02-863000-9

Feed Your Kids Right The Lazy Way
By Virginia Van Vynckt
0-02-863001-7

Cut Your Spending The Lazy Way
By Leslie Haggin
0-02-863002-5

Stop Aging The Lazy Way
By Judy Myers, Ph.D.
0-02-862793-8

Get in Shape The Lazy Way
By Annette Cain
0-02-863010-6

Learn French The Lazy Way
By Christophe Desmaison
0-02-863011-4

Learn Italian The Lazy Way
By Gabrielle Euvino
0-02-863014-9

Learn Spanish The Lazy Way
By Steven Hawson
0-02-862650-8